D1806755

Imagining Human Rights

Imagining
Human Rights

—

Edited by
Susanne Kaul and David Kim

DE GRUYTER

ZiF Zentrum für interdisziplinäre Forschung
Center for Interdisciplinary Research
Universität Bielefeld

ISBN 978-3-11-037619-7
e-ISBN (PDF) 978-3-11-037661-6
e-ISBN (EPub) 978-3-11-038729-2

(cc) BY-NC-ND

Dieses Werk ist lizenziert unter der Creative Commons Attribution-NonCommercial-
NoDerivatives 3.0 Lizenz. Weitere Informationen finden Sie unter
http://creativecommons.org/licenses/by-nc-nd/3.0/.

Library of Congress Cataloging-in-Publication Data
A CIP catalog record for this book has been applied for at the Library of Congress.

Bibliographic Information published by the Deutsche Nationalbibliothek
The Deutsche Nationalbibliothek lists this publication in the Deutsche Nationalbibliografie;
detailed bibliographic data are available on the internet at http://dnb.dnb.de.

© 2015 Walter de Gruyter GmbH, Berlin/Boston
Cover Photo: Kalliopi Lemos, Wooden Boat with Seven People, 2011, from the exhibition
Navigating in the Dark; Photography Rowan Durrant
Typesetting: Dörlemann Satz GmbH & Co. KG, Lemförde
Printing and binding: Hubert & Co. GmbH & Co. KG, Göttingen
♾ Printed on acid-free paper
Printed in Germany

www.degruyter.com

Acknowledgments

This volume originates in a conference titled "The Imagination of Human Rights" and held at Bielefeld University. Funded by the *Zentrum für interdisziplinäre Forschung* (ZiF) and the *Deutsche Forschungsgemeinschaft* (DFG), the event took place on June 28–30, 2013. We would like to thank these institutions for their invaluable support. During the conference, the Bielefeld *Institut für Weltgesellschaft* and the Department of History co-sponsored the public debate between Hans Joas and Samuel Moyn and we want to acknowledge their support as well. We express our sincere gratitude to the ZiF team especially director Ulrike Davy. Without their generous support, both the conference and the volume would have been infeasible. We would like to thank Gertrud Grünkorn and Juliane Schiffers for guiding us thoughtfully through the publication process. Last but not least, we thank Kalliopi Lemos for taking part in an academic conference and giving us permission to print an image of her work *Wooden Boat with Seven People* (2011) on the front cover.

December 2014   Susanne Kaul and David Kim

Table of Contents

Susanne Kaul and David Kim
Introduction:
Imagining Human Rights

For about six weeks in the fall of 2011, visitors to the Crypt Gallery in London had the rare opportunity to bear witness to an unusual underground world in several senses of the term. Deep below the surface, in the basement of St. Pancras Church, the London-based Greek artist Kalliopi Lemos had transformed the early nineteenth-century burial crypt into a ghostly passage for life-size wooden boats and animal-like creatures. Made of smoothly bent metal, birds, snakes, and bees animated this selectively lit space, while their motions had been suspended at various stages of life. Here, time seemed to have stopped or at least slowed down, as the installation presented a contemporary staging of the Acheron from ancient Greek mythology. Isolated from the hubbub of the urban metropolis above ground level, this imaginary interstititial space constituted an otherworldly world where life and death, movement and stillness, land and sea, history and mythos converged precariously in the twilight of passing.

Given the originally sacred location of this exhibition, which was titled *Navigating in the Dark*, visitors likely associated what they saw or heard with some sort of modern-day interpretation of life after death caught between disparate worlds. They probably felt transported to a liminal space beyond the fullness of life, where *zoë* – bare life – outweighed *bios* in the sense of absolute human vitality. As Giorgio Agamben famously explains in *Homo Sacer*, the Greek word for *life* comes in these two fundamentally different forms, the former representing "the simple fact of living common to all living beings (animals, men, or gods)" and the latter standing for "the form or way of living proper to an individual or a group" (1998, p. 1). Whereas bare life marks the lowest and thus common denominator for every living being on earth, life in its fullest sense entails the social belonging to a polity. In the case of Lemos's installation, this inspiration was both there and nowhere to see. On those seemingly stranded fragile boats were shadowy figures who appeared at once lost and determined, both hopeful and in suffering (see the front cover). Some of them appeared to be whispering in secrecy, while others were sitting silently with their heads slightly lowered. These variously still motions alerted spectators to the hidden dangers of navigating on high seas, traveling through international waters or being suspended in the dark. These absent-present figures represented the countless – and thus nameless – immigrants, asylum seekers, and boat people who regularly traveled across the ocean on overcrowded makeshift boats. In this underground world, these ghostly anonymous figures confronted visitors from another biopolitical world with hardly registered stories whose cruelty Étienne Balibar had described as being "'worse than death'" (2004, p. 115). Agamben had likewise referred to such extreme suffering as "*ein lebensunwertes Leben*": a life not worth living (1998, p. 137).

That Lemos drew attention to this dire, yet mostly invisible problem on the peripheries of land and sea – more specifically, on almost opposite shores of Europe – made one point clear. On the surface, the exhibit seemed to thrive upon a careful play of differences, but in actuality it split the very heart of Europe. The influx of illegal migrants from Africa and the Middle East to which Lemos was creatively alluding tested the core of European unification as a radically democratic opening of boundaries. On the continent where modern democracy had rediscovered its ancient dream, the tragedy that occurred in international waters under police surveillance, in darkness, away from public eye contradicted the inviolable dignity of personhood guaranteed by the European Convention for the Protection of Human Rights and Fundamental Freedoms and reaffirmed by the Maastricht Treaty. In inviting visitors to walk through an imaginary scene of such contradiction, Lemos's installation highlighted the obscure crisis in European citizenship.

Navigating in the Dark raises critical questions about common and divergent points of departure for interrogating the limits of common humanity in the twenty-first century. Instead of conceptualizing human rights as divisible subjects of investigation, it begs for answers that come from multiple disciplinary, historical, and geopolitical perspectives. What does it mean to empathize, if not to identify, with others who have succumbed to dark odysseys under nationally circumscribed police surveillance? How do the arts and letters engender public spheres where their suffering might properly be registered or where spectators can possibly engage in a productive conversation about migration, integration, and citizenship? What age-old myths of humankind exist to contest the abuse of social outcasts in global modernity? If human rights are considered inviolable norms of justice at international scales, why is it that the number of their violations within national boundaries has steadily increased in modern history? As Emilie Hafner-Burton documents, the number of human rights abuses, including torture, murder, political imprisonment, censorship, and political rights has grown since 1918 and this record is even specific to countries that have ratified the International Covenant on Civil and Political Rights (2013, p. 3). And beyond the geopolitical scope of Europe, where do private citizens and singular communities stand in relation to the utopias of common humanity? While Lemos has drawn upon her artistic creativity to query these and other inhuman features of modern society, scholars of human rights are called to address them from rigorously interdisciplinary perspectives.

Imagining Human Rights is an interdisciplinary volume, which originates in the increasingly urgent desire to address international human rights and violations thereof in the intersection of the humanities and the social sciences. The essays collected here show from a variety of disciplinary perspectives and within different historical contexts how critical it is to engage in interdisciplinary conversations about the origin and language of human rights, personal dignity, redistributive justice, and international solidarity. Together, they show why a close examination of human rights does not do without a genuine attempt to partake in cultural, historical, philosophical, psychological, and sociological deliberations at once.

The volume consists of one conversation and eleven essays. These contributions to the diverse and rapidly expanding field of human rights examine a wide range of pertinent issues, including the validity of normative grounds for human rights claims, the inadequacy of human psychology for responding to mass violence, the genealogy of human rights in global history, and the efficacy of humanitarian aid in the so-called developing world. They are written in various combinations of philosophical deliberation, historical examination, and psychological, legal or aesthetic analysis, and they illustrate how the currency of human rights is not to be confused with some sort of self-evidence or straightforwardness. *Imagining Human Rights* is the first collection of essays that ambitiously responds to this precarious nature of human rights.

All but two of the essays were presented in shorter versions at the interdisciplinary conference "The Imagination of Human Rights" in the city of Bielefeld on June 28–30, 2013. Co-sponsored by the German Research Foundation (*Deutsche Forschungsgesellschaft*) and the Center for Interdisciplinary Research (*Zentrum für Interdisziplinäre Forschung*) at Bielefeld University, the gathering offered a unique occasion for bringing together a transatlantic group of experts on human rights under the provocative heading of imagination. In recognition of the fact that human rights is a subject of investigation cutting through aesthetic, ethical, historical, sociopolitical, philosophical, legal, and psychological considerations, the conference sought to facilitate a much needed dialogue across disciplinary boundaries, a dialogue that had rarely been pursued to the same extent at one place. Represented in this initial working group were psychological, literary, filmic, historical, juridical, philosophical, and sociological studies of human rights.

The title of this volume deliberately links with Lynn Hunt's seminal historiography, namely *Inventing Human Rights* (2007). Hunt argues in her award-winning book that the idea of human rights originates in eighteenth-century France where Enlightenment writers such as Rousseau and Richardson appeal to affective identifications between reader and character "across class, sex, and national lines"

(Hunt 2007, p. 38). Hunt asserts that their epistolary novels mobilize empathy for public good, as fictional characters appeal to readers' imagination to make sense of passionate claims to personal dignity. In Pamela, for instance, a servant girl becomes a model of personal autonomy because she expresses inner feelings in personal letters. Thus, Hunt concludes, readers learn to register the suffering of others in literary imagination. She goes on to say how intensely Rousseau's and Richardson's contemporaries – men and women alike – reacted to the novels, and that even military officers identified with the fictional heroines (Hunt 2007, p. 47).

The essays collected in this volume complicate Hunt's argument by clarifying further how critical the concept of imagination is for thinking through the problem of human rights across disciplinary boundaries and by elaborating on the heterogeneity of human rights talk in modern history. It is true that affective labor and literary imagination are pivotal for current debates on this vast topic, but the volume seeks to offer nuanced and contentious analyses of human rights, as well as the kinds of conceptual, imaginative, and practical solutions they solicit to intolerable cruelties. By discussing global hunger, posttraumatic reconciliation, the resettlement of refugees, psychic numbing, and international solidarity, the contributors set the stage for an intellectual encounter that exposes the strikingly complex problem of human rights in the twenty-first century.

The volume begins with a special conversation between sociologist and philosopher Hans Joas and historian and legal scholar Samuel Moyn because their different accounts of human rights in modern history exemplify the best of interdisciplinary analyses on this contentious topic. In *The Sacredness of the Person*, Joas contends that Émile Durkheim's notion of the sacredness of the person, along with Talcott Parson's conception of value generalization, offers an informative way of synthesizing the history of human rights beginning with the abolition of torture in the eighteenth century and culminating in the Universal Declaration of Human Rights of 1948. While dispelling certain myths of the genesis of the Universal Declaration of Human Rights after World War II, Joas documents a wide range of cultural traditions, ethical commitments, and political negotiations in drafting that symbolic foundation. By contrast, Moyn emphasizes how the long history of human rights is inscribed in far more contingent and conflicting terms. For him, this universal moral precept does not acquire its international dimension until the 1970s following decolonization. Both in *The Last Utopia* and in this debate, Moyn does not go so far as to deny the importance of human rights movements prior to this turning point, but he uncovers for modern consciousness the fragility of human rights especially in the Western welfare state. The conversation between these scholars goes through fascinating twists and turns in intellectual history, legal thought, and philosophical analysis and we hope that its transcription serves as an enriching complement to reading *The Sacredness of the Person* and *The Last Utopia* side by side.

Titled "Claiming Human Rights," *Section One* investigates whether human rights can be considered universal concepts, and if so, what moral and legal claims they make, what origins they have, what justifications they invoke, and what political and psychological conditions they require for realization. The methodological approach of this section concerns the normative dimension of human rights imagination, as well as the historicity of human rights activism. The *Section Two* is titled "Human Rights in Imagination" and it focuses on aesthetic questions and the function of imagination in human rights discourse. It explores how the arts and letters, including new media, engage with human rights, and how fiction generates empathy for those in suffering.

In Chapter One, philosopher Thomas Pogge defines the concept and the main function of human rights in modern society. For him, governments must protect the rights of citizens and respect the rights of those with whom they interact. Under such conditions, human rights claims help authorize international organizations when they intervene in governments that fail to meet their responsibilities. However, Pogge observes that the prospect of realizing human rights looks rather bleak. Therefore, he suggests that we conceive of human rights less as a matter of moral imagination and more as a practical tool for preserving basic freedom, and that we assign human rights central roles in intergovernmental negotiations through which supranational institutional arrangements are designed. Pogge illustrates how human rights might realistically be fulfilled in two examples: one in the field of pharmaceutical provision (medical access for the poor), the other in regard to investment capital and tax revenues (financial transparency in the international tax system). While contesting national nepotism, Pogge proposes a global impartiality requirement confined to human rights as a step toward the higher ideal of *cosmopolis*.

In Chapter Two, psychologists Paul Slovic and Daniel Västfjäll examine the assumption that people can imagine the statistics of human rights violations and act on this basis. In their behavioral research, they argue that numbers fail to trigger the compassion that is required for motivating action, and that for this reason people and governments repeatedly ignore mass murder. Slovic and Västfjäll explain this insensitivity to lifesaving and the corresponding disability to respond adequately to mass murder as a failure of imagination. They contend that people fail to make sense of the loss of life as the number increases and that human beings are unable to rely upon moral feelings in order to engender proper action; instead, they need to ensure that reason and analysis are equally employed. It is on this rational basis that human beings must cultivate moral intuition and design new legal and institutional mechanisms for enforcing an effective response to genocide and mass atrocity.

While most scholars consider the validity of human rights to be a matter of fact and they think about ways of avoiding human rights violations, philosopher Rüdiger Bittner in Chapter Three revisits questions of epistemic status and political stake in human rights imagination. He interrogates the "self-evidence" of human rights that Thomas Jefferson and his fellow campaigners have proclaimed since the eighteenth century. He sees in the history of human rights (including the ideas of natural law and natural right) a history of errors and he claims that it is not justified to grant people rights just because of their humanness or reasonability. Moreover, he contests the idea that human rights are part of the social imaginary or that they exist at all. From his perspective, only people imagine, but a society at large does not. Thus, human rights are not even real in shared imagination. Since there are no persuasive arguments for the existence of human rights, the question arises what good human rights talk is. Bittner's answer to this question is that it is no good because it directs attention only to people's suffering, and not to the process that brings about this pain. It fails to engender activism in an effort to change this process.

In Chapter Four, David Kim concentrates on Foucault's notion of "international citizenship" to examine what it means to hold governments accountable for human rights violations. According to Foucault, Kim explains, standing together in solidarity and naming and shaming the responsible – and this is what the concept of *parrhesia*, or telling the truth, entails – is not only a moral duty but also a universal right since governments use physical force to monopolize power. Kim pursues the question of telling the truth or speaking truth to power in relation to transformative politics. In doing so, he compares Foucault's critical return to *parrhesia* to Kant's notion of *Aufklärung*, or Enlightenment.

The following two contributions are case studies of human rights violations and they pay special attention to issues regarding humanitarian aid and political intervention. In Chapter Five, Lora Wildenthal examines the first decade of the Society for Threatened Peoples (*Gesellschaft für bedrohte Völker*) to show how its re-imagining of human rights was innovative in the context of 1970s West German human rights activism. As the Society broadened its engagement from Biafra to other causes, it emphasized genocide and group rights. Controversially, it placed German victims of human rights violations (notably ethnic German expellees) in the same group rights framework as the many non-German groups with which it worked. This sparked confrontations with the West German Left, which the Society countered with emphasis on the concept and reality of genocide in state socialist as well as capitalist states. Wildenthal concludes that the organization successfully imagined threatened peoples by establishing new criteria for human rights violations and by transforming the human rights scene for West Germans in West and unified Germany.

Chapter Six is Nina Berman's investigation of humanitarian work in contemporary Kenya. Berman highlights the ways in which "contraband charity" – that is, humanitarian activity outside of official channels – carries contemporary global inequality caused by a humanitarian mindset rooted in missionary activities of the colonial era. Using the example of the Diani area, Berman explains that developments associated with beach tourism and the real estate market have transformed a largely self-sustaining community into an overwhelmingly impoverished population. While Germans have played a crucial role in this development, many humanitarians do not understand the reasons for the poverty they encounter. Berman's discussion sheds light on the intricate interplay between economic globalization and neoliberal charity.

Chapter Seven marks the beginning of *Section Two* where the focus lies on image and imagination and their role in contemporary discussion of humanitarian aid and crisis. Here, Sebastian Wogenstein shows how theater raises questions about the idea of human rights including its institutional framework, and how it reveals the realities of power that are all-too-often eclipsed by institution-focused human rights discourse. His literary examples revolve around the French Revolution. Following Jacques Rancière, Wogenstein describes the way in which plays speak to us as "dissensus." It questions fundamental common-sensical assumptions and highlights a qualitative function of theater that differs from what Richard Rorty and Lynn Hunt propose about literature and its ability to produce empathy in the reader.

In Chapter Eight, Oliver Kohns investigates the imaginary status of human rights and the role of fiction in the enforcement of human rights via an interpretation of Franz Werfel's novel *The Forty Days of Musa Dagh* (1933). The 1789 Declaration of the Rights of Man and of the Citizen establishes a normative political fiction in stating that men are born free and equal in rights. Human rights become a utopian program here and it depends on the possession of citizenship. Again following Rancière, Kohns investigates the imagination of human rights as an aesthetic issue in political discourse. On this basis, he analyzes the relationship between human rights and the narrative genre of the *Bildungsroman* and he applies this relationship to Franz Werfel's novel as a political intervention in human rights violation.

In Chapter Nine, philosopher Michael Bösch and literary scholar Susanne Kaul examine the ways in which human rights are "staged" by the Truth and Reconciliation Commission in South Africa, and how this staging in commemorative juridical culture is represented in Gillian Slovo's novel *Red Dust* (2000) and its filmic adaptation by the same title in 2004, and in Antjie Krog's book *Country of*

My Skull (1998) and John Boorman's adaptation thereof in 2004. The thesis of this contribution is that the effectivity of the commission's work was limited partly because apartheid was declared a taboo issue, and partly because the hearings were sometimes misused as a mere instrument of amnesty without repentance or reconciliation. According to Bösch and Kaul, the power of fiction especially in film is to engender empathy and to make a large audience familiar with what is at stake.

Elizabeth Anker's essay in Chapter Eleven addresses two crucial challenges that have accompanied the achievements of human rights: first, the exclusion of citizenship, meaning that refugees and unauthorized migrants lack protection of a sovereign state; second, the aim of human rights to safeguard the human body from injury, which implies a relegation to the state of dehumanization. In her reading of Alejandro González Iñárritu's 2010 film *Biutiful*, Anker contends that the film's subject matter, as well as its aesthetics, enact an embodied human rights imaginary especially in reference to the large number of dead and dying bodies, which helps to maintain a highly specific appreciation for human rights. Anker draws upon Merleau-Ponty's phenomenologic reflections about embodiment to substantiate a critical mindset for fighting human rights violations and their corresponding theoretical assumptions.

The last chapter of this volume offers Artemis Manolopoulou's in-depth knowledge of Greek sculptor and installation artist Kalliopi Lemos. It traces her personal trajectory on the basis of political work and self-understanding as an international migrant. Manolopoulou recapitulates Lemos's presentation in Bielefeld about issues concerning physical and psychological displacement and the mistreatment of human dignity and she gives vivid examples of the ways in which art awakens a common feeling of humanity or inspires people to imagine a better world.

Bibliography

Agamben, Giorgio (1998): *Homo Sacer: Sovereign Power and Bare Life*. Translated by Daniel Heller-Roazen. Stanford: Stanford University Press.

Balibar, Étienne (2004): *We, the People of Europe? Reflections on Transnational Citizenship*. Translated by James Swenson. Princeton: Princeton University Press.

Hafter-Burton, Emilie (2013): *Making Human Rights a Reality*. Princeton: Princeton University Press.

Hunt, Lynn (2007): *Inventing Human Rights: A History*. New York: W.W. Norton.

Joas, Hans (2013): *The Sacredness of the Person: A New Genealogy of Human Rights*. Translated by Alex Skinner. Washington: Georgetown University Press.

Moyn, Samuel (2010): *The Last Utopia: Human Rights in History*. Cambridge: The Belknap Press.

Hans Joas and Samuel Moyn

The Sacredness of the Person or *The Last Utopia*: A Conversation about the History of Human Rights[1]

This chapter is a slightly revised transcript of the conversation between Hans Joas and Samuel Moyn at the University of Bielefeld on June 28, 2013. The public event was moderated by David Kim.

DK: We have invited Hans and Sam to engage with the audience in an interdisciplinary dialogue about the genealogy of human rights. This event is a valuable extension of our three-day-long conference because it exemplifies the best of interdisciplinary approaches to the history of human rights today.[2] In *The Sacredness of the Person*, which has recently appeared in English translation with Georgetown University Press, Hans crisscrosses between sociology, religion, history, and philosophy.[3] In *The Last Utopia*, Sam guides his readers through history, law, and political science.[4] My own training is in cultural and literary studies, so I hope that this conversation will shake things up in exciting ways.

To warm us up for the discussion, I have asked Hans and Sam to begin by saying a few words about their books. The questions that I have shared with them in advance include the following: what were their points of entry into the history of human rights? How did their work evolve in the course of reading and writing? And what was the crux of their main argument? Afterward, I would like to raise a set of questions and ask others to join me as well. So without further ado, Sam, please begin.

SM: It is a great privilege to be here. I have heard the term "debate" used in the last few hours to refer to this event, but I want to make clear at the start that I am

---

1 The editors would like to thank Mark Phillips and Adam Orange, Ph.D. students in German Studies at Michigan State University, for their assistance with transcribing the recorded event.

2 Co-sponsored by the Center for Interdisciplinary Research (*Zentrum für Interdisziplinäre Forschung*) at Bielefeld University and the German Research Foundation (*Deutsche Forschungsgemeinschaft*), the conference involved scholars of human rights from the social sciences and the humanities and it took place at Bielefeld University on June 28–30, 2013.

3 Hans Joas, *The Sacredness of the Person: A New Genealogy of Human Rights*. Washington, DC: Georgetown University Press, 2013.

4 Samuel Moyn, *The Last Utopia: Human Rights in History*. Cambridge, MA: Belknap Press, 2010.

not approaching it at all in that way. For one thing, I would lose. But the main reason is that I found Hans's book quite educational and stimulating. I have little in it with which I disagree, although perhaps a few points of distinction to draw out. I actually think that the books are about somewhat different topics, so what I thought I would do instead of giving you a genealogy of my book was to say a few words about some big differences between these two accounts of where human rights came from. I want to start by saying that Hans and I begin with a very similar fundamental premise, and that is: a historical understanding needs to incorporate an intellectual history of concepts and norms, but must go far further. Where we diverge is where we go, what we are trying to explain when we say we are trying to think historically about human rights, and then how we explain it. That said, I would maintain that our arguments are generally compatible.

My main premise in *The Last Utopia* is that we need a history that's oriented not simply to the normative substance of human rights, but also to two other major factors. The first one I'll call *cultural salience* and the second I'll call *political scale*.[5]

One of my main concerns in the book is to consider and even to measure how present or salient the idea of human rights was in philosophy or politics or the public sphere from time to time and from place to place. And I think it's at this point that a big difference between us enters. Generally, Hans thinks that once there's a politically important text on the table like the French Declaration of the Rights of Man and Citizen of 1789 or the Universal Declaration of Human Rights of 1948, there cannot be any doubt that human rights are already culturally central. Then he takes up the task of explaining this centrality: "How did this centrality come about?" By contrast, I doubt that a text is enough. I agree that we must move from norm to text, but human rights are about much more than just the text in which norms are announced and the political processes that lead to those text. I won't say much about the French Revolution unless we come back to it, but my main starting point in thinking about this topic is the following observation: the Universal Declaration of Human Rights seems to have been by and large ignored in its own time, whereas it's now central to our moral consciousness. For that reason, when it comes to historicizing this salience or centrality of human rights today, I don't think we can stop with the text of the Universal Declaration precisely because it seems to have stimulated little – whether philosophically or mobilizationally – in its time. This explains why our books are so different in their chronological coverage. Hans doesn't go beyond 1948, whereas I think almost

---

5 For more on these terms, see Samuel Moyn, "Substance, Scale, and Salience: The Recent Historiography of Human Rights." *Annual Review of Law and Social Science* 8 (2012): 123–140.

everything of interest happens after that date, although a lot might depend on how much is in the word "almost." In case you haven't read it, which I assume is almost universal here, my book emphasizes the later Cold War origins of the salience or prominence of human rights in culture.

My case is also furthered by my concern for thinking about political scale. The second fundamental premise in the book is that if we haven't described and explained *international* human rights politics as opposed to domestic citizenship politics, then in my view we haven't begun to think about what human rights mean to us now. And, among other things, I think this internationalization – or scalar leap of rights from domestic spaces to the globe – is one of the central distinguishing features of human rights, as we understand them now. And if we haven't historicized this scalar leap, then we will have omitted something quite significant.

Much of my book is about that problem. It involves a contrast between rights and domestic citizenship contexts, and rights in the form of international human rights politics. And it's in part for that reason that I emphasize the global South so heavily in my book. Again, this material is largely absent from Hans's book – up until the presence of a few actors in 1948 who are involved in formulating the Universal Declaration. In my view, however, the Universal Declaration of Human Rights was still compatible with an imperial world and most of its framers understood it in that way. The major anticolonial and decolonizing movements of history after World War II seemed to be very different in their aspirations, their stated norms, and their mobilizational strategies than international human rights movements today. Understanding the intervening forms of anticolonialism as predecessors to contemporary human rights seems to me utterly central – not least since human rights are primarily today a project directed towards the suffering in the formerly colonized world. If we haven't understood how they've become that postimperial project, then we won't have understood much about human rights.

Lastly, I'm very concerned – I think in contrast to Hans again since I'm not mentioning all the things we share – by economic context. Or to put it differently, I'm very interested in the relationship between what I'll call welfarism and rights. In my approach, the Universal Declaration of Human Rights in the 1940s is primarily offering one idiom for national welfarism, as I call it. In my understanding, this was the victorious ideology of World War II. It encapsulated ideologically how states should govern themselves and what sort of citizenship they should offer their citizens. And that's why, given the priority of welfarism, economic and social rights were so consensually central to human rights ideas in the 1940s.

But if that's true, I see something disturbing about our world. The era of international human rights politics – the age of that scalar leap I talked about – seems to be not a welfarist age anymore. Indeed, it seems to be one in which human rights are prominent, but we've headed, unlike after the 1940s, into a world that has some of the greatest inequalities both within and among nations that the globe has ever seen. I think the history of human rights should put this disturbing fact center stage. What, I wonder, is the relationship between the rise of international human rights and the collapse of domestic welfarism ideologically? These two developments have the same chronology and the question is whether they're related in deep ways and are not just companions across the same timeline.

So finally, for all those reasons, I don't see human rights history either as a triumphalist celebration – and Hans doesn't either, I know; nor do I develop anything like what he very interestingly calls *affirmative genealogy*. Now I want to make clear that it wasn't my goal to be destructively genealogical in writing the book and I differ there with some of my Marxist friends. I think human rights remain really the sole uplifting political idiom that we have left in a very dreary world, after the crisis of many other idioms we preferred first in the West and around the world. Human rights are remainders from the history of idealism, even if we decide that we need to transform it now. And that means that the point of the history of human rights should be in part to emphasize their disturbing features and abject failures so far, so that we can face the future as clearly as possible.

DK: Thank you, Sam. Hans?

HJ: I have a double task now, I think. First, I would like to respond to the questions David posed to us, and then I will briefly comment on the similarities and dissimilarities between the two books, as I see them. So, first, on what David has asked us to answer: "What was the point of entry into your study on the history of human rights?" I said in the preface to my book – quite clearly, I think – that the idea emerged from two earlier books, namely one that is called *The Genesis of Values* where I've developed – whether it is convincing or not I have to leave it to my readers – a kind of theory that is intended to explain how we develop our value commitments, in what experiential contexts we experience something as self-evidently good or evil. And in another book, which is called in its English translation *War and Modernity*, I explain the experience of violence, the long-term consequences of the experience of violence, and the problems of the articulation and interpretation of the experience of violence.[6] At a certain point, I had

---

6 Hans Joas, *The Genesis of Values*. Chicago: University of Chicago Press 2000; Hans Joas, *War and Modernity*, trans. Rodney Livingstone. Cambridge: Polity, 2003.

the idea of bringing these two projects together. If I don't bring them together, the processes of the emergence of value commitments always sound as if they were exclusively based in what I call "enthusiastic experiences," which people consider to be totally positive. So I'm interested in the interplay between such enthusiastic, positive experiences and the experience of violence – be it on the side of the perpetrator or on the side of the victim.

Now I think logically, in a certain sense, that I had two options in this situation: first, one could examine the influence of the experience of violence on people's value commitments – for example, within the context of Fascism and Nazism, how people generalize their experience of violence into a worldview that the only thing that counts is to be strong – struggle for survival, so to speak; second, one could study the history of violence in light of the possibilities that are available to find a way out of the spiraling escalation of violence, to produce some sort of positive experience in the midst of these horrifying experiences of violence. That led to my interest in the interplay between the history of violence in the 19th and 20th centuries and the history of human rights as one such potential way out.

Now I use, as a shorthand formula for my particular description of the history of human rights, the term "sacralization of the person." I say *person*, and not individual, to avoid a certain misunderstanding. For the sacralization of the individual can easily sound like the self-sacralization of the individual and that is an important topic in contemporary sociology of religion. People say: "The only thing that is sacred to me is 'I,' myself." And that's clearly not what I mean. So I chose the notion of *person* that also plays an important role in the philosophy of Max Scheler, Emmanuel Mounier, and others. Sacralization and sacredness: I use these terms in a value-neutral sense, as scholars such as Émile Durkheim, Marcel Mauss, Nathan Söderblom and Rudolf Otto have done since 1900. I emphasize this point because there is a constant suspicion that talking about sacredness means somehow smuggling into the picture some religion, some religious faith. That's not what I mean. That's at least a totally different question. How religious one has to be, that for me is a totally different discourse. What I mean here is – maybe we just bracket the term "sacredness" for a moment –, but what I'm aiming at is the history of human rights not as a legal history mostly, nor as a history of ideas mostly, although of course it is also a history of ideas and a legal history, but as a history of profound cultural transformation. I say a profound cultural transformation in three dimensions: in regard to values, and that of course also implies intellectual discourse: what is good, what can be defended as good, and so on; in regard to practices, when practices may change without much intellectual discourse, people just become more sensitive to something, they are more easily motivated by something than they are in another phase of history; and of course in regards to institutions, and among institutions, legal institutions are perhaps the most important ones.

But my whole approach is "experientialist," not "culturalist," and I put an enormous emphasis on the dynamics of experience, and on the dynamics of the articulation of experience. For me, this notion of sacredness and sacralization is very handy because I am interested in experiences that have two features, to use a more analytic language. They must be affectively intense. It's not just "I have an opinion, ok?" and you say "No, I have a different opinion." They are affectively intense. There is an element – on the phenomenological level of the experience – of what I call "subjective self-evidence." That means: I *personally* have the feeling that I have recognized something as good or evil and I *personally* don't have the feeling that I need any argumentation to prove that that feeling is justified. I emphasize *personally* because I'm not irrational to say: "We don't need argumentation. It's just a gut feeling or something like that." No, I want to do justice to the empirical fact – and I think it is an empirical fact – that even in processes of argumentation we are mostly guided by pre-theoretical, pre-argumentative experiences of self-evidence, and that we have to grasp this element of the phenomenology of the emergence of value commitments. Now I did that in the book very selectively only in regard to four historical cases: the emergence of the main declarations of the late eighteenth century and the emergence of the 1948 Declaration as two specific events; and as two drawn-out processes the abolition of torture in Europe during the 18th century and the abolition of slavery mostly in the United States during the 19th century.

Here, a first brief response to David's questions: I see my own book as being totally selective – thus, not as an exhaustive study of the history of human rights. When I end in the year 1948, I do not make the claim that the history of human rights should end in that year. And I do not study the consequences of these codifications, as you have said – and you are right, I fully agree with you –, but somebody should study the consequences of the codification. So I have nothing against that, but one can ask the question: "How did that codification come up?" I mean that this is part of a larger question. Another element I should emphasize here is: it is selective even in the sense that I do not say these four narratives or these four stories form one grand narrative of the history of the sacralization of the person. No, these are four stories. There is no master process of sacralization of the person. There are other processes, other sacralizations, of the nation, etc.

Now on David's second question: I think it was relatively easy for me to do research on and write the first three chapters and the last one on the drafting of the 1948 Declaration. These are the sociohistorical chapters. Chapters Four and Five were much more difficult. And I think it makes sense to highlight these two chapters very briefly. The most misunderstood one is Chapter Five. I deny in the first three chapters that we can derive human rights from Christian roots. But I'm also writing as a Christian, so in the historical-sociological parts, I would say, I have to ask myself the question: "Is there any evidence for the Christian roots?" My answer to that is: "There is no such root." So I go on to say: when an interesting cultural innovation like the idea of the sacredness of the person comes up, all religious traditions, all secular-intellectual or political traditions, including the Christian one, somehow have to define their relationship to this cultural innovation. Hence, I try to describe that at a certain point those Christians who did not position themselves in opposition to human rights started to look for elements in the Christian tradition, elements that allowed them to say: "This is what we have always already wanted to say, but we were just not able to articulate it well enough." And what they discovered are the two elements of the Christian, and partly also of the Jewish, tradition: first, human beings are created in the image of God; and second, we are the children of God. These are the two basic elements.

Now I know that some people – I know that from reviews – read Chapter Five as a place where I am being totally self-contradictory. They believe that in the first three chapters I deny any Christian roots and in Chapter Five I somehow smuggle the Christian roots back in. No! I'm just being honest. As a Christian and as a historical sociologist, I say what I think about the history of human rights. That is, from the perspective of historical sociology *and* from my Christian convictions. And if I were a Muslim author, I would say that somebody would have to write Chapter Five in such a way that this idea related to the Muslim tradition. And if you are a secularist, you have to do exactly the same and explain how this idea is connected to your utilitarianism, Kantianism, existentialism or whatever your philosophical conviction is.

Now this is getting too long, so maybe I don't say anything about Chapter Four in which the idea of "affirmative genealogy" appears. But let me make one short remark. I called it neither Kant nor Nietzsche, and a very benevolent person told me: "You should have said Kant *plus* Nietzsche." For what happened was I alienated all the Kantians and all the Nietzscheans simultaneously. But if I had said "Kant *plus* Nietzsche," both the Kantians and Nietzscheans would have loved me. So that was clearly a mistake.

Now let me turn to the discussion with Sam. I agree with Sam that there are many similarities. I would emphasize as the main similarity that we both emphasize contingencies, that we are both skeptical of teleological historiography. I would like to take issue with your usage of the term "church history," though. I think this is unfair to contemporary church historians. They are very serious scholars. They do not write the history of the church in a simplistic, hagiographical sense, as you seem to assume. But I also agree with you that in a certain sense there is no controversy. We have written two books about two different topics.

Now the controversy possibly arises because you do not simply make the claim that you are writing a book about the history of human rights after 1970, but you emphasize very strongly the discontinuity in the history of human rights.

Instead of arguing about all sorts of historical detail, I would like to make a more constructive proposal and maybe you can respond to it at some point. I personally think that there are three breakthroughs in the global history of human rights and one can clearly distinguish the three from each other. But a complete history, so to speak, has to do justice to all three of them. So the first I would say is – in my language – the emergence of moral universalism in the Axial Age. There is a point in history when religious and philosophical ideas came up, that what defines the good is not what is good for us in the sense of a somehow limited community – tribe, state, family, religious community –, but for all human beings, maybe even including all future human beings. I follow Karl Jaspers and a few of you might know that I've just published a book in the US with Robert Bellah on the Axial Age.[7] This is more global than just speaking about Greek philosophy and Hebrew prophets, for example, although they clearly belong to that story. So, from the Axial Age onward, from 600 before Christ and onward, we have in different civilizations, religions, and philosophies the articulation of basic ideas of moral universalism. Their emergence is connected to the problems of the archaic state. I don't have the time to explain what I mean, but I have to mention that because I think all these phases are somehow connected to phases of the history of state formation.

The second breakthrough is connected to the history of the early modern and absolutist state and leads from the moral philosophies and religious articulations of universalism to state-based codifications and that happened in the 18th century. You are totally right to say, of course, when you emphasize in your book that it's always on the level of the state: Yes! But it was an attempt to codify and to institutionalize certain ideas that had been around since the Axial Age. And what happened after the Second World War in the 1948 Declaration, but with much more force later is an institutionalization that is not restricted to the nation-state, but the attempt to develop international mechanisms that oblige the individual states. That was a reaction, first, to the totalitarian state and, then, to the colonial state. So in that sense what I have done in this particular book is mostly about phase two, and what you have done in your book is mostly about phase three. And I think that I have done in other publications, and will do in other publications, something on phase one. The real history would have to bring

---

7 Robert N. Bellah and Hans Joas, eds. *The Axial Age and Its Consequences*. Cambridge: Belknap Press, 2012.

the three things together. How do actors in the second phase relate to the ideas of the first phase? Do they see themselves in continuity with the axial religious innovations or do they position themselves against – but in the sense of we are more axial than – the axial innovations. And the same is true for the third phase: how exactly do we describe the institutionalizations in-between? What is the relevance of natural law doctrines for medieval law and so on? But there could be an integration of the different perspectives and you have been very polemically attacked because of your exclusive emphasis on the third phase. Now in my picture I have been similarly polemically attacked because of my main emphasis on the second phase. People say: it's just ridiculous to deny that there were ideas of universalism around Plato or Jesus Christ, as if I had ever had any motivation to deny that. Okay, I think I will leave it there.

DK: Thank you so much for the wonderful outlining of your arguments and for the resonances and disagreements. Sam, would you like to respond to Hans's remarks?

SM: I would like to respond to Hans's opening statement.

DK: Yes, please go ahead.

SM: Most of what you say sounds sensible to me. I'll just make two broad points – sticking again with where I disagree against the background of general agreement. One is about the background of the experience of violence, which is emphasized in a chapter of Hans's book.

In contrast to Hans, I think that appealing to violence as a predicate for values is an incredibly weak explanation of them – on the grounds that it seems to be behind a huge profusion of possible value commitments. To make this point, we can stop the clock in the 1940s and ask: "What was the normative response to World War II and the violence that it unleashed?" After all, most people found both horrendous, although they were not yet concerned with the Holocaust in particular. If you'd like to take this point about the Holocaust up, I'd be happy to do so. One response was realism about power politics. The United Nations was not founded on principles of justice, but the states came together, with the Allies leading them, and founded what was a great power organization. Some, at the time, felt it was a reversion to the Concert of Europe after Napoleon. It's true that human rights were mentioned in the UN Charter, but the declared goal of the organization to this day is peace rather than justice. So that was one response to the violence. And it's only in our day that the charter is being reread to incorporate concerns for justice and episodes like the invention of the responsibility to protect.

More broadly, I think the main normative response to World War II was the huge ascendancy of nationalism, which, indeed, the postwar peace ended up promoting as the globally normative political form that it had never been before. If we take the European continent even in the east where many Jews lived, anti-fascism was an exceptionally powerful response ideologically to World War II, and maybe the most directly internationalist response to the Holocaust at least for a few years. Just on the basis of these examples, it seems as if, whether at that moment or frankly at any point in history, violence underdetermines any possible value response; it doesn't necessitate a commitment to human rights, let alone international human rights.

I broadly agree, in part for that reason, with Hans's notion of a human rights history that has many phases and integrates continuity and discontinuity. I didn't have a chance to respond to David's initial questions, but I was reacting polemically to a historiography that emphasized the age-old continuous evolution of human rights and I wanted to show that a powerful case could be made to the contrary, but in the end I take it as obvious that, for example, when we come to the idea of a formal individual right or the content of some human rights we have today, we are dealing with very old items in the Western repertory. Nothing in our time would have happened without the Universal Declaration of Human Rights, even if it was re-appropriated later in very unexpected ways. I think my point was primarily that the continuities that are there are obvious and boring and the discontinuities are interesting and compelling.

I think I would disagree about some of the specifics of Hans's presentation – of the stages that he lays out. It's very controversial, for example, to claim that before the Axial Age there were just parochial moral cultures mired in tribe and family. Students of the human-animal border, just to take a very interesting case, insist that the implicit idea of humanity as a species-concept must be far older than the Axial Age. More importantly, the idea of the formal unity of the human type, like the moral significance of membership, seems to be a gateway to a huge profusion and controversy amongst various universalisms that would follow. It's a gateway to Christianity and all the other universalistic religions. Indeed, I understand history as late as the Cold War as a contest of moral universalisms. It's not as if moral universalism, like violence I discussed before, does anything more than establish a massive, open field for the contestation of different visions. Accordingly, my own argument is that many of these had to collapse in their appeal before human rights became the straightforward or intuitive form of cosmopolitanism.

When we come to the early-modern state, I would go a bit further than saying that the formulation of universalistic rights norms occurred because of various reasons at the state level. Rather, my deeper point, at least as I understood it, is that rights are connected to the erection of sovereignty, including borders. What were the Americans and Frenchmen trying to do when they announced human rights in 1776 and 1789? They were trying to gain sovereignty – to erect it on the ruins of empire and absolute monarchy through the tools of violence – and that just seems utterly different than what human rights mean today. Now they're about the qualification of sovereignty or the subjection of sovereignty or subordination to global legal and other technologies.

1948, I think, is clearly an important moment. Yet I myself would want to tell, as I indicated in my opening remarks, a more melancholy story, in which in 1948 the world had a brief moment of consensus around national welfarism. The colonial world wanted it, too, and that was why decolonization happened. Our time, in stark contrast, is the time of the collapse of national welfarism and it seems to me that international human rights could be more a symptom of this loss, rather than a grand breakthrough. But I recognize this is a very controversial argument to make.

DK: If I may interject for a brief moment – and I will let you respond to Sam's note in a brief moment. I would like to ask you to consider the following, as you respond to Sam's note, and that is: I would like you to theorize – and I think cultural studies scholars would be very interested in that – how you envision the process of sacralization and then that of utopianization. I think that might help us look beyond the disagreements. Because in your book, you say that you take much more seriously into consideration the concept of inclusion in a Foucauldian sense to think about, let's say, the process of cultural transformation, such that it's almost like a Hegelian *Aufhebung*, where you do take some vital concepts of the Axial Age, but you don't take them as such; instead, you transform them – you leave off some parts and you include new meanings – and they undergo some kind of universalization in very affective ways, in very experiential ways. If that is true – if that describes on a theoretical level the process of sacralization – I would like Sam to tell us: at what point do you say utopianism has happened? What describes the past utopia? What describes the present utopia? How do those transitions happen?

HJ: First, just as a clarification. I did not say that the experience of violence leads to a commitment to universalist values. On the contrary, I said that normally it leads to revenge or to the formation of a worldview in which revenge is justified, or maybe to power political realism, but retrospectively we can select those historical cases in which this did not happen, but people derived from an experience of violence the conviction that there must be a way out, as I have said before, of the spiraling escalation of violence. And then it is justified, I would say, in an affirmative genealogy to study those cases and it's not an objection to this study to say: These are rare cases – yes! That is exactly the reason why I'm interested in them! Not because I think they are representative in any quantitative sense. Nazism – you know what I am saying, but you didn't do full justice to the following distinction in your book – the importance of Nazism for the discussions of 1945 and the importance of the Holocaust. And I agree with you that the Holocaust was not crucial, but I think people like Johannes Morsink and others have convincingly shown that Nazism in the sense of some tyranny that is aggressive, enslaves other peoples and so on, was crucial for the debates. So it's remarkable that the relative neglect of the Holocaust was not just a phenomenon of this committee. It was a much wider phenomenon. Third, I agree with you – and that was Karl Jaspers's point when he developed his idea of the Axial Age or when he invented the term – that we live with a plurality of universalisms, that all the attempts of, let's say, Christians or Enlightenment rationalists who say "I am the universalist, the others are not universalists" are wrong. There are Buddhist universalists. This, again, does not mean everyone is a universalist. What I'm saying is: what we need politically is a coalition of all universalists, be they Christian, Buddhist, Jewish, secular, this or that. Against all non-universalists, be they Christian, Buddhist, as in Myanmar, or secular. So we live with a plurality of universalisms.

Now I disagree with what you say about collapse. If you include in your argument for a moment Christian proponents of human rights, then you will see that they have not become proponents of human rights because they think that their Christian faith has collapsed. So what you are saying may be true for a certain generation – I would say, mostly of former leftists – but it's certainly not generalizable. And even the choice of the word "utopia" for me is totally unconvincing. For me, at least, human rights is not a utopia. I want to live in a society where there is no torture. But that is a kind of minimal standard. I would never say that I live in a utopian society because there is no torture here. It can be a society with extreme social inequality and ecological problems and everything is very far from utopia. I think these two things are connected, to be honest. You somehow argue in a way that is very far from what has been, for example, the Christian worldview for a very long time. That is, there will never be a utopia on earth. That human beings will remain tempted to do evil things for all imaginable futures and that we need the law to prevent them from doing that. But that we need not only the law, but also value-related education, for example, religious education for that purpose. And if I'm right in regard to that, I think this main narrative that led to the title of the book, that this is somehow a utopia, and somehow the most important thing for this is this exhaustion of earlier utopian imaginations, I would not deny that it is true for certain groups, so to speak, and some people. But I think you're overgeneralizing.

SM: I want to concede that the notion of utopia in my title of the book is woefully undertheorized. I had something very simple in mind: I wanted to have a good title. But I mainly had in mind the pedagogical experience from which this book arose, which is, confronting young students today, who come to university and want to save the world, or at least make it better. I think making it better has some utopian features; you don't have to want to save, transform, and utterly perfect it to be a utopian. And I asked myself why it was that, in their generation, human rights were the sole version of idealism and activism in which they would engage. This fact marks out their generation from all those that preceded it in history. I wondered: "What were the historical circumstances in which this transformation could have come about?" I often talk to my students about the 1960s and 1968 at Columbia University where I have taught and I show them pictures of what happened. And no one said the words human rights as part of student activism. Though they certainly wanted a better world, they thought about it and mobilized in its favor in profoundly different ways.

I do, however, want to concede Hans's point about Christianity. I think the vast majority of proponents of human rights in the 40s – not that there were many – were Christians in transatlantic affairs. To me, actually Christianity, especially on the European continent, has gone through a world-historical collapse. It might not have reached Hans, but the transformation and decline of Christianity is a remarkable event in world history, and, to me, is actually very germane to understanding the centrality of human rights, though it is only one feature of this centrality. Now, it is not obvious whether this secularization of human rights involved the rise of a truly non-partisan set of beliefs that's compatible with Christianity, or a mere version of Christianity that has survived the collapse of churchgoing. But I wouldn't want at all to exclude Christians from the story of the collapse of prior belief systems, although I do agree my model is best applicable to the secular left.

HJ: Did you really just call the Vatican II a collapse? I mean, you can complain ...

SM: Vatican II paradoxically set the stage for the collapse of West European Christianity in both its old and its renovated forms.

HJ: ... that it didn't have enough consequences, but at the time it was a revitalization ...

SM: Of course. It was.

HJ: ... rejuvenation – not experienced as collapse.

SM: True, but that was a long time ago.

HJ: Yes, okay, but then we have to become more specific, I would say.

SM: Right, this is a detailed topic.

HJ: Yes, yes. I'll leave it aside.

Another potentially controversial thing in the book, and also in your own summary here, I do not agree with your relatively dismissive way of speaking about national self-determination both in regard to liberal nationalism in the 19th century, and in regard to the anticolonial movement. I mean, for me, it is easy to imagine that somebody says, even if my highest goal is human rights, what we need first is national self-determination. I fully agree that not all the people who were in favor of national self-determination were ever really in favor of human rights, so to speak, but that national self-determination can be a presupposition for human rights. I personally think you do not take that seriously enough in your book.

Now to your question: you know, when I'm speaking about sacralizations, whether in the past or today, I do not say sacralization of the person is the only one. The idea comes from Émile Durkheim – I think Durkheim sacralized two things simultaneously: the French nation and the human person. If you do that – sacralize two things simultaneously while being intellectually consistent –, then you have to say: "How do they relate to each other?" And I think his way of relating these two things to each other was to say, France is the nation of human rights. To be a French patriot or even nationalist means to do something for the sake of human rights. But that is not necessarily the case and people live with enormous tensions. And I had in *Die Zeit* – I think one or two weeks ago – I had an article that was based on a dinner conversation I had in Charlottesville, Virginia, where the host asked me: "Do you think that human rights are now stabilized?" And I said: "No, I don't think so. For example, I see a constant tension between the demands of, let's say, national security and human rights – sacredness of the person." And only because he really exerted some pressure, I mentioned Guantanamo. Then, he said: "In Guantanamo we defend the human rights of our American citizens." And if he hadn't been my host, I would have said, this shows that you have never understood the basic idea of human rights. But if we take this person as in any sense representative, it is deeply depressing. It means that some people, in a serious tension between two values that they both take very seriously, may decide in favor of the *other* one and say: "Under these circumstances torture is justified." I imagine the same to happen in Germany – I should add – if we experienced a similar attack like on 9/11. So I'm not saying this is American, that here everything is much more stabilized. It's a different experiential background in that sense, at the moment. But this makes me rather pessimistic. So at the same time, of course, sensitizing effects of these processes that led to the institutionalization of human rights may go on to change the mentality in regard to gay marriage, but at the same time, people may, in a trade-off, reduce their support for human rights. So in that sense, I'm not really optimistic for the future.

DK: Questions please.

Audience: The example you gave about Guantanamo illustrated perfectly what I think Sam Moyn wants us to consider, namely the distinction between citizenship rights and human rights. In a way what you're pursuing is an idealist account of the development of rights that goes through the various stages, but until today we are still stuck to the notion of citizenship rights, which are based in nation-state rights. And human rights to this day are not enforceable – universal human rights on a global scale – and that is a rather recent development. There's an argument that under the International Criminal Court and so forth, there are attempts to institutionalize them. And so far, we do not have a legal framework to enforce human rights. So I think that maybe we could try to work with this distinction between citizenship rights and human rights. I mean when the French invented human rights for themselves, at the same time they had the *code noir* in the colonies. That is true for all the European colonial powers that their notion of citizenship rights was always based on exclusivity. And, of course, it didn't include women – it didn't include other non-Christians, etc. So I think we should really try to be a bit more careful with our terminology when we talk about what kind of rights we're really addressing here because the universalism of earlier times was not the universalism that exists today.

HJ: I agree with everything you say and realize that you think it somehow contradicts what I said before and that is a mystery.

Audience: No, no. I thought your example illustrates perfectly that tension between...

HJ: Yes, there is this tension!

Audience: ... between Americans trying to protect their citizenship rights and the notion of human rights.

HJ: I see, let's say, an ambiguity in the notion of citizenship rights. You could say: "We declare that all men are created equal. But of course, here, when we codify that, we can only do so in the framework of our own state." But if you declare: "These are the rights of Englishmen," then you do not even assume that they should be institutionalized in the other states as well – it's just the English tradition then. So in that sense, I see a difference between England and the United States in the late 18th century and you could apply this distinction to all cases. And what I would say to this guy in Charlottesville is, of course, that he, let's say, reparticularizes the American understanding even of citizenship rights. So it's not citizen rights versus human rights. One distinction is codification on the national level and implementation mechanisms versus codification on the supranational and international level – that's one distinction. It's not the same distinction as the distinction between citizenship rights and human rights.

SM: I think you've made the point that the distinction helps us get historiographically at the novelty of supranational human rights politics. I think Hans is confused when he says I'm dismissive of national self-determination. In fact, I want to rehabilitate nationalism and the experience of citizenship politics – to reclaim them from the relative decline in prestige which both have suffered. I actually trace that loss to decolonization. In my understanding, Adolf Hitler didn't convince the world to give up on nationalism. Indeed, it seems as if at the time of the Universal Declaration rights were reaffirmed as having their basis first of all in a properly governed national welfare state. It was really later, with decolonization, when nationalism as the primary conduit and device of the propagation of rights globally came into disrepute. And I think this fact is very telling, because it suggests that only when people we Westerners once ruled got national sovereignty or rather claimed it for themselves, sometimes through violence, sovereignty suddenly became problematic. And we developed new devices that were no longer formal, imperialist devices to police their conduct. And that's, I think, a pretty big part of the history of human rights, especially of post-Cold War human rights.

But framing things my way also helps us see that whatever salience human rights have achieved, it's not because they've definitely changed real outcomes for humanity. No one would ever ask whether nationalism made a difference, or whether the experience of citizenship made a difference in world history. And yet, a mere ten years ago, Oona Hathaway could write an article called "Do Human Rights Treaties Make a Difference?" Recently, a new book has come out by Beth Simmons that proves that they have helped at the margins.[8] But the amazing

---

8 Oona A. Hathaway, "Do Human Rights Treaties Make a Difference?" *Yale Law Journal* 111, no. 8 (June 2002): 1935–2042; Beth A. Simmons, *Mobilizing for Human Rights: International Law in Domestic Politics* (Cambridge: Cambridge University Press, 2010); see also Samuel Moyn, "Do

fact is that the debate had to take place at all, because we would never deny the emancipatory role of nationhood and the quest for citizenship within nations in world history. By contrast, human rights politics seem to be a very narrow form of mobilization. The Americans didn't name and shame George III only. The Frenchmen didn't name and shame their king; they claimed their citizenship through a refounding of sovereignty. Human rights politics, as we know them, seem to be much less effectual. Indeed, that is my main complaint, and my reason for historicizing them in a more negative, or, let's say, deconstructive way, even if I don't mean to be destructive. Because my complaint about international human rights is that they don't seem to have found any politically effective form that gives them the emancipatory force that national self-determination at least for awhile had in spite of all the terrible things that nations have also done – to their own people and other people.

Audience: Maybe, well, I'm not sure, but it sounds very much like the point is where the mechanism of reverting human rights on those who claim them for themselves – that's the point where the systematic difference may be. Or at least it is an important point for making human rights internationally or universally valid. I mean, if the United States says, for example, we are furthering human rights all over the world, but they maintain Guantanamo for safeguarding their people from terrorist attacks. So the reciprocity, which forms part of a universalist construction of the human rights thought, is not given. The United States attacks Nicaragua. The International Court has a judgment on the United States and says, well, they are guilty of crime against humanity and, then, there is no reaction. Why? Because there is no enforcement, and there is no will to put forth human rights as human rights, which are really *human* rights, and have this logic of reciprocity.

SM: I do agree that you are getting to a pretty fundamental difference between our approaches, which I think should be out there, just so that people can decide whether they're compatible or incompatible. Both Hans and I think we need to take the norms of human rights and connect them to something else, for the sake of understanding their genesis and why they were directed in some ways against some countries and not others and so forth.

Human Rights Treaties Make Enough of a Difference?" in Conor Gearty and Costas Douzinas, eds., *Cambridge Companion to Human Rights Law* (Cambridge: Cambridge University Press, 2012).

Hans gives us a sociological context, drawing on classics and social theory and ransacking them for any insight the history of social theory as we know it – Durkheim, Weber, and so forth – might have to bring to bear on the history of these norms. And then he stops the clock in 1948. But to me, what truly matters is what happens to these norms in our time, which is, by the way, what also has to explain our own contemporary scholarly interest. It may be true that in the historiography of human rights we can cite Georg Jellinek (1895), as Hans does, but recall that Jellinek's book concerns one declaration; and as far as I know, it the sole book ever to think about the French Revolution in terms of human rights until our time.[9] The truth is that there was no human rights historiography until ten years ago. And so, to me, it's not the sociological context that's motivating us as scholars to think about where they came from, but really the postwar, including the great power context. So I think that's a pretty big difference.

HJ: This is really empirically wrong, if I may say that. No, I mean simply on this level of Jellinek's book, there was a huge international controversy. I have several files at home with hundreds of pages of contributions. And it's not true that there has been a historiography only in the past ten years. I mean there were books at least in German republishing important papers from this 1900 controversy in the 1950s or 60s. I could give you a whole bibliography. Émile Durkheim wouldn't have been able to develop what he said if it hadn't been for a certain context. There was a lively debate about the history of human rights around 1900. And that does not fit into your picture, but you cannot deny that it *was* there.

SM: That's a fair point.

Audience: I do not see so much difference between the two approaches, because if the sacralization of the person is a sacralization of every person, accepted by every person, and reverted on every person, so what's the differences? How this idea is applied, and who applies it, and the power structures, which are behind plight and which are behind the legal systems we have and the political contradiction – you know, the story.

---

9 Georg Jellinek, *Die Erklärung der Menschen- und Bürgerrechte: ein Beitrag zur modernen Verfassungsgeschichte* (Leipzig: Duncker und Humblot, 1895). The contemporary classic on human rights in the French Revolution is Lynn Hunt, *Inventing Human Rights: A History* (New York: W.W. Norton, 2007).

HJ: Sam has – now you could say – a more precise or narrower understanding of human rights with the emphasis on international institutions and international social movements. I could grant that because my main concept is the sacralization of the person and that does not necessarily take on a legal form. I tried to describe why people – let's say, around 1700 – didn't find torture a good thing, but nor were they terribly motivated to abolish it, and why this changed in the course of the 18th century. And for that argument, it is in a certain sense completely irrelevant whether they use the word "human right" or not. I would include that in such a history irrespective of the vocabulary the actors used. But, of course, if you defend a very narrow understanding, then it becomes important whether they said that, whether they articulate their ideas in those terms. If not, it does not belong to the narrative. Both things are justified. I mean, you can write a conceptual history of the notion of human rights. Then this is totally justified. But if you think in terms of a cultural transformation in which every person is respected as a person, then it doesn't make sense to restrict yourself to this literal meaning. So, in that sense, it's not controversial again!

SM: What you say makes a lot of sense. I just want to be clear that, no matter what importance one grants to post-1948 developments, one would of course need not simply an intellectual history but an experiential genealogy – affirmative or not – of things like the French Declaration of the Rights of Man and Citizen and the Universal Declaration. Where the controversy comes in is what importance that has for explaining global human rights politics today. On the narrow issue, torture was not abolished in the 18th century. It was a familiar part of imperial rule until the 1950s, 60s, and 70s, when the...

HJ: The empire ...

SM: That is to say, the whole world.

HJ: Yes, yes – I agree!

SM: And finally Amnesty International had its campaign against torture in the early 1970s. This was a transformative event for *global* norm-setting – although, of course, as we know, when it comes to my country, and many of its partners in the war on terror, the practice is still not gone. So the "consensus" we're speaking about has to be detailed, and often it's at a purely normative level. And with regards to the larger picture, it seems to me that the sacralization story works for a few places early in history, but not for the globe after 1945, when one needs some other account. And so the compatibility would have to be sought on that basis I think.

DK: And I think I have a perfect quote here. This is a quote from Sam's book. I would think that it speaks directly to Hans's book right now. He writes: "As time passed after World War II" – and this is Sam once again – "such personalism more and more simply rephrased anti-communism and Western unity, rather than offering a philosophy of global amity. There was no serious promotion by European international lawyers of human rights as a wider project, as the European convention signaled values without bringing a serious legal regime into being." And so this is the point where Sam thinks about the importance of social movement and its impact on international lawyers.

Here comes my question that follows up. Hans on the other says that by affirmative genealogy of human rights, he means a certain work of translation, shifting – and he also calls it generalization of values, experiences, subjective evidence, after Jürgen Habermas and Talcott Parsons. And I think this is toward the end of your book where you make a few observations in regards to what happens much more in contemporary times. So, the first question for Sam is: Do you think that Hans's model – that is, sacralization of personhood – explains what happens with international lawyers beginning 1977? If not, why not? And the analog of that question for Hans would be: what shape does that social movement take, as it undergoes a certain universalization of values for the dignity of the individual being? So that we get a more concrete sense of the political actors who are operative in that universalization. Perhaps that's another way of fine-tuning some of the historical differences, as you pursue your different disciplinary approaches to the history of human rights.

SM: As I've indicated already, I don't think the sacralization of the person is a very useful concept for explaining the details of history after 1945 – whatever its use is before. I'm officially going to be neutral about whether Hans successfully explains the ancient prehistory of post-1945 human rights politics. All I want to commit to saying right now is that I can't see the value of the concept for explaining what happens since.

What happens since, it seems to me, has to do in part with some of the topics Hans takes up in his last chapter. But I would cast the "generalization of values" in a different way. I don't think the UDHR should be seen, as he does, as coming about thanks to moment of multicultural communion, mainly because almost nobody from around the world was in the room – and those who were there were diplomats trained in Western universities as, by the way, many diplomats to this day are. We shouldn't think of the UDHR as a popular or grassroots product. It's a product of diplomatic elites that only later found the backing of social movements even in the North Atlantic under very different circumstances. It's actually very hard to say even today whether human rights have found a global backing at all.

On a new part of the website *Open Democracy* called "Open Human Rights," some political scientists have recently tried to investigate empirically, rather than just believe in, the global salience of human rights ideas.[10] And they've concluded that to date it remains an exceptionally elite set of norms in the global South. This finding, of course, doesn't mean that human rights don't have a grand future ahead of them.

In my view, however, it was for good reason that after 1945 nationalism remained prestigious and emancipatory for a long time – the Jews wanted it in Israel, all of the many peoples under empire wanted it and pursued national self-determination for the sake of individual protection, but also as a project of collective emancipation. When the 1970s dawned, the most significant challenge to the Western hegemony that had led to empire was the New International Economic Order (NIEO) proposals, which offered a plan to redo the world order – and especially the economic world order. But the NIEO was destroyed. It doesn't seem as if human rights politics, as we know them, are waiting to happen after 1945, until these really surprising events intervene and I don't see the sacred having much to do with it.

HJ: First, just to be clear, because you mentioned torture in European colonies, I fully agree with that. But I had said the abolition of torture in Europe.

SM: Precisely.

HJ: I did not say on a global scale. And actually, I've even written a new manuscript on exactly that.[11] I'm interested in destroying this European triumphalism – we abolished torture, when it's not true for the European colonies. This has at least become the European self-understanding. To David: Please, the two terms value generalization and affirmative genealogy have very different meanings. Affirmative genealogy refers to this question of how do we, in view of our ideals, reconstruct history in a non-teleological way, so that those ideals are not this necessary result of the historical processes, but nevertheless we defend them as our ideals, see them in all their contingency, but defend them. This is about the role of historical reconstruction in such a quasi-normative argumentation,

---

10 James Ron et al., "The Struggle for a Truly Global Human Rights Movement," *Open Democracy*, http://www.opendemocracy.net/openglobalrights/james-ron-david-crow-shannon-golden/struggle-for-truly-grassroots-human-rights-move.
11 Hans Joas, *Slavery and Torture in a Global Perspective: Human Rights and the Western Tradition*. Leiden: Brill, 2014.

whereas value generalization refers in Parsons to a dialogue between the representatives of different value systems and how they discover surprisingly, so to speak, that they share more, how they reinterpret themselves, re-articulate their convictions, in a way that... – okay, I would need more time to illustrate that.

Now your question about social change after 1945 or 1948 and whether this notion makes sense. I would say, it makes more sense the more you think of unintentional processes of cultural change. Let's say, in Germany, the relations between medical doctors and their patients changed in the direction of more respect for the autonomy of the decision of the patient about his or her own body. This is not mostly – certainly not at first – a change in law. And maybe not even so much a consequence of intellectual discussions about that. It's a kind of gradual, almost unnoticed change. Or, at least, there are such cases. I mean, if you show me that this is not the case; that there was an intense debate – I missed it – that may be. But I think that nobody can deny that there are such changes, with regard to parental attitudes to their children, to sexual rapprochement or such processes. I think we need some term for such, let's say, intuitive change of cultural attitudes. So that's part one.

And the other thing is, of course, your question aimed at social movements. There I would like to, if I may, refer to my chapter on the abolitionist movement, where I mention three elements for the explanation: one again is sacralization, but only one. And sacralization in the sense of, let's say, some Christians discovered that their Christian conviction should always have meant: abolish slavery. But it didn't and other Christians didn't share this. But for them, this was a kind of revelation. William Lloyd Garrison: I don't want to live one more day under the conditions of slavery. I have recognized what the absolute evil is: slavery. And so I will do everything to abolish it. I think for this process such quasi-religious terms like sacredness, revelation and so on really make sense. Now, I say in the book, this has to be connected to processes of a much more rational kind – for example, of the cognitive attribution of responsibility: what can I do about it? This is not sacralization, of course, and I don't call it sacralization. But that is the empirical study of facts, for example, and how am I connected to these facts.

I've recently used the following example, I'm deeply convinced that there are terrible labor camps in North Korea, but I have no idea what I can do about them. If you show me that my shoes have been produced in a North Korean labor camp, things change for me; they change cognitively. I've been against these labor camps before, but I had no idea what to do. And that may mean that now I have some idea what to do. And there come in organizational questions, like the role of transnational advocacy networks. So for a model of a social movement you need much more than this notion of sacralization, but sacralization remains an important part. Because you won't have an intense movement that moves people, so to speak, without such revelations and such important emotional foundations or whatever.

Audience: I think there is one important point in talking about the social movements – it is the dialectics of resistance, which took place during the 1990s. There was a big debate, you surely remember, about the validity of the human rights question in Asian cultures and among indigenous peoples. In Latin America, for example, in the beginning of the 90s, members of indigenous peoples in resistance would not accept human rights, the human rights discourse. But then, during their resistance, they took up more and more human rights laws and brought them into their own strategies. Consequently, the concept of the person is important here because they did not take up the European, individualist formulations, but they took up the sense of personhood and the way they culturally understood personhood. Now, the debate is going on about the rights of tribes.

HJ: The European tradition is also much more pluralist. It's not just liberal individualism. And Sam has written a very good article on personalism. Also, I would say, this in itself is pluralist. And I use the term person. But that does not mean that I share all of the convictions of earlier authors for whom the concept of person was crucial. But all this is totally complex, of course.

I would just like to conclude by saying, of course, yes, we disagree in our descriptions of the drafting process of this 1948 Declaration. Of course, I mean, empirically, you are right. This was a diplomatic elite, but what else was to be expected? I'm against saying, since this man from Lebanon was Christian, or since the Chinese had already spent time in the Western world, they are not authentic representatives – that I wouldn't buy. Because I think this is a kind of essentializing now of the non-European in the sense of: we only take those people from Asia seriously who have never been in a Western country, never come into contact with Western thinking. No. It was an elite phenomenon. But it was a productive process of communication between people with very different religious and philosophical backgrounds. Of course only very, very limited. Again, I'm not saying that whenever these people come together, something positive comes out of that. But in rare cases – and we should look at these rare cases – something positive comes out of that. And I think that 1948 was such a case. It was positive.

SM: Just very briefly in conclusion, I just want to say to the audience that, of all the things I loved about Hans's book, I think his sketch of a theory of affirmative genealogy is perhaps the most pioneering and provocative, because it is applicable to the sociology of any value formation. Which of course then raises the question, which it is applied to. And presumably, we have to know why we're not giving an affirmative genealogy of nationalism anymore, but human rights. And I purport to have tried to address that question.

DK: On that note, we have already extended the discussion for ten minutes. So I think, on that note, it's time to thank our two speakers for their wonderful engagement. Thank you so much for joining us.

Section One: **Claiming Human Rights**

Thomas Pogge
The Progressive Potential of Human Rights

We might begin reflection on the progressive potential of human rights by looking at the role that human rights are supposed to play within the present international order. Here two main functions stand out. First, human rights are meant to constrain and inform the conduct of political authorities: of governments and their various domestic and international agencies and organizations. Governments must *respect* the human right of those living under their authority and of others they may interact with. Governments must *protect* the human rights of members of their state against internal and external threats from crime, war, civil war and terrorism, from natural catastrophes including epidemics and human-made ecological disasters, and from threats to the economic preconditions for meeting the basic needs of the state's members. Insofar as these efforts to respect and protect prove insufficient, governments must also *provide* for their citizens any missing objects of human rights, for example food aid in the event of a flood or a drought.[12]

Second, human rights are also supposed to motivate and guide the design of an international back-up regime of governments that step in with assistance, incentives and compulsion when one state's political authorities are unable or unwilling to meet their human rights-based responsibilities to respect, protect or provide. Various existing international governmental organizations and arrangements can be seen as elements of such a regime: the UN Security Council with its Chapter-7 authority to use coercive measures, including military force, to deal with "any threat to the peace, breach of the peace, or act of aggression" (UN Charter 1948, Art. 39, 41, 42); the World Health Organization (WHO) with its mechanisms for responding to the outbreak of epidemics; the World Food Program (WFP) delivering emergency food aid to famine-stricken regions; and the UN Framework Convention on Climate Change (FCCC) charged with averting a major human-rights catastrophe caused by the warming of our planet as a result of excessive greenhouse gas emissions.[13]

---

12 This respect-protect-provide triad goes back to Henry Shue's seminal book *Basic Rights*, which argues that each basic right gives rise to three distinct correlative duties: to avoid depriving, to protect from deprivation and to aid the deprived (Shue 1996, p. 60). Shue's typology entered official UN discourse in the 1980ies through Philip Alston and Asbjorn Eide (Alston 1984, pp. 162, 169–174; see generally Alston and Tomaševski 1984).
13 My sketch of the accepted role or function of human rights essentially follows Charles Beitz' two-level model according to which human rights are urgent interests, with (a) primary responsi-

With this being the prevailing understanding, the objects of human rights are amply protected in our world, protected by a sequence of "waves of duties."[14] Are human rights then also amply fulfilled in our world? As Amnesty International keeps reminding us, "torture is flourishing in at least three quarters of the world's countries" (Amnesty International 2014, back cover). And the state of social and economic human rights can only be described as appalling. According to the latest official figures, of the 7.3 billion people alive today, 842 million are officially counted as undernourished (FAO, IFAD and WFP 2013, pp. 8, 42), well over 1 billion lack adequate shelter (Rolnik 2014, p. 1), 748 million lack safe drinking water (Too-Kong 2014, p. 47), 1.8 billion lack adequate sanitation (Too-Kong 2014, p. 45), over 1.2 billion lack electricity (World Bank 2013, http://go.worldbank.org/6ITD8WA1A0), more than one-third lack reliable access to essential medicines (Nyanwura and Esena 2013, p. 208), 781 million over age 14 are illiterate (UNESCO 2013, www.uis.unesco.org/literacy/Pages/literacy-data-release-2014.aspx), and 168 million children aged 5 to 17 do wage work outside their household – often under slavery-like and hazardous conditions: as soldiers, prostitutes or domestic servants, or in agriculture, construction, textile or carpet production (ILO 2014, www.ilo.org/global/topics/child-labour/lang--en/index.htm).

We must conclude, then, that human rights fulfill both of their functions rather poorly. Many governments are unwilling or unable to realize human rights within their territory. And international responses to the remaining massive human rights deficits are discordant, selective and unreliable: the powerful (the U.S., Russia, and China) are routinely exempt from sanctions and the marginal are routinely left unprotected (the people of Libya and Syria recently, or the victims of the genocide in Rwanda). What should we conclude from these facts about the plausibility of the prevailing understanding of human rights?

It depends on how we conceive of human rights. We might conceive of them as a central piece of political morality, and of morality as a purely passive system of timeless universal standards to be used to assess, from an imagined extra- or post-historical standpoint, the relevant occurrences in human history: the conduct and character of human agents, human rules and various pertinent states of affairs. On this conception, it is no fault of our evaluative standards that the world falls far short of them – that, in particular, governments fail to meet

---

bility for their fulfillment assigned to the state to which each person belongs, and (b) other states assigned preventive or remedial responsibilities for improving states with a poor human rights record (see Beitz 2009, pp. 108ff).

14 This language is suggested in Waldron (1989, pp. 503, 510). See also Shue (1996, p. 156) and Pogge (2009, p. 113).

their primary and secondary responsibilities. Alternatively, we might conceive of human rights, and perhaps of morality more generally, as practical tools in the struggle to achieve a world in which all human beings live in the firm knowledge that they can securely enjoy certain basic freedoms and securely meet their basic needs. On this alternative conception, we might well conclude that this tool has worked poorly and that we should at least explore ways of adapting our morality to make it more effective at achieving what, by its own lights, matters.

Staying with this latter conception of human rights, why have the rhetoric and legal apparatus of human rights not been a more effective tool in their realization? How can we change this tool or its use so as to make it more effective? One prominent response to these questions involves rethinking the ambitiousness of our list of human rights. Thus, some scholars have argued that by unsystematically recognizing too many human rights, the UN has drawn attention away from the most urgent ones, generally diluting the importance people assign to human rights considerations.[15] Arguably, then, even the expansive set of human rights currently recognized would be better realized if we were officially committed to only a substantially smaller subset of them.

Unconvinced that this diagnosis gets to the heart of the problem, I will here explore a different adaptation of the way the human rights tool is deployed. The basic idea is to apply this tool in a new place: to fight for a central role for human rights in the intergovernmental negotiations through which supranational institutional arrangements are designed.

The last thirty years have seen the rapid emergence of a dense network of global institutional arrangements that now profoundly influence international interactions and also reach deep into the inner lives of national societies. In shaping these institutional arrangements, the more powerful governments, especially those of the United States and its main allies, have played a dominant role. In exerting this influence, these governments were in turn heavily influenced by their most powerful constituents: large investors and the leaders of powerful multinational corporations, industry associations, banks and hedge funds. It is then unsurprising that this rapidly emerging global order reflects the interests of these highly privileged agents. They do not, to be sure, intend any harm to the poor. But they do try to increase their own share of global income, and, insofar as they succeed, the shares of poorer segments of the human population must decline. As the poor are least able to exert political influence – especially on suprana-

---

15 This point about human rights inflation is made in different ways by Cranston (1973), Wellman (1999) and Orend (2002). See also Griffin (2008) who emphasizes especially the lack of a systematic rationale for the rights currently included.

tional institutional design decisions – it is to be expected that their needs and interests are systematically disregarded. Global institutional arrangements generate a severe headwind against the global poor, a headwind that existing efforts by governments to fulfill their various waves of duties are woefully insufficient to neutralize. We see this when we observe that socio-economic inequality has been rising globally and in most countries, causing severe poverty to persist as the poor are unable to participate proportionally in global economic growth. In the 1988–2008 period, for instance, the income share of the poorest 30 percent of the world's population has shrunk from an already minuscule 1.52% to an even tinier 1.25% of global household income.[16]

What I am asking for, then, is that we stop thinking of supranational rule making as a morality-free zone in which it is acceptable for partisan government representatives to strike bargains for mutual advantage. Instead, we should recognize and highlight the fact that everyday supranational rule making, notably in the economic sphere, has profound effects on human rights fulfillment around the world. And we should accept the principle that supranational institutional arrangements should be shaped so that human rights are fulfilled insofar as this is reasonably possible. Can such a change be effected? And if so, how?

The change can be supported by appeal to the venerable core document of the post-World War II human rights movement, the 1948 *Universal Declaration of Human Rights*. Article 28 reads: "Everyone is entitled to a social and international order in which the rights and freedoms set forth in this Declaration can be fully realized." This Article clearly calls for human rights to be applied to the design and reform of our international order. What difference would it make if the most powerful governments took this Article to heart and allowed their supranational rule making to be constrained by the imperative of human rights fulfillment?

Let me illustrate the difference this could make with two examples: the new international rules governing pharmaceutical innovation, which systematically deprive poor populations of access to advanced medicines, and the rules governing international accounting and taxation, which systematically deprive poor populations of investment capital and tax revenues.

---

16 In the same period, the richest five percent of the world's population succeeded in expanding their share of global household income from 42.87% to 45.75%. Data kindly provided by Branko Milanovic, City University of New York. The cited income shares are based on market exchange rates, not purchasing power parities.

First Illustration: Pharmaceutical Patents and the Health Impact Fund

The current system of pharmaceutical provision is shaped by Annex 1C of the WTO Agreement covering Trade-Related Aspects of Intellectual Property Rights (TRIPS) (WTO 2014, www.wto.org/english/docs_e/legal_e/27-trips_01_e.htm). Innovators are rewarded through national patents that give them exclusive rights on the manufacture and sale of their new medicines for at least 20 years.

Given the prevailing enormous economic inequalities, this system leads to exorbitant mark-ups that make patented medicines unaffordable to a majority of humankind. It also steers pharmaceutical research away from diseases concentrated among the poor and toward the development of maintenance drugs and close substitutes ("me-too drugs"). Additional inefficiencies arise from massive deadweight losses and wasteful expenditures on countless patents and patent litigation, competitive advertising and counterfeits.

The system could be greatly improved by adding a second reward track for pharmaceutical innovators. The Health Impact Fund (HIF, see www.healthimpactfund.org) is a proposed pay-for-performance scheme that would offer innovators the option to register any new medicine, thereby undertaking to make it available, during its first 10 years on the market, at or below cost. The registrant would further commit to allowing, at no charge, generic production and distribution of the product after expiration of this reward period.

In exchange, the registrant would participate during that decade in fixed annual reward pools divided among all registered products according to their measured health impact. The size of these pools could be chosen to incentivize an appropriate number of important research and development (R&D) projects. At its minimum size of $6 billion annually, the HIF might support some 25 new medicines at any time, with two or three entering and leaving each year.

Since the strength of the incentives depends on secure long-term funding, the reward pools would ideally be financed through a sizable endowment fed from contributions by states (proportional to their gross national income), international agencies, NGOs, foundations, corporations, individuals, and estates. Such contributions to the HIF would produce vastly greater health gains per dollar than the $600 billion that humanity is now spending each year on patented medicines. This is so because of the HIF's much greater efficiency. The HIF would avoid the bias in favour of maintenance drugs by fully rewarding health gains achieved by preventative and curative drugs. It would discourage the development of me-too drugs by rewarding them only insofar as they produce health gains beyond those achieved by their similar predecessors. It would motivate registrants to care not about mere sales but about health gains: a registrant would focus its marketing on patients who can really benefit from its product and would try to ensure that its medicines are widely available, competently prescribed and optimally used. Additional dramatic advantages in efficiency would arise from avoiding deadweight losses (no mark-ups), counterfeiting (with the genuine item widely available at or below cost, making and selling fakes is unprofitable) and expensive litigation (generic firms would lack incentives to compete, and registrants would lack incentives to suppress generic products and might therefore not even bother to file for patents in most national jurisdictions). Through all these efficiency gains and lower drug prices, the HIF might well pay for itself, allowing contributors to realize offsetting savings in national health systems, insurance premiums, insurance payments, direct pharmacy purchases and foreign aid.

The most important reason for the HIF, however, is that it would end the exclusion of the world's poor from advanced medicines and would thereby make a major contribution to the realization of human rights. The HIF would stimulate the development of new high-impact medicines especially against the now-neglected diseases of the poor, which it would turn into some of the most lucrative pharmaceutical R&D opportunities. And the HIF would promote access to all registered medicines by limiting their price to the lowest feasible cost of manufacture and distribution, by motivating registrants to sell to the very poor even below cost in order to earn additional health impact rewards and by encouraging efforts, even in the poorest populations, to ensure that medicines are optimally used.

Second Illustration: Curtailing Illicit Financial Outflows from the Less Developed Countries

On the prevailing understanding, the first-line responsibility for the large human-rights deficits remaining in the less developed countries lies with the governments of these countries. But the task is large and most of these governments are poor. While the industrialized states have annual revenues in the order of $20,000 to $50,000 per citizen, India has annual revenues of barely $200 per citizen and many other governments are poorer still. These large international discrepancies are due to two factors: the *per capita* gross domestic products of poor countries are much smaller; and these countries also raise a much smaller proportion of their GDPs as government revenues, typically under 20% as compared to an OECD average of well over 40%.

Through sophisticated efforts, wealthy citizens of poor countries, and corporations operating there, escape taxation to an extent that would be unthinkable in an affluent country with political clout and a highly sophisticated and well-funded tax administration. Boston Consulting Group estimates that 33.3% of all private financial wealth owned by people in Africa and the Middle East and 25.6% of such wealth owned by Latin Americans – some $2.6 trillion in total – is kept abroad; while the analogous estimates for North America and Europe are 1.8% and 7.9%, respectively (Boston Consulting Group 2013, pp. 4, 11). To collect taxes on the income and capital gains generated by this wealth, poor countries must largely rely on the honesty of their taxpayers as they lack access to information about their citizens' overseas holdings.

Multinational corporations (MNCs) also massively escape taxation typically by creating additional subsidiaries in tax havens and then letting their poor-country subsidiaries contract with their tax-haven subsidiaries into money-losing arrangements involving trade mis-invoicing, abusive transfer prices as well as inflated consulting and intellectual-property fees (Hearson and Brooks 2012). These arrangements diminish the taxed profits of the poor-country subsidiaries while increasing the untaxed profits of the tax-haven subsidiaries. Global Financial Integrity estimates that corporate tax abuse accounts for 80% of all illicit financial outflows from less developed countries, or about $4.7 trillion during the 2002–11 period and $760 billion in 2011 alone (Kar and LeBlanc 2013, pp. iii, vii, x). This amount is five or six times the sum total of all official development assistance flowing into these countries during the same periods (http://mdgs.un.org/unsd/mdg/SeriesDetail.aspx?srid=569&crid=). Christian Aid calculates that, through these profit- and tax-diminishing capital outflows, governments of less developed countries have lost tax revenues in the order of $160 billion annually – or about $2.5 trillion for the Millennium Development Goals period (2000–2015). "If that money was available to allocate according to current spending patterns, the amount going into health services could save the lives of 350,000 children under the age of five every year" (Christian Aid 2009, p. 3).[17]

Four groups of agents bear direct responsibility for the human rights deficit that results from poor countries' inability fully to collect reasonable taxes. First, the secrecy jurisdictions and tax haven countries (including Switzerland, Singapore, Ireland, the UK and the US) that structure their tax and legal systems so as to encourage tax abuse and also typically protect bank secrecy against the tax authorities of less developed countries. Second, the individuals and corporations that erode the tax base of poor countries by using tax havens to dodge

---

17 There are many pressures toward improving current government spending patterns in poor countries, which are often distorted by corruption, bloated security apparatuses and indifference to the poor. Insofar as such efforts are succeeding, additional revenues would have an even larger human rights impact than Christian Aid is calculating.

taxes on their wealth and profits. Third, the bankers, lawyers, accountants and lobbyists who devise, implement and "legalize" these schemes. Fourth, powerful rich-country governments that allow their own country to serve as a tax haven for foreign MNCs, facilitate the tax dodging of their MNCs abroad,[18] or oblige tax havens to cooperate with their own tax enforcement efforts without ensuring that poor-country governments receive similar cooperation.[19]

The key to reducing the tax gap and consequent human rights deficits in the poor countries involves reform of the international tax system toward global financial transparency. The most promising and realistic elements of such a reform can be gleaned from a Delphi study involving iterated inputs from 29 illicit financial flows experts from various backgrounds, including academia, NGOs, the private sector and multilateral institutions (Payne, Rowe, Bolger and Shubert 2014). This study revealed overwhelming expert support for reforms that would increase financial transparency at both the domestic and global levels. In particular, there is consensus that all governments should agree to mandate (a) disclosure of the ultimate beneficial owners of companies and of the controlling parties of trusts and foundations, (b) public country-by-country reporting of profits and other tax-relevant information by multinational enterprises, (c) automatic exchange of tax-relevant financial information by national tax authorities worldwide, (d) public reporting on funds paid to governments for the extraction of natural resources and on the use of those funds and (e) tough sanctions, including jail time, for professionals who facilitate illicit financial flows, for instance senior officers of global banks, accounting firms, law firms, insurance companies and hedge funds. In addition, governments should jointly commit to (f) harmonizing anti-money laundering regulations internationally and (g) carrying out clear, reliable, frequent and timely public fiscal reporting as well as opening up their

---

18 An example are the "tax holidays" periodically granted by the US Congress, such as the *American Jobs Creation Act* of 2004, which enabled US-based MNCs to repatriate profits accumulated in tax havens at a discounted 5.25% – instead of the usual 35% – tax rate (Alexander, Mazza and Scholz 2009). A coalition of 93 corporations spent $282.7 million on a concerted effort to get this Act passed by the US Congress, and these same corporations then repatriated over $200 billion while realizing a total of $62.5 billion in tax savings – $221 of tax savings for every $1 they had invested in lobbying. The losses fell mostly on the populations of the less developed countries from which these MNCs had shifted their profits into tax havens; without the prospect of tax holidays in their home country, MNCs would have little to gain from such profit shifting.

19 Even the OECD's new landmark model agreement on automatic exchange of financial information is likely to exclude many less developed countries from its benefits because they lack the resources to set up the data collection arrangements required to qualify as a reciprocating partner.

fiscal policy-making process to public participation. Such financial transparency would greatly reduce illicit financial flows that, by draining less developed countries of capital and tax revenues, constitute a great impediment to sustainable development. Such transparency would additionally protect human rights also by curtailing the activities of criminals such as terrorists, money-launderers, and traffickers in persons, drugs and weapons.[20]

The two case studies illustrate how important existing supranational institutional arrangements can realistically be reformed so as to make them much less hostile to human rights fulfillment.[21] They begin to show that a substantial part of the horrendous current human rights deficit is traceable to how governments have shaped this emerging global order during the globalization period. The illustrations also bring out that we, the governments and citizens of the more affluent countries, are not mere bystanders to the deprivations suffered by the world's poor, but – through our foreign policies and especially our governments' role in shaping international rules and practices – are active participants in the non-fulfillment of their human rights. With some 18 million people dying prematurely each year from poverty-related causes, this may well be the largest, though not the gravest, human rights violation in human history. We must end it as quickly and decisively as we can by structuring, in accordance with Article 28 of the Universal Declaration, the rules of international cooperation so as to realize human rights insofar as this is reasonably possible.

---

20 For more on human rights and tax justice, see IBAHRI 2013.

21 Additional case studies could easily be supplied. Grandfathered into the WTO Agreement, protectionist policies by the affluent countries, especially in agriculture, continue to unfairly deprive poor populations of export opportunities. The absence of effective pollution regulation enables the richer countries to undermine living conditions in the poorer countries without providing reasonable compensation. The absence of substantial global labor standards organizes a race to the bottom in which poor countries, to attract foreign investment, must offer ever more exploitable workforces. Recognizing rulers on the basis of effective power alone as entitled to borrow money and sell natural resources on "their" country's behalf enhances the staying power of oppressive rulers and encourages coups and civil wars to captures these spoils. A largely unregulated international arms trade further aggravates these problems. These additional cases are discussed in Pogge 2008.

Integrating Human Rights into a Large Vision of Historical Progress

Many find the above human rights argument for global institutional reform compelling. But many also find that the argument leaves them cold, that the vision of a future world in which human rights are fully realized is not a sufficiently inspiring ideal that can truly capture our imagination. By design, human rights define a minimal threshold below which no human being should be reduced. A world in which human rights are fully realized can therefore still fall short in many ways, even in regard to political justice – for instance, it could be a world of very large and ever-increasing social, economic and political inequalities. To make the human rights argument practically and politically successful, we may then need to embed it in a richer vision of a future world that our efforts to realize human rights here and now can contribute to. I will try to do this here by describing a higher ideal that lies beyond the vision of a human-rights-compliant world order and, while still being realistic, can provide more inspiration for us to struggle for progress toward human rights and beyond.

What I have in mind is the extension to the global plane of an ideal that is familiar in domestic settings: the ideal of anti-nepotism. On reflection, this is actually quite a surprising element of ordinary moral thinking. Human beings can form very close bonds with one another: the bond between a parent and her child, for example. And it is very natural, then, for people who stand in such a very close relationship to give it much special weight: for a mother, say, greatly to prioritize her child over other people to whom she has a much slighter attachment or none at all. To be sure, the special weight a mother may give to the needs and interests of her child is not unlimited; but it is nevertheless quite substantial. It is all the more remarkable, then, that ordinary morality strictly limits the scope of any such partiality: there are certain contexts in which she may give even quite important interests of her child no special weight at all. When she makes decisions as principal of a high school, for instance, it would be wrong – *unfair* – of her to give greater weight to her own child's interest in good grades than to the analogous interest of other pupils. The same is true when she holds a public office that involves the awarding of government contracts.

The same is true even when she merely exercises the office of citizen, when she weighs in, for instance, on the question whether and how affirmative action should be continued in her country. In this context it would again be unfair of her if she based her public statements on private reasoning such as the following: "I love my children and, if they were girls or black, I would of course speak up in support of affirmative action. But in fact my kids are both white boys who would be taxed to fund an affirmative action effort that would also erode their competitive advantage over girls and non-white kids. For the sake of my children, I will therefore use my political voice in opposition to affirmative action programs." Even opponents of affirmative action would find such reasoning morally deficient: it is widely agreed that, in their public pronouncements and electoral decisions about matters of legislation and institutional design, citizens ought to set aside their private commitments and loyalties to focus exclusively on social justice and the national good.

This piece of ordinary moral thinking is surprisingly demanding. The requirement is not merely that, in cases of conflict or competition, one should give more weight to the demands of one's public roles – as parliamentarian or citizen, as judge, principal or procurement officer – than to any reasons arising from one's private roles. The requirement is rather that, in exercising one's public roles in designing and applying the rules and procedures of one's national society, one ought to be strictly impartial by giving no extra weight whatsoever to the needs and interests of one's own children, spouse, parents and friends for example. Acting in such an official role, one is to treat its demands as providing what Joseph Raz has called exclusionary reasons, that is, strong first-order reasons combined with second-order reasons to set aside other first-order reasons that would otherwise have competing relevance to one's conduct decisions (Raz 1990, ch. 1.2).[22]

It is remarkable that, in many national societies, such an impartiality requirement associated with certain roles and performances has come to be internalized and honored to the extent that it is. Centuries of social struggle on different continents and in diverse cultures have preceded this civilizational achievement. Crucially important to the historical outcome is the plain fact that, in any historical period, societies that were ahead in terms of internalizing a strong national impartiality requirement had a substantial competitive advantage over societies that were behind. By interfering with an efficient, merit-based division of labor, nepotism is a serious drag on a society's ability to solve its problems and to hold its own against other societies.

Let me try to sketch such a strong national impartiality requirement in a little more detail. Its guiding idea is that the basic rules of a society as well as its pol-

---

22 The faithful execution of such official roles would be slightly less demanding if its responsibilities were thought of as merely taking lexical priority over the occupant's private loyalties and commitments, which could then still serve as tie breakers among otherwise admissible options. If her son put in a bid that is exactly as good as that of another bidder, a procurement officer could then favor the bid of her son because he is her son. Our commitment to impartiality is such that, even in this case, we tend to feel better about the mother if she tosses a coin or disqualifies herself from the decision.

icies and officials ought to be *fair* by showing equal concern for the needs and interests of all members of this society. This implies various procedural and substantive requirements on national political organization. On the procedural side it implies that those who are bound by national rules enforced upon them within the national territory ought to be able to play an equal role in the formulation of these rules and of the institutional arrangements implementing and enforcing them. It would be clearly incompatible with citizens' equal moral standing, for example, if some society's laws were made by an assembly whose members were elected by male citizens alone or through a system of weighted voting that favors whites or males, for instance, or those who pay more taxes or live in thinly populated areas. Absent a compelling reason for giving more weight to the judgments of some citizens than to those of others,[23] some broadly democratic national system of government is required by the commitment to moral equality.

Somewhat more controversial is the idea that the moral equality of citizens places not merely formal but also material constraints on procedures of collective decision making. John Rawls argues, for instance, that the moral equality of citizens is violated by a society that does not maintain the fair value of the political liberties – a society like the United States, for instance, whose political competition is in large part funded and shaped by private campaign contributions.[24] Though formally satisfying the one-person-one vote requirement, the US in fact more closely approximates a one-dollar-one-vote system in which political outcomes are routinely auctioned and purchased through lobbying.

In addition to such (formal and material) *procedural* implications, the equal moral standing of citizens is widely believed also to entail *substantive* constraints on the legislative output of national political processes. These substantive constraints can again be classified as formal or material. A law barring an ethnic, religious or linguistic minority from higher education, for instance, would be widely

---

23 A compelling case can be made for the exclusion of children from democratic decision making: some rare exceptions notwithstanding, children are generally lacking the knowledge, experience and judgment requisite to making sound political decisions, and their interests are typically better protected by the political rights of their adult relatives as well as by their own future political rights.

24 See Rawls 1971, sec. 82, and especially Rawls 1993. Rawls would have regarded the US Supreme Court's judgments in *Citizens United v. Federal Election Commission* (558 U.S. 310, 2010) and *McCutcheon v. Federal Election Commission* (572 U.S. __, 2014) as flagrant violations of his first principle of justice: "Each person has an equal claim to a fully adequate scheme of equal basic rights and liberties, which scheme is compatible with the same scheme for all; and in this scheme the equal political liberties, and only those liberties, are to be guaranteed their fair value" (Rawls 1993, p. 5).

condemned as a *formal* violation of the moral equality of the members of the excluded minority. The *material* constraint such equal moral standing imposes on legislative outputs might be generally stated as the demand that the design of a society's social and economic institutions ought to reflect equitable trade-offs among the needs and interests of different population segments. Theorists differ on how to specify this demand. A weak version, which would probably be widely accepted in contemporary political philosophy, might be this. In the choice between two candidate national legislative outcomes, N_1 and N_2, if the representative groups that would do better with a decision in favor of N_1 are (i) larger, (ii) worse off[25] *and also* (iii) more strongly affected by the outcome than the representative groups that would do better with a decision in favor of N_2, then the basic commitment to moral equality requires that N_1 be chosen over N_2.[26] A national legislature making the opposite choice cannot credibly claim to be recognizing the losers as the moral equals of the winners, to be attaching as much importance to the needs and interests of the former as it is attaching to the needs and interests of the latter.

As I have sketched it, this national impartiality requirement may well be more detailed and determinate than the widely shared moral view I was trying to characterize. The fact remains that, in many countries, the moral commitment to such a national impartiality requirement is widespread and highly effective – partly through corresponding criminal law but mainly through internalization and informal sanctions – in keeping nepotism at bay. National impartiality requirements ground a defeasible presumption in favor of equal treatment that, though easily defeated in many contexts, is quite powerful in the absence of defeating reasons.

The formation of a highly influential global institutional order makes it highly appropriate to promote the emergence of a widespread moral commitment to an analogous *global* impartiality requirement. Its basic rationale would be that the fundamental equality of all human beings demands that, insofar as human agents are involved in the design or administration of global rules, practices or organizations, they ought to disregard their private, local *and national* commitments and loyalties to give equal consideration to the needs and interests of every

---

25 The intended meaning of (ii) is: those who would do better with a decision in favor of N_1 would do worse under N_1 than those who would do better with a decision in favor of N_2 would do under N_2. Together, (ii) and (iii) entail that, even under N_1, those who would do better with a decision in favor of N_1 would do worse than those who would do better with a decision in favor of N_2.
26 This demand is a very weak version of the Pigou-Dalton condition familiar to economists.

human being on this planet.[27] In these special contexts, agents ought to be guided exclusively by agent-neutral considerations.[28]

We might begin to specify such a global impartiality requirement by sketching analogues to the four implications of national impartiality explored in the preceding section. First, the equal moral standing of all human beings implies that global decision making ought to be designed so that all human beings are enabled to play a role in the formulation of global rules and of the global institutional arrangements that are implementing and enforcing these rules (procedural-formal). Second, in analogy to Rawls's fair-value requirement, moral equality implies, that global decision making ought to afford even to poorer, more vulnerable human beings opportunities to exert real political influence which do not fall far short of the corresponding opportunities enjoyed by wealthy and privileged people around the world (procedural-material).[29] Third, moral equality implies that all should be able to participate in global institutions, such as markets and communications, on equal terms (substantive-formal). Fourth, the moral equality of all human beings also implies that decisions about global rules must meet the analogue of the weak demand: in the choice between two candidate global agreements, G_1 and G_2, if the representative groups that would do better with a decision in favor of G_1 are (i) larger, (ii) worse off *and also* (iii) more strongly affected by the outcome than the representative groups that would do better with a decision in favor of G_2, then the basic commitment to moral equality requires that G_1 be chosen over G_2 (substantive-material). An international summit or rule-making body reaching the opposite decision cannot credibly claim to be recognizing the losers as the moral equals of the winners, to be attaching as much

---

27 I discuss this global impartiality requirement in Pogge (2008, ch. 5). Central to that book is, however, a weaker account of global justice: global institutional arrangements must be designed to fulfill human rights insofar as this is reasonably possible. Beyond this requirement, those involved in the design of global institutional arrangements would be free to give special weight to the (other) interests of their family, friends or compatriots.

28 Fully developed, this prescription would extend equal concern also to future generations. Those who, weighing in on matters of global institutional design, give priority to the needs and interests of members of their own generation over the needs and interests of the members of future and past generations act on reasons that are subtly agent-relative.

29 This condition could in principle be met by international decision making in a world of broadly democratic states where it is through their elected government's appointed emissaries, delegates or negotiators that individuals exert political influence upon the formulation of global rules and of the global institutional arrangements that are implementing and enforcing these rules. The condition is not met in our world, of course, where the political influence one US billionaire can exert on global institutional design is vastly greater than that of a million poor citizens of Niger or Haiti.

importance to the needs and interests of the former as it is attaching to the needs and interests of the latter.

Needless to say, present global political decision-making does not remotely satisfy any of these demands; and the supranational analogue of nepotism is so widely taken for granted that there is not even a word for it. The dominant view is that those involved in the creation and revision of international laws, treaties, agreements, or conventions or of intergovernmental agencies and organizations are morally permitted (and perhaps even required) robustly to advance the interests of their home country in such negotiations. This dominant view is tolerant of such national partiality even in regard to the interpretation, application and enforcement of international laws, treaties, agreements and conventions and in regard to the daily operation of intergovernmental agencies and organizations.

To be sure, heads of UN agencies and members of the WTO Appellate Body are expected to follow the relevant international rules and to give weight to the legitimate interests of countries other than their own. But it is widely expected and accepted that such persons give disproportionate weight to the interests of their own country and its governing elites. And in the context of such wide acceptance, these persons do in fact often and blatantly favor their home country in ways that would be met with near-unanimous condemnation at the national level. National governments consequently expend considerable efforts on filling important such positions with a compatriot. Consider the extreme length to which the US government regularly goes to ensure that the President of the World Bank will be one of their own. This effort stands in stark contrast to the effort that the government and citizens of Texas expend toward ensuring that the US President will be someone from Texas. The difference cannot be explained by the greater power and influence of the President of the World Bank – on the contrary! Rather, the difference is primarily explained by the fact that state officials and citizens throughout the US know that the President of the United States *will* not and politically *could* not substantially favor the interests of his or her home state; whereas government officials and individuals around the world well understand that the President of the World Bank will run the Bank to promote US economic and political interests and US ideological commitments, and that such conduct will be expected and accepted by the global elites and replicated by other intergovernmental officials and national governments.[30]

---

30 In light of the huge discrepancy between the sketched demands of a global impartiality requirement and such common practices and perceptions, one might wonder whether a commitment to the moral equality of all human beings really leads to the global impartiality requirement with the four implications I have outlined. Such doubts might be substantiated in two distinct

A global impartiality requirement is then, relative to the *status quo*, a quite radical proposal and yet also one that is quite obviously continuous with the national impartiality requirements that are widely accepted – at least in word if not always in deed – in the more developed societies. Its widespread acceptance around the world could slow and perhaps even reverse the inequality spiral discussed earlier, and such acceptance is politically not unrealistic once people understand that supranational institutional arrangements and governance organizations have become highly influential in their distributive effects and rather similar in their authority and functioning to national institutional arrangements and governmental agencies. As in the corresponding national historical processes, moral insight can be reinforced by a prudential appreciation of the collective costs imposed by national nepotism.

What we cannot count on in the global case, though, are the competitive pressures that have probably played a substantial role in the historical achievement of an unnatural but now (in some countries) widely accepted national impartiality requirement. It is clear enough that the global governance structures that have grown by leaps and bounds in the decades since the end of the Cold War – infested as they are with national nepotism – will not be able to solve the challenges facing human civilization. Foremost among these challenges are the threats posed by nationally controlled advanced weapons and other dangerous technologies, the threats of ecological catastrophe through climate change or resource depletion and the threats posed by supranational lobbying which results in inefficient and unstable supranational institutional arrangements that can lead to massive economic collapse. If humanity is to master these existential challenges, we must learn to reject national nepotism and to expunge it from our supranational rule making and international organizations. Given the magnitude of the threats, it would be good if we could get on with this learning before disaster strikes.

---

ways. One can argue that even in regard to national political decision making, mere moral equality does not have any of the implications most political philosophers believe it to have. Alternatively one could argue that whatever implications moral equality has for national political decision-making lack analogues in the realm of global political decision making. One would then have to explain, case by case, why moral equality should have a certain implication at the level of national politics without having the analogous cosmopolitan implication at the level of global politics. A paradigmatic effort in this vein is Nagel (2005), pointing to certain special features of intra-societal cooperation that supposedly make principles of egalitarian distributive justice applicable within, but not beyond societies. A general problem for such arguments is that they must explain why such principles apply even to societies in which the special features are absent: to societies divided by caste, class or religion, for instance, in which the rulers make no pretensions to ruling in the name or for the benefit of all.

Now rules, procedures and other institutional arrangements are not living, accountable creatures who could be expected to conform themselves to moral standards. Rather, their character and effects depend on the human agents who formulate, shape, design, interpret, apply, enforce, obey, violate, undermine or ignore them. Thus, moral prescriptions about what criteria rules and practices ought to meet must ultimately be cashed out as moral prescriptions addressed to human agents and, specifically, to the conduct of human agents in regard to such rules and practices. And similarly for moral prescriptions addressed to collective agents such as governments and international organizations. The global impartiality requirement is ultimately, then, a differentiation in the standards of moral assessment applying to the conduct of individual human agents. While they may and should give priority to their near and dear in their personal conduct and to their home country when they represent it in a fairly structured competitive context, they must be required to be suitably impartial in contexts where they – as individuals or in some official role or on behalf of a state or enterprise – contribute to the formulation, interpretation or implementation of global rules and procedures. In such contexts, their sole concern must be that these rules and practices, collectively, are *fair*, that is, justifiable by reference to the equally-weighted needs and interests of all human beings. This requirement is strong and extensive enough to ensure that, if most of us honor it, then the ensemble of supranational institutional arrangements will have the requisite impartiality, organizing a genuine *cosmopolis* in which countries, enterprises and individuals can cooperate and compete on a level playing field.

Given the high priority human rights enjoy over other human needs and interests, a global institutional order that is fair as defined would be one under which human rights would be realized insofar as reasonably possible – though such a global order would also go far beyond mere universal human-rights fulfillment. We might plausibly seek to approach such a *cosmopolis* by starting with a weaker impartiality requirement confined to human rights: insofar as human agents are involved in shaping and implementing supranational institutional arrangements, they must give equal weight to the human rights of all human beings and, in particular, no special weight to the human rights of their compatriots. This preliminary and weaker impartiality requirement would require persons, in the relevant contexts, to give to the human rights of non-compatriots as much weight as they give to the human rights of compatriots, while still allowing them to prioritize other needs and interests of their own country and compatriots.

The global impartiality requirement, the global analogue to anti-nepotism, reinforces then the demand of Article 28 for a global order in which the still enormous human rights deficits of the present would be overcome and human rights be fully realized. But it depicts such a global order not as humanity's ultimate end but as a stepping stone toward the higher ideal of a universal *cosmopolis* that would include all human beings as equals in that it would be governed by institutional arrangements and officials firmly committed to giving equal weight to the needs and interests of all human beings worldwide.

Bibliography

Alexander, Raquel M., Stephen W. Mazza and Susan Scholz (2009): "Measuring Rates of Return on Lobbying Expenditures: An Empirical Case Study of Tax Breaks for Multinational Corporations," *Journal of Law and Policy* 25, pp. 401–57.

Alston, Philip (1984): "International Law and the Right to Food." In: Eide, Asbjorn, Wenche Barth Eide, Susantha Goonatilake, Joan Gussow and Omawale (Eds.): *Food as a Human Right.* Tokyo: United Nations University Press.

Alston, Philip, and Katarina Tomaševski (Eds.) (1984): *The Right to Food.* Dordrecht: Martinus Nijhoff Publishers.

Amnesty International (2014): *Torture in 2014: 30 Years of Broken Promises.* New York: Amnesty International.

Beitz, Charles (2009): *The Idea of Human Rights.* Oxford: Oxford University Press.

Boston Consulting Group (2013): *Global Wealth 2013: Maintaining Momentum in a Complex World,* www.bcg.de/documents/file135355.pdf (December 14, 2014).

Christian Aid (2009): *False Profits: Robbing the Poor to Keep the Rich Tax-Free,* www.christianaid.org.uk/Images/false-profits.pdf (December 14, 2014).

Cranston, Maurice (1973): *What Are Human Rights?* London: Bodley Head.

FAO, IFAD and WFP (2013): *The State of Food Insecurity in the World 2013. The multiple dimensions of food security.* Rome: UN Food and Agriculture Organization.

Griffin, James (2008): *On Human Rights.* Oxford: Oxford University Press.

Hearson, Martin, and Richard Brooks (2012): "Calling Time," Action Aid, www.actionaid.org.uk/doc_lib/calling_time_on_tax_avoidance.pdf (December 14, 2014).

IBAHRI (International Bar Association's Human Rights Institute) Task Force on Illicit Financial Flows (2013): *Tax Abuses, Poverty and Human Rights,* www.ibanet.org/Human_Rights_Institute/TaskForce_IllicitFinancialFlows_Poverty_HumanRights.aspx (December 14, 2014).

Kar, Dev, and Brian LeBlanc (2013): *Illicit Financial Flows from Developing Countries: 2002–2011.* Washington: Global Financial Integrity, http://iff.gfintegrity.org/iff2013/2013report.html (December 14, 2014).

Nagel, Thomas (2005): "The Problem of Global Justice." In: *Philosophy and Public Affairs* 33, pp. 113–47.

Nyanwura, Edmund Mohammed, and Reuben K. Esena (2013): "Essential Medicines Availability and Affordability: A Case Study of the Top Ten Registered Diseases in Builsa District of Ghana." In: *International Journal of Scientific and Technological Research* 2. No. 8, pp. 208–19.

Orend, Brian (2002): *Human Rights: Concept and Context.* Peterborough, Ont.: Broadview Press.

Payne, Rachel, Gene Rowe, Fergus Bolger and Esther Shubert (2014): *Policy Options for Addressing Illicit Financial Flows: Results from a Delphi Study.* New Haven: Academics

Stand Against Poverty, http://academicsstand.org/2014/09/policy-options-for-addressing-illicit-financial-flows-results-from-a-delphi-study/ (December 14, 2014).

Pogge, Thomas (2008): *World Poverty and Human Rights: Cosmopolitan Responsibilities and Reforms*. 2nd edition. Cambridge: Polity Press.

Pogge, Thomas (2009): "Shue on Rights and Duties." In Beitz, Charles, and Robert Goodin (Eds.): *Global Basic Rights*. Oxford: Oxford University Press, pp. 113–30.

Rawls, John (1971): *A Theory of Justice*. Cambridge, MA: Harvard University Press.

Rawls, John (1993): "The Basic Liberties and their Priority." In: Rawls, John: *Political Liberalism*. New York: Columbia University Press, lecture VIII.

Raz, Joseph (1990): *Practical Reason and Norms*. Princeton: Princeton University Press.

Raquel Rolnik (2014): *The Right to Adequate Housing*. Geneva: Office of the United Nations High Commissioner for Human Rights.

Shue, Henry (1996): *Basic Rights: Subsistence, Affluence, and US Foreign Policy*. 2nd edition. Princeton: Princeton University Press.

Too-Kong, Tessa (Ed.) (2014): *The Millennium Development Goals Report 2014*. New York: United Nations.

Waldron, Jeremy (1989): "Rights in Conflict." In: *Ethics and International Affairs* 99, pp. 503–19.

Wellman, Carl (1999): *The Proliferation of Rights: Moral Progress or Empty Rhetoric?* Boulder, CO: Westview Press.

Paul Slovic and Daniel Västfjäll

The More Who Die, the Less We Care
Psychic Numbing and Genocide[31]

A defining element of catastrophes is the magnitude of their harmful consequences. To help society prevent or mitigate damage from catastrophes, immense
effort and technological sophistication are often employed to assess and communicate the size and scope of potential or actual losses. This effort assumes that
people can understand the resulting numbers and act on them appropriately.

However, recent behavioral research casts doubt on this fundamental assumption. Many people do not understand large numbers. Indeed, large numbers have
been found to lack meaning and to be underweighted in decisions unless they
convey affect (feeling). As a result, there is a paradox that rational models of
decision making fail to represent. On the one hand, we respond strongly to aid a
single individual in need. On the other hand, we often fail to prevent mass tragedies – such as genocide – or take appropriate measures to reduce potential losses
from natural disasters. We believe this occurs, in part, because as numbers get
larger and larger, we become insensitive; numbers fail to trigger the emotion or
feeling necessary to motivate action.

We shall address this problem of insensitivity to mass tragedy by identifying
certain circumstances in which it compromises the rationality of our actions and
by pointing briefly to strategies that might lessen or overcome this problem.

Background and Theory: The Importance of Affect

Risk management in the modern world relies upon two forms of thinking. Risk as
feelings refers to our instinctive and intuitive reactions to danger. Risk as analysis
brings logic, reason, quantification, and deliberation to bear on hazard manage-

---

31 This work draws on the material from Paul Slovic and Daniel Västfjäll (2013): "The More Who
Die, The Less We Care: Psychic Numbing and Genocide". In: *Behavioural Public Policy*. Edited by
Adam Oliver. Cambridge University Press. Reproduced with permission.

This material is based upon work supported by the Hewlett Foundation, and by the
U.S. National Science Foundation under Grant Nos. SES-1024808, SES-1227729, and SES-
1427414. Any opinions, findings, and conclusions or recommendations expressed in this material are those of the authors and do not necessarily reflect the views of the Hewlett Foundation or
the National Science Foundation.

ment. Compared to analysis, reliance on feelings tends to be a quicker, easier, and more efficient way to navigate in a complex, uncertain, and dangerous world. Hence, it is essential to rational behavior. Yet it sometimes misleads us. In such circumstances we need to ensure that reason and analysis also are employed.

Although the visceral emotion of fear certainly plays a role in risk as feelings, we shall focus here on the "faint whisper of emotion" called affect. As used here, affect refers to specific feelings of "goodness" or "badness" experienced with or without conscious awareness. Positive and negative feelings occur rapidly and automatically; note how quickly you sense the feelings associated with the word joy or the word hate. A large research literature in psychology documents the importance of affect in (1) conveying meaning upon information and (2) motivating behavior. Without affect, information lacks meaning and will not be used in judgment and decision making.

Facing Catastrophic Loss of Life

Risk as feelings is clearly rational, employing imagery and affect in remarkably accurate and efficient ways. But this way of responding to risk has a darker, non-rational side. Affect may misguide us in important ways. Particularly problematic is the difficulty of comprehending the meaning of catastrophic losses of life when relying on feelings. Research reviewed below shows that disaster statistics, no matter how large the numbers, lack emotion or feeling. As a result, they fail to convey the true meaning of such calamities and they fail to motivate proper action to prevent them.

The psychological factors underlying insensitivity to large-scale losses of human lives apply to catastrophic harm resulting from human malevolence, natural disasters, environmental degradation, and technological accidents. In particular, the psychological account described here can explain, in part, our failure to respond to the diffuse and seemingly distant threat posed by global warming as well as the threat posed by the presence of nuclear weaponry. Similar insensitivity may also underlie our failure to respond adequately to problems of famine, poverty, and disease afflicting large numbers of people around the world and even in our own backyard.

Genocide and Mass Atrocities: The Scope of the Problem

Over the past century the world has been shocked to learn of many horrific incidents of mass collective violence. The Holocaust of World War II stands out and, in recent years, atrocities in Rwanda, the Balkans, and Darfur have gained the world's attention. Today, humanitarian catastrophes in Syria and the Middle East are in the news.

Yet, these memorable cases are only a small part of the problem, as shown in Table 1. Mass atrocities, defined as the intended death of at least 1000 non-combatants from a distinct group in a period of sustained violence (Ulfelder and Valentino 2008), are not rare. Since 1900, 201 distinct cases resulted in an estimated 84 million fatalities, an average of about 470,000 each! The atrocities death toll is comparable to interstate wars and vastly greater than that from terrorism.

Table 1: Comparative measures of seriousness for state-sponsored mass atrocities (genocides and mass killings), intrastate and interstate wars, and terrorism.

Conflict Type	Number of Distinct Cases	Time Period	Seriousness	
			Total estimated fatalities for the cases	Estimated fatalities per case
Mass Atrocities	201	1900–2012	84,183,410	470,298
Interstate Wars	66	1900–2007	30,698,060	465,122
Excluding WW I and WW II	64	1900–2007	5,485,122	85,705
Intrastate Wars	228	1900–2007	5,469,738	28,1922
Terrorism (Domestic and International)	113,113	1970–2012	241,480	2

Tab. 1: Comparative measures of seriousness for state-sponsored mass atrocities. Slovic (2015) Pending Copyright Approval From Oxford University Press
Source: Adapted from Anderton (in press).

In addition to the stunning frequency and scale of mass atrocities, what stands out in historical accounts of these abuses is the inaction of bystanders. In her prizewinning book "A Problem from Hell: America and the Age of Genocide,"

Samantha Power documented the inadequacy of the U.S. Government's response to numerous genocides dating back to 1915 (Power 2003). She concluded:

> "No U.S. president has ever made genocide a priority and no U.S. president has ever suffered politically for his indifference to its occurrence. It is thus no coincidence that genocide rages on" (Power 2003, p. xxi).

Nowhere is the problem of apathy and inaction more starkly apparent than in the Darfur region of Western Sudan. Since February 2003, hundreds of thousands of people in Darfur have been murdered by government-supported militias, and millions have been forced to flee their burned-out villages for the dubious safety of refugee camps. This has been well documented (Hamilton 2011; Reeves 2007). And yet the world looks away.

The United Nations (UN) General Assembly adopted the Convention on the Prevention and Punishment of the Crime of Genocide in 1948 in the hope that "never again" would there be such odious crimes against humanity as occurred during the Holocaust of World War II. Eventually, some 140 states would ratify the Genocide Convention, yet it has rarely been invoked to prevent a potential attack or halt an ongoing massacre. Darfur has shone a particularly harsh light on the failures to intervene in genocide. As Richard Just (2008) has observed,

> ... we are awash in information about Darfur. ... [N]o genocide has ever been so thoroughly documented while it was taking place ... but the genocide continues. We document what we do not stop. The truth does not set anybody free. ... (p. 36).
> [H]ow could we have known so much and done so little? (p. 38).

Affect, Analysis, and the Value of Human Lives

This brings us to a crucial question: How should we value the saving of human lives? An analytic answer would look to basic principles or fundamental values for guidance. For example, Article 1 of the UN Universal Declaration of Human Rights asserts that "[a]ll human beings are born free and equal in dignity and rights."[32] We might infer from this the conclusion that every human life is of equal value. If so, then – applying a rational calculation – the value of saving N lives is N times the value of saving one life, as represented by the linear function in Figure 1.1a.

---

32 Full text available at: http://www.un.org/en/documents/udhr/

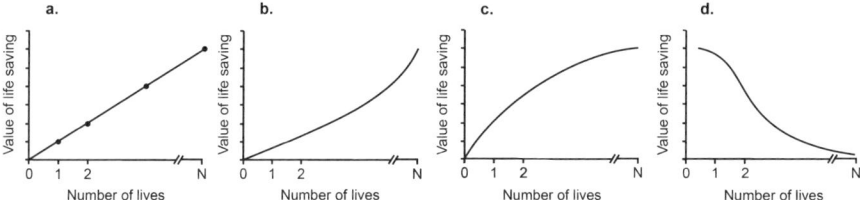

Fig. 1: Normative Models where (a) every life is of equal value and (b) large losses threaten group or societal descriptive models of (c) psychophysical numbing and (d) psychic numbing and the collapse of compassion. Source: Slovic (2007).

An argument can also be made for judging large losses of life to be disproportionately more serious because they threaten the social fabric and viability of a group or community (see Figure 1.1b). Debate can be had at the margins over whether one should assign greater value to younger people versus the elderly, or whether governments have a duty to give more weight to the lives of their own people, and so on, but a perspective approximating the equality of human lives is rather uncontroversial.

How do we actually value human lives? Research provides evidence in support of two descriptive models linked to affect and intuitive thinking that reflect values for lifesaving profoundly different from those depicted in the normative (rational) models shown in Figures 1.1a and 1.1b. Both of these descriptive models demonstrate responses that are insensitive to large losses of human life, consistent with apathy toward genocide.

The Psychophysical Model

There is considerable evidence that our affective responses and the resulting value we place on saving human lives follow the same sort of "psychophysical function" that characterizes our diminished sensitivity to changes in a wide range of perceptual and cognitive entities – brightness, loudness, heaviness, and wealth – as their underlying magnitudes increase.

As psychophysical research indicates, constant increases in the magnitude of a stimulus typically evoke smaller and smaller changes in response. Applying this principle to the valuing of human life suggests that a form of psychophysical numbing may result from our inability to appreciate losses of life as they become larger. The function in Figure 1.1c represents a value structure in which the importance of saving one life is great when it is the first, or only, life saved but diminishes as the total number of lives at risk increases. Thus, psychologically, the importance of saving one life pales against the background of a larger threat: We may not "feel" much difference, nor value the difference, between saving 87 lives and saving 88.

Fetherstonhaugh, Slovic, Johnson, and Friedrich (1997) demonstrated this potential for psychophysical numbing in the context of evaluating people's willingness to fund various lifesaving interventions. In a study involving a hypothetical grant funding agency, respondents were asked to indicate the number of lives a medical research institute would have to save to merit receipt of a $10 million grant. Nearly two-thirds of the respondents raised their minimum benefit requirements to warrant funding when there was a larger at-risk population, with a median value of 9,000 lives needing to be saved when 15,000 were at risk (implicitly valuing each life saved at $1,111), compared to a median of 100,000 lives needing to be saved out of 290,000 at risk (implicitly valuing each life saved at $100). Thus respondents saw saving 9,000 lives in the smaller population as more valuable than saving more than ten times as many lives in the larger population. The same study also found that people were less willing to send aid that would save 4,500 lives in Rwandan refugee camps as the size of the camps' at-risk population increased.

In recent years, vivid images of natural disasters in South Asia and the American Gulf Coast, and stories of individual victims there, brought to us through relentless, courageous, and intimate news coverage, unleashed an outpouring of compassion and humanitarian aid from all over the world. Perhaps there is hope here that vivid, personalized media coverage featuring victims could also motivate intervention to halt the killing.

Perhaps. Research demonstrates that people are much more willing to aid identified individuals than unidentified or statistical victims. But a cautionary note comes from a study in which Small, Loewenstein, and Slovic (2007) gave people who had just participated in a paid psychological experiment the opportunity to contribute up to $5 of their earnings to the charity Save the Children. In one condition, respondents were asked to donate money to feed an identified victim, a seven-year-old African girl named Rokia. Respondents in a second group were asked to donate to Rokia, but were also shown statistics of starvation in several African countries – millions in need. Unfortunately, coupling the statistical realities with Rokia's story of need reduced contributions to Rokia by about 40%!

Why did this occur? Perhaps the presence of statistics reduced the attention to Rokia essential for establishing the emotional connection necessary to motivate donations. Alternatively, recognition of the millions who would not be helped by one's small donation may have produced negative feelings that inhibited donations. Note the similarity here at the individual level to the failure to help 4,500 people in the larger refugee camp. The rationality of these responses can be questioned. We should not be deterred from helping 1 person, or 4,500, just because there are many others we cannot save!

In sum, research on psychophysical numbing is important because it demonstrates that feelings necessary for motivating lifesaving actions are not congruent with the normative/rational models in Figures 1.1a and 1.1b. The nonlinearity displayed in Figure 1.1c is consistent with the devaluing of incremental loss of life against the background of a large tragedy. It can thus explain why we don't feel any different upon learning that the death toll in Darfur is closer to 400,000 than to 200,000. What it does not fully explain, however, is apathy toward genocide, inasmuch as it implies that the response to initial loss of life will be strong and maintained, albeit with diminished sensitivity, as the losses increase. Evidence for a second descriptive model, better suited to explain apathy toward large losses of lives, follows.

The Collapse of Compassion

American writer Annie Dillard (1999) reads in her newspaper the headline "Head Spinning Numbers Cause Mind to Go Slack." She writes of "compassion fatigue" and asks, "At what number do other individuals blur for me?"[33]

An answer to Dillard's question is beginning to emerge from behavioral research. Studies by social psychologists find that a single individual, unlike a group, is viewed as a psychologically coherent unit. This leads to more extensive processing of information and stronger impressions about individuals than about groups. Consistent with this, a study in Israel found that people tend to feel more distress and compassion and to provide more aid when considering a single victim than when considering a group of eight victims (Kogut and Ritov 2005). A follow-up study in Sweden found that people felt less compassion and donated less aid toward a pair of victims than to either individual alone (Västfjäll, Slovic, Mayorga, and Peters 2014). Perhaps the blurring that Annie Dillard asked about begins for groups as small as two people.

The insensitivity to lifesaving portrayed by the psychophysical-numbing model is unsettling. But the studies just described suggest an even more disturbing psychological tendency. Our capacity to feel is limited. To the extent that valuation of lifesaving depends on feelings driven by attention or imagery, it might follow the function shown in Figure 1.1d, where the emotion or affective feeling

---

33 She struggles to think straight about the great losses that the world ignores: "More than two million children die a year from diarrhea and eight hundred thousand from measles. Do we blink? Stalin starved seven million Ukrainians in one year, Pol Pot killed two million Cambodians. ..." (Dillard, 1999, pp. 130–131).

is greatest at $N = 1$ but begins to fade at $N = 2$ and collapses at some higher value of N that becomes simply "a statistic" (Västfjäll et al., 2014). Whereas Robert J. Lifton (1967) coined the term psychic numbing to describe the "turning off" of feeling that enabled rescue workers to function during the horrific aftermath of the Hiroshima bombing, Figure 1.1d depicts a form of psychic numbing that is not beneficial. Rather, it leads to apathy and inaction, consistent with what is seen repeatedly in response to mass murder and genocide.

Perhaps both psychophysical and collapse valuations are activated within the same decision context as the number of lives at risk increases, resulting in a hybrid, inverted U-shaped function such as that shown in Figure 2. There is considerable evidence for a value function following such an inverted U-shaped function (Grant and Schwartz 2011; Reutskaja and Hogarth 2009; Smith 1983). For example, food consumption often follows this trajectory where the value of initial food intake is very high. After attaining some level of satiation, further food intake may no longer be attractive. Importantly, at some point (that may vary with individuals and over time and contexts) the value of further intake is going to decline, perhaps precipitously (Blundell et al., 2009). We believe that such a model describes how we respond to life valuation as well and thus contributes to the failure to respond adequately to genocide and mass atrocities (Västfjäll et al., 2014).

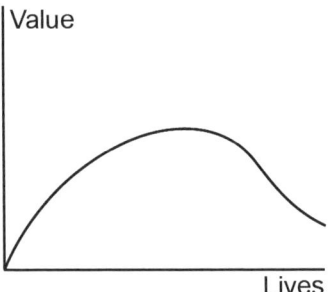

Fig. 2: A psychophysical-collapse function describing the value for saving lives. Adapted from Västfjäll et al. (2014).

The Failure of Moral Intuition

Thoughtful deliberation takes effort. Fortunately, evolution has equipped us with sophisticated cognitive and perceptual mechanisms that can guide us through our daily lives efficiently, with minimal need for "deep thinking."

For example, the natural and easy way to deal with moral issues is to rely on our intuitive feelings We can also apply reason and logical analysis to determine right and wrong, as our legal system attempts to do. But, as Jonathan Haidt (2001), a psychologist at the University of Virginia, has demonstrated, moral intuition comes first and usually dominates moral judgment unless we make an effort to critique and, if necessary, override our intuitive feelings.

Unfortunately, moral intuition underlies the descriptive models of lifesaving described above, where the importance of saving lives lessens or even declines as the number of people at risk increases. As a result, intuition fails us in the face of genocide and other disasters that threaten human lives and the environment on a large scale. We cannot trust it. It depends upon attention and feelings that may be hard to arouse and sustain over time for large numbers of victims, not to mention numbers as small as two. Left to its own devices, moral intuition will likely favor individual victims and sensational stories that are close to home and easy to imagine. Our sizable capacity to care for others may be demotivated by negative feelings resulting from thinking about those we cannot help. Or it may be overridden by pressing personal and local interests. Compassion for others has been characterized by social psychologist Daniel Batson as "a fragile flower, easily crushed by self-concern"(Batson, O'Quin, Fultz, Vanderplas, and Isen 1983). Faced with genocide and other mass tragedies, we cannot rely on our intuitions alone to guide us to act properly.

What Should We Do?

Behavioral research, supported by common observation and the record of repeated failures to arouse citizens and leaders to halt the scourge of genocide and to prevent thousands from perishing in natural disasters, sends a strong and important message. Our moral intuitions often seduce us into calmly turning away from massive losses of human lives, when we should be driven by outrage to act. This is no small weakness in our moral compass.

Educating moral intuitions

A natural response to the growing awareness of our insensitivity to problems of scale is to consider ways to educate moral intuitions. But how can we modify our gut instincts to better understand and respond to problems large in scope? This is not an easy question to answer, but we can speculate about possible ways forward.

One way of infusing intuition with greater feeling is by changing the way we frame information. The affective system primarily deals with the here and now and with concrete images. We speculate that reframing a large-scale problem may be a way of increasing affect, attention, and action. For instance, "800,000 killed in the last 100 days" can be broken down and reframed as "1 life lost every 11 seconds." Both the 1 life lost and the near-time horizon of "every 11 seconds" induce accessible images and thus are likely to create more affect and different information processing (Trope and Liberman 2003).

More generally, if statistics represent "human beings with the tears dried off," tears and feeling can be increased by highlighting the images that lie beneath the numbers. For example, organizers of a rally designed to get Congress to do something about 38,000 deaths a year from handguns piled 38,000 pairs of shoes in a mound in front of the Capitol (Associated Press 1994). Students at a middle school in Tennessee, struggling to comprehend the magnitude of the Holocaust, collected six million paper clips as a centerpiece for a memorial (Schroeder and Schroeder-Hildebrand 2004). In this light it is instructive to reflect on the characterization by Holocaust survivor Abel Hertzberg: "There were not six million Jews murdered: there was one murder, six million times."

When it comes to eliciting compassion, psychological experiments demonstrate that the identified individual victim, with a face and a name, has no peer, providing the face is not juxtaposed with the statistics of the larger need (Small et al., 2007). But we know this as well from personal experience and media coverage of heroic efforts to save individual lives. The world watched tensely as rescuers worked for several days to rescue 18-month-old Jessica McClure, who had fallen 22 feet into a narrow abandoned well shaft. Charities such as Save the Children have long recognized that it is better to endow a donor with a single, named child to support than to ask for contributions to the bigger cause.

The face need not even be human to motivate powerful intervention. A dog stranded aboard a tanker adrift in the Pacific was the subject of one of the most costly animal rescue efforts ever (Vendantam 2010). Hearing this, columnist Nicholas Kristof (2007) recalled cynically that a single hawk, Pale Male, evicted from his nest in Manhattan, aroused more indignation than two million homeless Sudanese. He observed that what was needed to galvanize the American public and their leaders to respond to the genocide in Darfur was a suffering puppy with big eyes and floppy ears:

> "If President Bush and the global public alike are unmoved by the slaughter of hundreds of thousands of fellow humans, maybe our last, best hope is that we can be galvanized by a puppy in distress".

Further to this last point, Paul Farmer (2005) has written eloquently about the power of images, narratives, and first-person testimony to overcome our "failure of imagination" in contemplating the fate of distant, suffering people. Such documentation can, he asserts, render abstract struggles personal and help make human rights violations "real" to those unlikely to suffer them. Who hasn't gained a deeper understanding of the Holocaust from reading Elie Wiesel's *Night* or *The Diary of Anne Frank*? Fiction, too, can create empathy and meaning. Barbara Kingsolver conveyed this rather elegantly:

> The power of fiction is to create empathy … . A newspaper could tell you that one hundred people, say, in an airplane, or in Israel, or in Iraq, have died today. And you can think to yourself, "How very sad," then turn the page and see how the Wildcats fared. But a novel could take just one of those hundred lives and show you exactly how it felt to be that person … . You could taste that person's breakfast, and love her family, and sort through her worries as your own, and know that a death in that household will be the end of the only life that someone will ever have. As important as yours. As important as mine. (Kingsolver, 1995, p. 231)

If the power of narrative and the personal story can be used to enhance the understanding of large numbers, we should think about how to use this to educate children about numbers. We teach children about the mechanics of operations such as addition, division, etc., but we do not teach them how to "feel the meaning" behind numbers that represent real life entities such as people and endangered species. Research in numerical cognition suggests that we have an "intuitive number sense" (Dehaene 1997) that allows us to represent and manipulate numerical quantities nonsymbolically (Peters, Slovic, Västfjäll and Mertz 2008). This number sense provides the conceptual basis for mapping numerical symbols onto their meaning (Dehaene 2001) and is present even in infants (Libertus and Brannon 2009). Yet, people fail to assign meaning to large numbers. The number sense initially develops to deal with precise representation of small numbers, while large quantities are only approximate representations (Feigenson, Dehaene, and Spelke 2004). The development of a nonverbal number sense, with the ability to approximate larger magnitudes, appears to depend on the input a child receives (Clements and Sarama 2007). Thus, children have the tools for understanding large numbers, but are not given sufficient knowledge on how to apply these tools to appropriately deal with real-world numbers. We believe that development of methods designed to help children "feel the meaning" of numbers might be an important way to combat psychic numbing. Maybe the intuitive number sense can be more tightly coupled with our moral sensitivities by educating children about the affective meaning of numbers.

From moral intuition to moral judgment

 If strategies to educate intuition and overcome psychic numbing are successful, there will be an upsurge of emotion that needs to be channeled into effective
action by national governments. Here is where moral intuitions need to be bol-
stered by moral judgment to design laws and institutions that commit states to
respond to mass tragedies, rather than being silent witnesses. And if education
of intuition proceeds slowly or not at all, maintaining the current level of psychic
numbing, the deficiencies of moral intuition point even more strongly to the need
for structured decision-aiding procedures and institutionalized mechanisms to
protect human rights. The former include sophisticated decision-analytic tech-
niques designed to clarify the relevant objectives and ensure that actions taken
are consistent with considered normative values for those objectives (Slovic,
Västfjäll, and Gregory 2012). For lifesaving values, the models in Figures 1a and
1b might be appropriate. Regarding institutional mechanisms, the Convention on
the Prevention and Punishment of the Crime of Genocide and the UN (1948) were
supposed to do this but they have repeatedly failed. Efforts to address this with
new treaties such as "responsibility to protect" (UN 2005) are urgently needed.

 Recognizing that international actors will resist laws that precommit them to
act to prevent or stop genocide, Slovic, Zionts, Woods, Goodman, and Jinks (2013)
have proposed a "softer" solution based on the intrinsic reasonableness of moral
judgments applied to the value of human life. Specifically, officials should be
required to publically deliberate and reason about actions to take in response to
genocide and other mass atrocities. Just as we expect government to proffer reasons
to justify intervention, we should expect and require public justification for decisions not to intervene to save human lives. This merging of intuition and deliberation may be achieved through the reporting requirements of a deliberation-forcing
regime that would likely ramp up pressure on governments to take action.

Conclusion

The stakes are high. Failure to overcome the numbing to which our moral intuitions are susceptible may force us to passively witness another century of genocide and mass abuses of innocent people, as in the previous century. Educating
intuitions through the use of images, narratives, and first person testimony holds
promise for infusing numerical data with emotional meaning. Laws and institutions, designed with an understanding of the shortcomings of intuitive response,
hold another vital key to meaningful interventions.

Bibliography

Anderton, Charles (in press): "Datasets and trends of genocide, mass killing, and other civilian atrocities". In: Anderton, Charles/Brauer, Jurgen (Eds.). *Economic aspects of genocide, mass atrocity, and their prevention*. Oxford, UK: Oxford University Press.

Associated Press (1994, September 21): "38,000 shoes stand for loss in lethal year". *The Register-Guard*, p. 6A.

Batson, Daniel/ O'Quin, Karen/Fultz, Jim/Vanderplas, Mary/Isen, Alice (1983): "Self-reported distress and empathy and egoistic versus altruistic motivation for helping". *Journal of Personality and Social Psychology, 45*, 706–718.

Blundell, John/De Graaf, Kees/Finlayson, Graham/Halford, Jason/Hetherington, Marion/King, Neil/Stubbs, Richard (2009): "Measuring food intake, hunger, satiety and satiation in the laboratory". In: David B. Allison, Monica L. Baskin (Eds.): *Handbook of assessment methods for eating behaviours and weight-related problems: Measures, theory and research* (2nd ed., pp. 283–325). Newbury Park, CA: Sage.

Clements, Douglas/Sarama, Julie (2007): "Early childhood mathematics learning". In: J. F. K. Lester (Ed.): *Second handbook of research on mathematics teaching and learning* (pp. 461–555). New York: Information Age.

Dehaene, Stanislas (1997): *"The number sense: How the mind creates mathematics"*. New York: Oxford University Press.

Dehaene, Stanislas (2001): "Précis of the number sense". *Mind & Language, 16*, 16–36.

Dillard, Annie (1999): *"For the time being"*. New York: Alfred A. Knopf.

Farmer, Paul (2005): *"Never again? Reflections on human values and human rights"*. Paper presented at the Tanner Lectures on Human Values, Salt Lake City, Utah. Retrieved from http://tannerlectures.utah.edu/_documents/a-to-z/f/Farmer_2006.pdf, visited on 10 December 2014.

Feigenson, Lisa/Dehaene, Stanislas/Spelke, Elizabeth (2004): "Core systems of number". *Trends in Cognitive Sciences, 8*, 307–314.

Fetherstonhaugh, David/Slovic, Paul/Johnson, Stephen/Friedrich, James (1997): "Insensitivity to the value of human life: A study of psychophysical numbing". *Journal of Risk and Uncertainty, 14*, 283–300.

Grant, Adam/Schwartz, Barry (2011): "Too much of a good thing: The challenge and opportunity of the inverted U". *Perspectives on Psychological Science, 6*, 61–76.

Haidt, Jonathan (2001): "The emotional dog and its rational tail: A social intuitionist approach to moral judgment". *Psychological Review, 108*, 814–834.

Hamilton, Rebecca (2011): *Fighting for Darfur: Public action and the struggle to stop genocide*. New York: Macmillan Publishers.

Just, Richard (2008, August): "The truth will not set you free: Everything we know about Darfur and everything we're not doing about it". *The New Republic, 239*, 36–47.

Kingsolver, Barbara (1995): *High tide in Tucson*. New York: HarperCollins.

Kogut, Tehila/Ritov, Ilana (2005): "The 'identified victim' effect: An identified group, or just a single individual?". *Journal of Behavioral Decision Making, 18*, 157–167.

Kristof, Nicholas (2007, May 10): "Save the Darfur puppy". *The New York Times. http://query. nytimes.com/gst/fullpage.html?res=9902EFD61731F933A25756C0A9619C8B63*, visited on 10 December 2014.

Libertus, Melissa/Brannon, Elizabeth (2009): Behavioral and neural basis for number sense in infancy. *Current Directions in Psychological Science, 18*, 346–351.

Lifton, Robert (1967): *Death in life: Survivors of Hiroshima*. New York: Random House.

Peters, Ellen/Slovic, Paul/Västfjäll, Daniel/Mertz, C. K. (2008): "Intuitive numbers guide decisions". *Judgment and Decision Making, 3*, 619–635.

Power, Samantha (2003): *A problem from hell: America and the age of genocide*. New York: Harper Perennial.

Reeves, Eric (2007): *A long day's dying: Critical moments in the Darfur genocide*. Toronto, Canada: Key Publishing House.

Reutskaja, Elena/Hogarth, Robin M (2009): "Satisfaction in choice as a function of the number of alternatives: When 'goods satiate' ". *Psychology & Marketing, 26*, 197–203.

Schroeder, Peter/Schroeder-Hildebrand, Dagmar (2004): *Six million paper clips: The making of a children's holocaust museum*. Minneapolis, MN: Kar-Ben.

Slovic, P. (2007): "If I look at the mass I will never act: Psychic numbing and genocide". *Judgment and Decision Making, 2*, 79–95.

Slovic, Paul/Vastfjall, Daniel (2013): "The more who die, the less we care: Psychic numbing and genocide". In A. J. Oliver (Ed.), *Behavioural public policy* (pp. 94–114). UK: Cambridge University Press.

Slovic, Paul/Västfjäll, Daniel/Gregory, Robin (2012): "Informing decisions to prevent genocide". *SAIS Review, 32*, 33–47.

Slovic, Paul/Zionts, David/Woods, Andrew/Goodman, Ryan/Jinks, Derek (2013): "Psychic numbing and mass atrocity". In: Eldar Shafir (Ed.): *The behavioral foundations of public policy* (pp. 126–142). NJ: Princeton University Press.

Small, Deborah/Loewenstein, George/Slovic, Paul (2007): "Sympathy and callousness: The impact of deliberative thought on donations to identifiable and statistical victims". *Organizational Behavior and Human Decision Processes, 102*, 143–153.

Smith, Barry (1983): "Extraversion and electrodermal activity: Arousability and the inverted-U". *Personality and Individual Differences, 4*, 411–419.

Trope, Yaacov/Liberman, Nira (2003): "Temporal construal". *Psychological Review, 110*, 403–421.

Ulfelder, Jay/Valentino, Benjamin (2008): *"Assessing risks of state-sponsored mass killing"*. http://ssrn.com/abstract=1703426, visited on 10 December 2014.

United Nations (UN) General Assembly (1948, December): "Convention on the prevention and punishment of the crime of genocide". http://www.un.org/en/preventgenocide/adviser/genocide_prevention.shtml, visited on 10 December 2014.

United Nations (UN) General Assembly (2005, October): "Resolution adopted by the General Assembly: 60/1. 2005 World Summit outcome". New York: Author. http://unpan1.un.org/intradoc/groups/public/documents/un/unpan021752.pdf. visited on 10 December 2014.

Västfjäll, Daniel/Slovic, Paul/Mayorga, Marcus/Peters, Ellen (2014): "Compassion fade: Affect and charity are greatest for a single child in need". *PLos ONE, 9*, e100115.

Vendantam, Shankar (2010): *"The hidden brain: How our unconscious minds elect presidents, control markets, wage wars, and save our lives"*. New York: Spiegel & Grau.

Rüdiger Bittner
On Invoking Human Rights When There Aren't Any

Human rights are supposed to be rights that human beings hold, not thanks to a particular legal transaction, like a declaration, a grant or a contract, but just thanks to their being human.

Doubts

Doubts about the existence of such rights are aroused by the fact that the idea of them has a questionable pedigree. Here is a sketch. In the late 18th century human rights, then called the rights of man, took the place of natural rights. This shift was largely one in terminology, not in substance, for natural rights were called natural precisely because people were similarly taken to hold these independently of any legal transaction. Also, natural rights were always understood to be held only by human beings, so that talking of human rights instead did not lead to a narrower domain of right-holders. In fact, talk of human rather than natural rights tended to widen the domain of right holders, because human rights were explicitly taken to be held by every human being, a point not commonly insisted upon in natural rights doctrines.

Natural rights theory, flourishing from the 16th to the 18th century, has its roots in medieval thought. The 12th century commentators on church law made the crucial step from the much older idea of natural law as the order of the world to the idea of a right held by a human individual, which is therefore often called a subjective right now, or with the useful German term, an *Anrecht* in contrast to *Recht*.[34]

Natural law in the objective sense in turn was first conceived by the Stoics who, taking up ideas from Heraclitus and the Sophists, saw the entire world as a big city and so as ordered by law.[35] Christian doctrine adopted this idea, making

---

34 For a helpful explanation of the difference between subjective rights and objective right, between *Anrecht* and *Recht*, see Geuss (2008), p. 60–67. For details of the genesis of the subjective rights idiom, see Tierney (1997), esp. chap. 2.
35 See Diogenes Laertius VII 87 and Philo Alexandrinus, de Ioseph II 46 (von Arnim 1903–1924, III 4 and 323).

god the law-giver of natural law, whereas the Stoics had not seen this law as imposed by someone, but as the rational order inherent in what there is.

This is a history of errors. There is no common law of things, which is right reason going through everything there is, as the Stoic Chrysippus taught, according to Diogenes' report just cited. We know of particular regularities holding for this or that sort of thing, but we do not know of substantive laws governing all there is. And were the physicists to come up with the "theory of everything", as it is called, it could not be claimed to be particularly reasonable. What is reasonable, given what we know right now, about light's travelling with the speed it does? Consequently, there is no reason to suppose that humans, since they are endowed with reason, are called upon to adjust their steps to that order of the world, as the Stoics also held, thus giving the law of the world both physical and ethical significance. Furthermore, Christianity's fragile compromise between its Hebrew and Greek legacies does not stand up: creation and rational order of the world do not fit together. Finally, individuals' rights do not make sense in a natural law framework. For under natural law some things just are right, and while some individuals may benefit from this or that being right, to speak in the subjective rights idiom of individuals' having its being right does not make sense.

So in fact there is no natural law as Thomas Aquinas conceived it, and neither are there the natural rights taught by John Locke and the other writers in the early modern period. No doubt European and American histories were importantly influenced by these ideas. False they are no less. To be sure, this tradition full of error might have suddenly born truth in the late 18th century. More likely is that an idea as steeped in its tradition as the idea of human rights merely continues those traditional errors under a new guise.

Problem

Doubts whether there are human rights are strengthened by the problem of limits. Human rights are humans' rights, but do ants for instance have rights too? If not, why does the human species have this particularity among the animals? The standard answer has been that humans alone have reason and therefore rights. Leaving aside the problem that some humans do not yet or no longer have reason, while allegedly covered by human rights, the central problem is the "therefore" in the preceding sentence. Even if reason is our speciality, matched by no other creature, why should that give us rights? Suppose that ants carry, relative to their own weight, heavier burdens than any other animal. Would that give them ant rights? If not, why does reasoning capacity count right-wise for more than carrying capacity? If ants do have rights, though, how about bacteria, leaves, winds, atoms? Somewhere, presumably, there will have to be a line separating right-holders from other entities, but wherever it is drawn, it will appear arbitrary. The trouble is that, for all the talk of natural rights, there is a tension between nature and rights. Rights are a privilege of those holding them, but within nature there are no differences of rank. It just does not make sense to say that birch-trees are higher than ducks in the order of nature, or conversely. Why then should humans enjoy such a higher standing?

True, one might refuse to draw such a line and give rights to whatever exists, but such an extension in effect relinquishes the concept of an individual's right. For violating such a right was supposed to be merely one kind of doing wrong, and if everything has rights, then any wrong will be a violation of somebody's or something's right, and the concept of an individual's right will no longer have any work to do.[36]

Arguments

Doubts whether there are human rights are confirmed, finally, by the fact that no good argument for their existence has been produced.[37] To give just two instances, one old, one new: Immanuel Kant, one of the first philosophers to speak expressly of "a right to which every human being by virtue of being human is entitled",[38] did not offer, in that passage or elsewhere, anything even pretending to show that there is such a right. And while James Griffin, in his recent book on human rights, does offer what he calls an account of them, he does not mean by that an argument showing that they exist. He is content to start with human rights as they are used in current discourse and to inquire "what higher principles one must resort to in order to explain their moral weight".[39] So he is arguing only from, not for human rights, which indeed is how the human rights literature generally proceeds.

Perhaps the thought is that the matter is too clear to need argument, but that is an error. It is not at all "self-evident", as Thomas Jefferson and his fellow deputies in the second continental Congress held[40], that humans as such have rights,

---

36 On this point see Thomson (1986), p. 13 f.
37 Here I follow MacIntyre (1981), p. 67.
38 Kant (1914), p. 237.
39 Griffin (2008), p. 29.
40 The declaration of independence (1776), para. 2.

let alone that they were endowed with them by their creator. In fact, by including the creator under the self-evident, the signatories of this important document show that they were not concerned to speak truly, but to warm the hearts of the right-thinking, for by 1776 it cannot have escaped them that serious people had rejected the idea of creation entirely. Self-evidence then being mere trumpeting, we need to see an argument before believing that humans have these rights. As no good argument has been given, the conclusion is, at least for the time being, that they do not have them.

Raymond Geuss has gone further and argued that a "'human right' is an inherently vacuous conception" on the grounds that for a right to exist there needs to be a specifiable and more or less effective mechanism of enforcing it in place, a condition not fulfilled in the case of human rights.[41] However, that condition appears too demanding. The process in the last few decades has gone the opposite way: first the rights were declared, then institutions beginning to enforce them were established. How good a job they have done is not the issue here.[42] The point is, to proceed in that order is not clearly preposterous.

Imagination

At this point it is tempting to settle instead for the imagination of human rights. Why care, it might be said, whether humans really have these rights? Whether or not they do, the rights are part of what some authors call the social imaginary, at least in the rich western countries, thus part of our social world. In that sense, they certainly are there, and it is too late to turn one's back on them, on grounds of non-existence.[43]

Yet there is no social imaginary. Society does not imagine. Neither does it remember, Halbwachs (1950) and Assmann (1992) to the contrary. People do these things or, more generally, people think and talk. Their thought and talk, though, does not form a unity, neither one per individual nor a society-wide one. It is all bits and pieces. To be sure, there are similarities and influences between these pieces, there are mixtures, oppositions, substitutions, and these processes are worth investigating in cultural studies. They just do not form a whole. Hence,

---

41 Geuss (2001), p. 143 f.
42 On this question see Campbell et al. (eds.), (2011).
43 This seems to be the reply emerging from Koschorke et al. (2007) as well as from Lüdemann (2004).

there is no such thing as society's self-knowledge[44] or society's *mise en scène* of itself,[45] ideas supposedly underwriting the specious singular of the phrase "the social imaginary" or indeed "collective imaginary".[46] Also, if there were such a thing, it would not be particularly important in social terms. Contrary to the tradition of Herder and Hegel, which, via Cornelius Castoriadis' work,[47] seems to captivate the friends of the social imaginary, it is not when a society comprehends itself, to repeat: as it does not, that it fully realizes itself. People's thinking and talking, of social and other matters, is mere "super-structure": perhaps more than just a dependent variable as in Marx, but certainly significant only within the context of economic and political processes. Leaving aside, though, the idealist leanings of these theories, the main point is that human rights are not part of the social imaginary, there being no such thing. The idea of human rights is just one idea floating around and thus as liable to being found empty as any other.

Still, even if human rights are merely imaginary, in the ordinary sense of the term, human rights talk need not therefore be a bad thing. We often speak of things that are merely imagined, and in many ways such talk can be helpful. We can give people a good time, we can guide and encourage them, we can even explain to them how things really are by telling them stories that represent things other than they really are; and sometimes our audience knows what we are doing, sometimes they don't, and often they don't care. On the other hand, works of the imagination can also be harmful. We can mislead, confuse and frighten people by telling them of things that do not exist. (Think of works of the religious imagination.) So with human rights not existing, it is still worth asking whether talk of human rights, imaginary though it be, helps or harms.

Long stories short

This talk certainly helps with abbreviation. You need not specify in detail what some dictator, army or organisation did to human beings in their power. You may summarily speak of the human rights of the latter having been violated, thereby also indicating the seriousness of what happened.

This is an advantage, but it can look bigger than it is. For among those who think that "human rights" refers to something, the precise extension of the term

---

44 Lüdemann (2004), p. 27.
45 Koschorke (2007), p. 62.
46 I am following here Kohns (2013).
47 Castoriadis (1975).

is controversial. That is to say, people disagree on whether such and such is a human right, as opposed to being a mere moral or mere legal right or even no right at all. Thus in using the abbreviation "human rights" for a certain set of moral concerns, you cannot be certain that your audience has in mind the same set. On the other hand, a core range of human rights, the rights, roughly, not to be killed, maimed, raped and tortured, are not in dispute, and mostly, when people speak without further specification of the violation of human rights, it is actions of these kinds to which they are referring.

Cutting long stories short has its drawbacks. Quick and easy abbreviations can make both speakers and listeners forget the weight of what is getting lumped together under them, and the expression "human rights violation" in particular lends itself to a clinically unconcerned way of speaking. But then virtually any description of serious abuse or neglect carries that danger, and to avoid abbreviations does not protect against being facile, or technical.

Truth

Those who invoke human rights speak of what is not there and thus fail to speak the truth. Is that a drawback? – In academic discussions it can be. It is no pleasure to be in a position like Kant's in the passage referred to above, enunciating a grand claim and then leaving the stage without offering the slightest support for it. However, given that human rights talk has caught on to the degree it has, one is at present fairly safe from being asked to justify speaking in these terms. Moreover, academia punishes mildly, and does so with good reason: people would not dare put forward new ideas if they really had to suffer for saying what is false.

Does it harm, then, not academically, but politically, to say what is false? – Not in general. Some political endeavours have come to a halt because of blatant lies told on their behalf, but these have concerned mostly plain matters of fact, like when someone knew what. In broader statements of political outlook and aims you can get away with just about any falsehood, provided the setting is right and the audience receptive. Ronald Reagan called the killers he sent to Nicaragua "freedom fighters", without his cause getting perceptibly damaged. Neither will the fact that there are no human rights prove a hindrance, at least under current conditions, to the efforts of those who struggle to have them respected.

Insincerity is different. People often damage their cause when they themselves think they are not speaking the truth. But this is not relevant here. Most of those invoking human rights do think there is something to invoke.

Interaction

Human rights talk suffers from a more serious problem than that of being about nothing. It does not describe what happens in political terms.

Human rights talk casts people as recipients. It says that being human they ought to receive such and such and ought not to have such and such done to them. When some people do not receive what they ought to receive, we can within the human rights script only state this lack: they go without something that is owed to them. And perhaps we can complain, before some court or to heaven: "Ach Gott, vom Himmel sieh darein" (Ah God, from heaven look onto this). But that is all: in terms of human rights there is no more to say than that some people did not receive what by right they should have received. Since human rights talk is mostly about people not receiving what they are due, the point can also be put thus: Human rights talk casts people as victims.

That is not a productive way to think of them. What is missing from the human rights picture is doers, it only contains "lackers". For in fact people's lacking something was brought about by other people's taking it away or in other ways preventing them from getting it or even by their own failure to hold on to it, and these things in turn were brought about by what still others did. That is to say, there is a story behind the lack, but talk of human rights having been respected or violated leaves that story out of sight. Not that anyone, friend of human rights or not, will deny that there is such a story. The point is, the story is only viewed in regard to its bringing about these results, in a kind of utilitarian spirit: what are the pay-offs? In this way, human rights talk remains, for all its insisting on rights, philanthropical, which is to say, concerned with rectifying what recipients receive. Thus it gives no footing to a political understanding, for that is all about the story behind the lack and about the direction in which it may be turned. Such a story always involves different parties. One can all by oneself lack what one is due, and so for that matter have what one is due, but what is really going on is that people exclude, suppress, exploit, torture, kill people, and so on, and these always take two, more than two, actually, since the power to do any of these things is owed to others. Human rights talk focuses on whether some human beings end up with the share they are due, but that is not the right focus for a political view of things, which is interested in the whole process that leads to people's holding this or that share.

Obligations

This is related to a line of argument that Onora O'Neill has long been pursuing. Back in 1986, she noted:

> "The vocabulary of rights has a complex formal structure, but is oddly remote from action."[48]

At that point she recommended replacing the vocabulary of rights with that of obligations, the latter being in any case more powerful, since some obligations, the imperfect ones, as for instance beneficence, do not have rights corresponding to them.[49] This last point may not stand up, however. Thomas Pogge argued convincingly that talk of obligations, imperfect no less than perfect ones, can be translated without loss into the rights idiom.[50] For while possible benefactors are not, under an imperfect obligation, bound to help some particular individual, they are bound to help some needy individual or other, to the extent they can. Hence a possible beneficiary can be understood to hold a corresponding right, not to be sure a right to receive help, but a right to be one of a group of individuals some of whom receive help, to the extent that benefactors are able to help. True, on this construction needy individuals who receive nothing because the basket is empty before it comes to them are not having their rights violated by these benefactors. That seems correct, though: as the benefactors did all they could, there is no claim left that could be brought against them.

Supposing that this is so and obligation talk does not extend more widely than rights talk, the more important question remains whether to speak in terms of obligations does remedy the defect of rights, whether with them we are indeed closer to action. It is doubtful that we are. In terms of obligations we state that one does or does not do what one should do, in terms of rights we state that one is or is not done to what one should be done to, and these are two ways of saying the same thing. The trouble with rights talk is not that it looks at actions from the receiving rather than the doer's end, but that it does not really look at actions at all, which is to say, at the processes leading to the distributions that rights talk then welcomes or deplores. And in that respect talk of obligations does no better. Taking actions from the opposite end, it likewise fails to look at the processes that lead people to do what in obligations talk they may then be praised or condemned for doing. Both rights and obligations talk remain committed to the "Ach

---

48 O'Neill (1986), p. 119.
49 O'Neill (1986), p. 104, (1989), p. 190. See also the more recent (2005).
50 Pogge (1992).

Gott, vom Himmel sieh darein"-perspective. God is not the point, to be sure, but the view from above that has us ask about what one did or what one underwent whether it was as it should be. And no longer to stay remote from action would instead mean to return to the horizontal perspective of looking at the conditions under which people's interactions take this form or that one, lead to this or that result.

Without rights

The "remote from action"-objection to human rights talk will appear unfair. Those who describe political events in terms of human rights' being respected or violated do not leave it at that, but certainly pay attention to causes of things' having gone this way and to prospects for them to go another way. Look at Thomas Pogge's proposal for changing the pharmaceutical market so as to provide access to medication for the poor.[51] Isn't that as horizontal as one could wish?

Yes, the interesting human rights literature goes political, but to the extent it does it no longer needs the appeal to human rights. Once we understand why and how exploitation, for instance, became the dominant social relationship in some country and also see how it might come to an end, people's right that it end has no longer any work to do. It can be dropped in theory: the understanding just sketched does not depend on there being such a right. It can be dropped in practice: those who fight exploitation need not rely on there being such a right. Think of what Karl Marx does in *Capital,* a Marx shorn, that is, of the claims of historical materialism. He tells us how capitalist exploitation works, how it became dominant in England and other European countries, how it might end and what people can do to advance its end. Whether this theory itself is true and empirically well founded is not the issue now. The point is, it does not have to appeal to a right of the exploited that exploitation end, nor for that matter to an obligation to work towards its end.[52] And what holds for exploitation, holds as well for the other social relationships in which people are violated in their alleged human rights.

Objection: Accounts that fail to appeal to rights or, equivalently, obligations are too weak. They do not provide reasons to fight exploitation, to stay with this example. Only people's having a right not to be exploited or people's having a duty to end exploitation provides such reasons. And these rights need to be

---

51 Pogge (2008).
52 See Wood (1981), chap. 9.

human rights for, as Marx himself insisted, states could easily be in the hands of the exploiters or their agents, so the rights granted by them may well not be strong enough to call for an end of exploitation.

The objection assumes that without rights or obligations in place, there are no reasons left to fight exploitation; more generally, that right and duty hold a monopoly on grounds for doing sensible things. If this were true, it would indeed be worrying that there are no human rights, because then there would be no reasons to do anything against what are called human rights violations. Clearly, though, this is not true. Witness Marx once again: he cannot have thought that, in dismissing "ideological cant of right" (*ideologische Rechts-Flausen*)[53], he deprived workers of reasons for fighting exploitation. In fact, one's being exploited can all by itself be a reason for somebody, oneself or someone else, to do something against it. One need not be called upon either by somebody's right or by one's own duty to do what under the circumstances is the right thing to do – and "right" now means neither "what somebody has a right to" (subjective right) nor "what is in accordance with the order of the world" (objective right). It just means "what in view of the circumstances it makes most sense to do".[54]

Perhaps it will be replied that lots of people think that exploiting others makes excellent sense, so to go by the criterion of what makes most sense to do is not safe, morally speaking. – True, but no criterion is. People can as easily be mistaken about their duties: Eichmann defended himself by appealing to the categorical imperative. Given, then, that a safe criterion is not to be had, the dispute is only whether, having determined as best one can the right thing to do under the circumstances, that result still needs to be cast in the mould of what one is bound by duty to do, or what treatment others have a right to; and it is hard to see why this should be necessary.

Or it may be replied that, while there may be reasons to do what makes most sense, independently of any backing by right or duty, such reasons are not effective, people do not act on them. – And on reasons backed by right or duty they do act? It is difficult to be confident that human rights talk improves matters; that thanks to our calling the horrors that people inflict on people a violation of what the latter are entitled to by being human, fewer people get killed, tortured, starved, raped and so on. It would seem, though this is admittedly mere guessing, that killers, torturers etc. and also their commanders change their ways, not on learning that they violate the rights of their victims, but on finding themselves

---

53 Marx (1974), p. 22.
54 This paragraph follows Foot's (2002b). However, she disavows that paper to some extent both in her (2001), chap. 1 and in (2002a).

in a situation that allows or invites a different response. And to figure out what changes it takes to have better alternatives for people than so called human rights violations requires precisely to go into the details of the antecedent stories that human rights talk, focussing on the victims, leaves unattended.

Attraction

If reference to human rights is useless or an obstacle for a political understanding, why has it become such a favourite both in the media and in academic talk, especially in the last few decades? Samuel Moyn suggested that the theme of human rights binds the utopian energies set free when the dominant ideologies of East and West lost their credibility by the end of the 1960's.[55] It is doubtful, however, that there was and is still such an undercurrent of utopian thought that could be tapped by human rights talk. Utopia belongs, Ernst Bloch's work notwithstanding, to the *ancien régime*. Why bother writing about Noplace or Goodplace, these being literal translations for "utopia"[56], if things can be changed right here, by revolution if need be? And revolutions do not need Utopia. The will to change a situation that has become intolerable is enough. Nor does the human rights movement actually show a utopian impulse. Its main effect so far has been an array of legal documents and institutions, and these are by their nature reformist in spirit, not utopian.

In fact, human rights talk may have become so attractive not in spite of, but because of its apolitical stance. In speaking of human rights, one need not get down into political business, into finding causes, means, alliances, prospects. One can just declare wrong what people underwent and in this way be done with it. There is comfort in the thought that all those gassed by the Nazis, burnt by US troops, starved by EU agricultural tariffs, and so on, can be imagined to have had, as it were, a document on them, saying that this must not be done to them; comfort certainly not for them, but for us watching what is happening around us. Think of Palmström in Christian Morgenstern's poem who, run down by a car and lying in hospital, checks the legal situation and concludes that what happened was only a dream, since cars were not permitted there, and what must not be cannot be.[57] Palmström may be taken to be satisfied by what he finds. In speaking

55 Moyn (2010).
56 Here I am indebted to Raymond Geuss, private communication.
57 Morgenstern (1947), p. 165 f.

of human rights we resemble him, not to be sure by declaring a dream what is happening, but by coping with it through restoring, in thought at least, the moral order of the world.

That human rights talk has grown exponentially may then be due precisely to the de-politicization of the last few decades. Citizens asserting that politics is theirs were last seen in western countries in the 1960's, and in various ways the respective states showed them who is master. Citizens learnt the lesson and by and large stayed home since then. Politics has become something that is done somewhere else and watched from afar, like the big sporting events, but it is not something one gets involved in oneself. Under such conditions human rights talk comes in handy. You side with the victims alright, so you are one of the good ones, but luckily you need not actually enter the political arena.[58]

Bibliography

von Arnim, Hans (Ed.) (1903–1924): *Stoicorum veterum fragmenta*, 4 volumes. Leipzig: Teubner.

Assmann, Jan (1992): *Das kulturelle Gedächtnis*. München: Beck.

Campbell, Tom et al. (Eds.) (2011): *The legal protection of human rights*. Oxford: Oxford UP.

Castoriadis, Cornelius (1975): *L'institution imaginaire de la société*, 4th edition. Paris: Seuil.

Foot, Philippa (2001): *Natural Goodness*. Oxford: Oxford UP.

Foot, Philippa (2002a): "Preface to 2002 edition". In: Foot, Philippa: *Virtues and vices*. Oxford: Oxford UP.

Foot, Philippa (2002b): "Morality as a system of hypothetical imperatives" (1972). In: Foot, Philippa: *Virtues and vices*. Oxford: Oxford UP.

Geuss, Raymond (2001): *History and illusion in politics*, Cambridge: Cambridge UP.

Geuss, Raymond (2008): *Philosophy and Real Politics*. Princeton, Oxford: Princeton UP.

Griffin, James (2008): *On human rights*. Oxford: Oxford UP.

Halbwachs, Maurice (1950): *La mémoire collective*. Paris: PUF.

Kant, Immanuel (1914): "Metaphysische Anfangsgründe der Rechtslehre" (1797). In: *Kant's gesammelte Schriften,* Vol. 6. Königlich Preussische Akademie der Wissenschaften (Ed.). Berlin: Reimer, pp. 203–372.

Kohns, Oliver (2013): "Die Politik des 'politischen Imaginären'". In: Oliver Kohns/Martin Doll (Eds.): *Die imaginäre Dimension der Politik*. München (Fink)

Koschorke, A. et al. (2007): *Der fiktive Staat. Konstruktionen des politischen Körpers in der Geschichte Europas*. Frankfurt (Fischer).

Lüdemann, S. (2004): *Metaphern der Gesellschaft. Studien zum soziologischen und politischen Imaginären*. München: Fink.

MacIntyre, Alasdair (1981): *After virtue*. Notre Dame: Notre Dame UP.

---

58 This paper benefitted from helpful comments by Sam Kerstein and the editors of this volume.

Marx, Karl (1974): "Randglossen zum Programm der deutschen Arbeiterpartei" (1875). In:
    Marx, Karl/ Engels, Friedrich: *Werke*, vol. 19, Berlin: Dietz, pp. 15–32.
Morgenstern, Christian (1947): *Alle Galgenlieder*. Wiesbaden: Insel.
Moyn, Samuel (2010): *The last utopia*. Cambridge, Massachusetts: Harvard UP.
O'Neill, Onora (1986): *Faces of hunger*. London: Allen.
O'Neill, Onora (1989): "Children's rights and children's lives". In: O'Neill, Onora: *Constructions
    of reason*. Cambridge: Cambridge UP.
O'Neill, Onora (2005): "The dark side of human rights". In: *International affairs* 81,
    pp. 427–439.
Pogge, Thomas (1992): "O'Neill on rights and duties". In: *Grazer philosophische Studien* 43,
    pp. 233–247.
Pogge, Thomas (2008): "Pharmaceutical innovation: must we exclude the poor?" In: Pogge,
    Thomas: *World poverty and human rights*, 2nd edition. Cambridge: Polity.
Thomson, Judith (1986): "A defense of abortion". In: Thomson, Judith: *Rights, restitution, and
    risk*. Cambridge, Massachusetts: Harvard UP, pp. 1–19.
Tierney, Brian (1997): *The idea of natural rights*. Atlanta: Scholars.
Wood, Allen (1981): *Karl Marx*. London: Routledge.

David Kim

The Cosmopolitics of *Parrhesia*:
Foucault and Truth-Telling as Human Right

This is my question:
At what price can subjects speak the truth about themselves?
Michel Foucault, "Structuralism and Poststructuralism"

Truth-Telling as Human Right

In June 1981, at the inaugural meeting of the United Nations International Committee Against Piracy, Michel Foucault appealed to the notion of "international citizenship" on behalf of Vietnamese boat people (Foucault 1984a, p. 22).[59] Following the Fall of Saigon some six years before, hundreds of thousands of Vietnamese had begun to flee the country by sea, but no government at the time was willing to halt their brutal and recurring victimization by pirates in the Gulf of Thailand and the South China Sea. Pirates had historically been considered "enemies of humanity" for their stateless status according to international maritime law and their "unpolitical," personally driven motives for assaulting members of any nation-state (Schmitt 2011, p. 28). Furthermore, the 1958 Convention on the High Seas, the 1974 International Convention for the Safety of Life at Sea, and the 1979 International Convention on Maritime Search and Rescue had specified that member states were required to aid people in distress at sea (UNHCR 2011).[60] And yet, help did not come from any government. So Foucault reminded his listeners in Geneva of their moral duty as international citizens, a duty that obligated everyone "to speak out against every abuse of power, whoever its perpetrator, whoever its victims." He said: "It is a duty of this international citizenship to bring always to the eyes and ears of governments the testimony of people's misfortunes for which it is not true that they are not responsible" (Foucault 1984a, p. 22). By recognizing the work of non-governmental organizations (NGOs) such as Amnesty International, Terre des Hommes, and Cap Anamur,

---

59 All translations are mine unless otherwise stated.
60 The three conventions provided an international framework for rescuing people in distress at sea regardless of citizenship, mode of transportation, and number.

Foucault put forth an ethical framework for confronting indifferent or idle governments in violation of or at least in disregard of international human rights. Since states refused to share political power with their citizens in confirmation of Max Weber's characterization of politics as a vocational "monopoly," Foucault contended that this "division of labor" in the public sphere was a universal condition under which individual subjects around the globe experienced a certain shared difficulty (Weber 1919, p. 4, p. 10). In fact, since governments distinguished themselves from other political associations by using physical force as a legitimate means to monopolize power, this distinction gave citizens everywhere "an absolute right to stand up and speak to those in power" (Foucault 1984a, p. 22). What entitled them to public opinion – and thus, to mobilizing shame – was the membership in an international community of commonly governed subjects: "After all, we are all of the governed and, for this reason, in solidarity" (Foucault 1984a, p. 22).[61]

On the surface, then, Foucault presented an adversarial or agonistic model of democracy, pitting the liberal emphasis on individual rights against the representational responsibility for commons. The title of his speech – "Facing Governments: The Rights of Man" – alluded to this universal opposition to state sovereignty. Since political regimes had abandoned the obligation to safeguard each and every citizen in the rapidly globalizing market economy, what Foucault suggested was the idea that only a persistent insistence on populist reason constructed an alternative public sphere where the plight of abused prisoners, political dissidents, refugees, and the poor could properly be heard.

Upon closer examination, though, Foucault's impassioned and somewhat hastily composed appeal to the notion of international citizenship turned out to be far more complicated. As he pointed out in succinct terms, the burden of monitoring human rights violations fell upon private individuals whose impatience with politics as usual led to international humanitarian initiatives. Such modes of resistance came from "indignant" individuals who despite having no qualification for representation joined hands across international borders in opposition to national governments. For Foucault, this status of non-representation was pivotal for claiming the right to say truth to power in neoliberal democracy: "So who appointed us? No one. And that is precisely what constitutes our right" (Foucault 1984a, p. 22).[62] Being governed and yet abused, ignored or neglected by state repre-

---

61 I borrow the term "mobilizing shame" from Thomas Keenan who draws upon Kant to argue that "*mobilizing shame* has Enlightenment roots" insofar as reason constitutes a faculty of public exchange that "exposes, reveals, and argues" (Keenan 2004, p. 436).
62 Jacques Rancière refers to Book III of Plato's *Laws* to specify how the seventh possible quali-

sentatives gave individual citizens both the right and the duty to stand together in solidarity. It grounded their moral obligation to tell the truth in international citizenship.

According to Foucault, international human rights groups managed to create "this new right – that of private individuals to intervene effectively in the sphere of international relations and strategies" and to refute "people's misfortune" as "a silent remainder of politics" (Foucault 1984a, p. 22). Although Foucault simplified human rights as the rights of speechless victims, victims who were unable to claim their rights as national citizens, he singled out Peter Beneson of Amnesty International, Edmond Kaiser of Terre des Hommes, and Christel and Rupert Neudeck of Cap Anamur as exemplary cosmopolitans who pressed states to take action and came first in offering their help to Vietnamese asylum seekers. While mobilizing passions at local and national levels, they exposed the untruth of public officials on the world stage. Acting upon their right as governed subjects, these private citizens told the truth about hypocrisy, lies, and broken promises by indifferent governments.

I have opened this essay with a close reading of Foucault's speech to address a broader issue he raises, namely truth-telling or *parrhesia* as a revolutionary practice in democracy and as an exercise in international citizenship. The origin of his intense interest in this speech act dates back to the second half of the 1970s when he began to work on ancient Greek modes of subjectivity and self-knowledge, coupled with public criticisms of the Gulag, the deportation of Klaus Croissant from France back to West Germany, and the widespread denunciation of the Iranian Revolution. As he reflected in one of his last interviews, Foucault was interested in statements of truth as opposed to scientific verifications and his intellectual trajectory moved accordingly from structures of power-knowledge to historical conditions under which political subjects considered themselves objects of critical inquiry. He explained this turn as follows: "This is my question: At what

---

fication for government is illustrative of this paradox. Four of the seven qualifications (*axiomata*) are traditional insofar as they are related to "positions of authority" (master and slave, parents and children) and "the difference of birth" (young and old, nobles and serfs). The fifth qualification has to do with "the principle of principles" and that is "the power of those with a superior nature, of the strong over the weak." The sixth qualification is grounded in science; it is "the power of those who know over those who do not." As Rancière goes on to say, Plato does not stop there. He adds a seventh one, which introduces a "paradox" to democratic rule. Here, "democracy is characterized by the drawing of lots, or the complete absence of any entitlement to govern." In other words, democratic rule originates in "the absence of entitlement" (Rancière 2010, p. 31).

price can subjects speak the truth about themselves?" (Foucault 1999, p. 444). For Foucault, telling the truth constituted a communicative – and thus essentially political – activity in which speaker and listener did not interact with each other on equal terms. Moreover, it was a deeply personal and courageous deed whose truth claim aimed to improve the speaker's life and the lives of others. As Foucault added, the problem with this risky practice was that a high price had to be paid; *parrhesia* was rarely possible for free. What concerns me in this essay is Foucault's critical valuation of veridiction in international solidarity with human beings who are equally governed, but whose rights as individual citizens are violated by governments in a spectacle of false claims and neoliberal policies. If humanitarian aid in the form of money is always already corrupt in a profit-driven coordination between governments and businesses, Foucault asks how telling the truth in its unembellished entirety intervenes in such hegemonic relations and strategies beyond politics as usual. What is it about this ethical practice in cosmopolitanism that has the potential to reject the lies of corrupt and irresponsible states and resists the instrumentalization of truth claims in theatrical public relations? Under what circumstances does *parrhesia* engender a truly transformative politics?

Although this investigation originates in the desire to understand more deeply the fluid concept of solidarity in European intellectual thought, I want to investigate Foucault's concern for human rights toward the end of his manifold life – basically, during the early 1980s – as a way of thinking through what Pheng Cheah has recently identified as variously alienating processes in global modernity, processes that compel individuals and communities "to radically rethink what it means to be human" (Cheah 2006, p. 3). At the risk of veering too far into the present, let us briefly revisit Cheah's study, *Inhuman Conditions*, before we examine the relevance of Foucault's unresolved struggle with *parrhesia* as a transhistorical category for a radically ethical or militant form of life under state surveillance.

Whether the impetus for a transformative horizon has to do with relentless capitalist exploitation, irresponsible technoscientific manipulation or excessive military violence is a central question for everyone to consider. For it determines the production of truth in modern politics. However, Cheah argues that the greatest challenge for humanity is the international division of labor after the end of the Cold War. He focuses on two correlating normative discourses to take issue with the dominant social-scientific presuppositions of humanism. One is that of cosmopolitanism and the other one is of human rights. "Both phenomena," Cheah asserts, "are generally viewed as placing actual and normative limits on the efficacy of national culture and the sovereignty of the nation-state, which is seen as particularistic, oppressive, and even totalitarian" (Cheah 2006, p. 3). As cosmopolitanism "erodes national parochialism and facilitates the arduous process of establishing a platform for transnational political regulation," what this ideal as "a form of collective consciousness" offers is a critical – and not strictly oppositional – distance from "the instrumentality of sovereign national states" upon which human rights depend for enforcement (Cheah 2006, p. 5). Thus, the nation continues to serve as an essential point of orientation for cosmopolitanism and the human rights regime.

By instrumentality Cheah means to suggest Max Horkheimer and Theodor Adorno's distinction of critical reason from instrumental reason, the latter being a blind, intoxicating, and abusive use of power in modern society. In contradistinction from this dehumanizing technology, which perverts progress and civilization into lethal weapons of destruction, Cheah conceives of cosmopolitanism as "a higher, self-recursive form of reason" whereby "the power to remake the world and ourselves" comes to fruition once again in rational terms (Cheah 2006, p. 6). If the Enlightenment notion of *Bildung* connotes a systematic formation of individual subjects free of fear and domination, Cheah understands cosmopolitanism to be an extension of this originally bourgeois pedagogy beyond the national body for the purpose of engendering a world community. It connotes, he writes, "a change in the *form* of the ordering of collective political life" to subsume cultural difference, national belonging, and historical particularity under common translocal interests (Cheah 2006, p. 8). Cheah concludes that this formative change takes place primarily through "symbols and images" (Cheah 2006, p. 6).[63]

I concur with Cheah that symbolism plays an essential role in mobilizing cosmopolitan solidarity or in shaming abusive governments, but as he admits, there is a key problem in this contestation. That is, a neat abstract separation between instrumentality and reason does not do justice to the fact that "neither human rights nor cosmopolitan solidarities can escape from being entangled within the

---

63 It is beyond the scope of this essay to explore Foucault's deep suspicion toward the visual as a principal mode of sense-making in Western culture. According to Martin Jay, Foucault does not completely ignore the difference between truth-telling and "truth-showing." For more information, see Jay (2008, p. 53). Andrew Herscher has also investigated the problematic use of satellite images not only for human rights advocacy, but also for interstate violence. He refers to this development as "'surveillance witnessing,'" that is, "a hybrid visual practice that has emerged at the intersection between satellite surveillance and human rights witnessing." Used by governments, businesses, and non-governmental organizations, this praxis compromises the work that human rights advocacy has historically given itself. See Herscher (2014, p. 473).

field of instrumentality" (Cheah 2006, p. 8) Since dignifying figurations of the human are bound to socioeconomic, military, and political technologies or, more generally speaking, to the various forms of *technê* in modern society, the challenge is to determine how symbols and images come in handy for engendering politically transformative actions at national and international levels. To be sure, the scarcity of material objects as modern-day technologies gives way to abundant immaterial objects – words and images, feelings and thoughts – as foundations of a radically alternative cosmopolitan economy, but even here "a paradoxical interplay between radical mutability and social inertia" rules, thus exposing a certain arbitrariness or risk in cosmopolitan life (Cheah 2006, p. 9). Although the impetus for rethinking the human in the age of globalization comes from a strong conviction in the human ability to remake the world, the kind of cosmopolitan solidarity of which Cheah speaks does not escape from the ambiguity, corruption or perversion of *technê* in modern society. Cosmopolitans have to wrestle with the unruly nature of words and images, and of feelings and thoughts, as they engage in political struggles between the state's instrumental reason and a person's critical reason.

Cheah's critique of human rights in the post-Cold War era is invaluable not least because he investigates the material conditions under which normative claims and universal aspirations impede globally humanizing projects. He points out that nationalism and cosmopolitanism do not oppose each other as much as they overlap with each other in the age of globalization, and that NGOs undermine simplistic North-South and East-West divisions in the new world disorder. He makes clear that non-Western governments do not oppose globalization per se, but that they object to Western models of development and aid: "The fight is between different globalizing models of capitalist accumulation attempting to assert economic hegemony" (Cheah 2006, p. 148). NGOs criticize this fight by bringing into view indigenous, feminist, ecocritical, and postcolonial perspectives, all of which urgently call for alternatives to market-driven, state-steered operations in global liberal capitalism. The challenge they face is a predominant figuration of the human in contemporary globalization talk, a representation that ultimately dehumanizes, excludes or rejects certain categories of humanity in the international division of labor or in the interest of national sovereignty. This challenge, Cheah concludes, is first and foremost for the humanities.

Cheah refers to Jürgen Habermas's concept of communicative action in the *Öffentlichkeit* as a place for engendering procedural democracy in pursuit of cosmopolitan solidarity and in protection of freedom and dignity. He also points out that this normative formulation presupposes "the relative autonomy of the political from the economic," an assumption that enables Habermas to conceive of power, but not money, in democratic terms (Cheah 2006, p. 47). As Cheah illustrates, though, power and money are inseparable in modern society; they are inextricably woven together into the fabric of market-driven neoliberal policies. "It is not completely true, as Habermas envisions, that collectively binding decisions are capable of regulating 'the actions of the administrative-bureaucratic state apparatus' because money is not subject to strict regulation" (Cheah 2006, p. 47). Does this mean that symbols and images bypass or cut through the dehumanizing technologies in late capitalism? Do they facilitate ethical practices in revaluing persons and things in global modernity? For Cheah, the answer is: no. In today's interconnected world, he believes that global capital permeates every sociopolitical relation and that cultural self-realization is always implicated in this instrumentalization. Although human rights and cosmopolitanism serve to safeguard unalienable, non-disciplinary definitions of the human on the foundations of individual freedom and personal dignity, both of them are partly thrown off by neoliberal prescriptions.

Cheah goes on to examine Kant's philosophical project – *Entwurf* – on perpetual peace to register "a shift from a merely voluntary ethical community of intellectuals to a world political community grounded in right" (Cheah 2006, p. 22).[64] He locates the emergence of Kant's modern cosmopolitan horizon in "a philosophical republicanism and federalism designed to reform the absolutist dynastic state" (Cheah 2006, p. 23). In the following pages, I want to take a slightly different route because Foucault similarly turns to Kant to clarify the definition of the human and offer a critical way out of being "just 'parts of a machine'" in modern society (Foucault 2010, p. 35). He concentrates on Kant's foundational essay "What is Enlightenment?" to grapple with the potential of opposing disciplinary constraints on humanity.[65] Instead of criticizing rationalism *tout court*, this detour enables the French philosopher to reveal how certain forms of rationality are practiced in Western societies.[66] It goes a long way in illuminating *par-*

---

64 For a critical examination of Kant's *Entwurf* in allusion to Abbé de Saint-Pierre's *Projet*, see Wood (1998, p. 66).

65 Foucault publishes a more polished, shorter and slightly different version of his text in 1984. See Foucault (1984b, pp. 32–50). In this essay, I refer mostly to his lecture because of its sustained connection between *Aufklärung* and *parrhesia*.

66 As David Macey points out, Foucault calls upon Maurice Agulhon, president of the Société d'Histoire de la Révolution de 1848, during a public debate in May 1978 to consider the same point of departure for a rigorously historical and philosophical inquiry into the penal system: "'Why not begin a major historical enquiry into the way the *Aufklärung* has been per-

rhesia as an ethico-political practice in world citizenship, as well as Foucault's philosophical conception of self vis-à-vis contemporary governmentality.

Kant's Aufklärung

Since money rules over every citizen, since no one lives outside of the force field of global capital, so to speak, Foucault calls attention to the ancient Greek notion of *parrhesia* (παρρησία), or what he describes as "true discourse in the political realm," as a radically democratic solution to the hegemonic logic of society (Foucault 2010, p. 6). He opens his 1983 lecture series at the Collège de France with a brief excursus of his intellectual trajectory in the history of thought and proceeds to explore how focusing on the concept of *parrhesia* illuminates revolutionary or subversive processes whereby private individuals transform into political subjects or universal subjects speaking as private individuals. Although Foucault invokes neither human rights nor cosmopolitanism, his study seeks to shed light on "the problem of the relations between government of self and government of others," a problem that he suggests affects every individual subject across time and space (Foucault 2010, p. 6). More specifically, Foucault identifies this problem as a matter of philosophy. For him, it is essentially a philosophical problem, one that concerns "the philosopher, the pedagogue," who is also "the writer (the qualified writer, translated into French as *savant*; *Gelehrter*; man of culture)," someone who has historically counseled the prince or has been responsible for enlightening the public (*Publikum*) (Foucault 2010, p. 6, p. 7).

At the heart of Foucault's lectures lies the Greek concept of veridiction, truth-telling (*dire-vrai*), free-spokenness (*franc-parler*) or saying everything (*dire-tout*) as a particular technology for "the constitution of [an] individual as subject for himself and for others" (Foucault 2010, p. 42). At first glance, this return to ancient Greece hardly seems relevant for modern politics, but Foucault asserts that nothing is further from the truth. It is true, he says, that everyone in the Greek *polis* has equal right to voice his opinion in public debate, but not everyone exercises this freedom due to lack of courage and virtue. Constitutive of citizenship, *isegoria* offers "the statutory right to speak," but *parrhesia* introduces an element

---

ceived, thought, imagined, exorcised, anathemised and reactivated in the Europe of the nineteenth and twentieth centuries? That might be an interesting piece of 'historico-philosophical' work. Relations between historians and philosophers could be 'put to the test'" (Macey 1993, p. 405).

of difference to this constitutional framework, producing "a certain ascendancy of some over others" (Foucault 2010, p. 157). This paradox is the reason why there are rulers who take action (*arkhein*) and others who receive action (*arkhesthai*). Although every (adult male) subject (*polites*) is equally free as citizen, the practical difference in equal political freedom poses two ethico-political challenges for the republic (*res publica*): first, political resistance requires that individuals leave behind their laziness, complacency or fear – Kant later describes this pre-enlightened state as "immaturity" (*Unmündigkeit*) – and tell the truth even at the risk of dying; second, this risky exercise of freedom of speech is not to produce another division of labor within the already divided, hierarchical order of democracy.[67] To interrupt the monopoly of power in Athenian democracy, private individuals have the double task of expressing their personal conviction in the public sphere and standing together without a leader, without anyone "walking at the head" (*arkhein*).[68]

Yet, Foucault does not discuss this topic for another week; instead, he goes on to introduce Kant's arguably ambiguous definition of *Aufklärung* as "a little epigraph" to the lengthy examination of *parrhesia* for the rest of the lecture series (Foucault 2010, p. 6). As he reminds his audience, Kant's essay appears in the *Berlinische Monatsschrift* in December 1784. In the November 1784 issue, one also finds Kant's *Idea for a Universal History from a Cosmopolitan Point of View* (*Idee zu einer allgemeinen Geschichte in weltbürgerlicher Absicht*) and more essays follow in the 1785 and 1786 issues. For Foucault, this mode of publication is important because it suggests that Kant has a specific "notion of public" in mind (Foucault 2010, p. 7). Whereas Foucault addresses the audience within an institutional context, which is open to everyone, Kant considers the journal to be an essential framework at the end of the eighteenth century for cultivating the pedagogical relationship between writer and reader.[69] Foucault also points

---

67 I refer to Kant at this point because he begins his essay with the following widely recognized sentences: "Enlightenment is man's emergence from his self-imposed nonage. Nonage is the inability to use one's own understanding without another's guidance. This nonage is self-imposed if its cause lies not in lack of understanding but in indecision and lack of courage to use one's own mind without another's guidance" ("Aufklärung ist der Ausgang des Menschen aus seiner selbstverschuldeten Unmündigkeit. Unmündigkeit ist das Unvermögen, sich seines Verstandes ohne Leitung eines anderen zu bedienen") (Kant 1784, p. 481).

68 As Rancière writes in his definition of politics, "the meaning of *arkhein*" is "to walk at the head." Consequently, he goes on to say, "if there is one who walks at the head, then the others must necessarily walk behind" (Rancière 2010, p. 30).

69 It is important to note that Foucault begins his first lecture with a complaint about the distance between himself and the public. The lecture series is open to everyone and, as such, it

out that Moses Mendelssohn's response to the same question "What is Enlightenment?" has appeared in the same journal only a few months earlier, indicating a coincidental crossing of the Protestant *Aufklärung* and the Jewish *Haskala* and signaling "not only the right, but also the necessity of an absolute freedom of not only conscience, but also of expression in relation to anything that might be a religious practice considered as a necessarily private activity" (Foucault 2010, p. 10). Last but not least, Foucault distinguishes Kant's philosophical deliberation on *Aufklärung* from every other work, as questions of genealogy or historical progress pave the way to public intervention in the present "for the first time" (Foucault 2010, p. 11). Foucault spells them out in the following three ways:

> The question focuses on what this present is. First of all, among all the elements of the present, the question focuses on the definition of one particular element that is to be recognized, distinguished, and deciphered. What is it in the present that currently has meaning for philosophical reflection? Second, the answer that Kant tries to give to the questions involves showing how this element is the bearer or expression of a process which concerns thought, knowledge, philosophy. Finally, third, within this reflection on this element of the present which is the bearer of or which reveals a process, what is to be shown is in what respect and how the person who speaks as a thinker, a *savant*, a philosopher, is himself a part of this process. But it is even more complicated than this. He has to show not only how he is part of this process, but how, as such, as *savant*, philosopher, or thinker, he has a role in this process in which he is thus both an element and an actor (Foucault 2010, p. 12).

Reflective of his own concern with the philosopher's role in the public sphere, Foucault works through Kant's essay to ask what it means to be a member of the "human community in general" and how the present connects him to a solidary project in particular (Foucault 1984b, p. 45). From his perspective, Kant is the first one in European intellectual history to examine how philosophy contributes to the realization of universal reason without giving rise to "dogmatism and heteronomy, along with illusion" (Foucault 1984b, p. 38). This explains why for Foucault *Aufklärung* is not a singular event tied to a philosophical tradition; rather, it constitutes "a critical attitude" that undergirds a philosopher's ideational position on political struggles between governors and governed (Macey 1994, p. 405).

Foucault builds upon this monumental work to formulate once again the philosopher's role in engendering and experiencing political change as one of many, which is to say, in solidarity. He says: "This 'we' has to become, or is in the process

---

involves Foucault's public use of reason. The opening remark makes clear, though, how difficult it is for him to resist private use of reason within the predetermined institutional context at the Collège de France.

of becoming, the object of the philosopher's own reflection. By the same token, it becomes impossible for the philosopher to dispense with an interrogation of his singular membership of this 'we'" (Foucault 2010, p. 13). The philosopher, the *savant*, the *Gelehrte* is directly responsible for addressing the public and shaping the present reality. Instead of blurring the singular in pursuit of the universal, the philosopher has to see things more clearly than others and show a way out of the unequal struggle between ruler and ruled in solidarity.[70]

Foucault argues that Kant defines *Aufklärung* "simply as '*Ausgang*,' as way out, exit, a movement" (Foucault 2010, p. 27). In quoting the Latin phrase *Sapere aude*, Kant also suggests the universal validity of *Aufklärung* as "man's way out from the condition of tutelage," tutelage being "'the inability to make use of his understanding without direction from another'" (Foucault 2010, p. 27, p. 26). At this point, Foucault specifies the vagueness of this definition, which leaves open the question of agency, the direction of such a transformative passage, as well as the precise nature of "man." "Should man be understood to mean the human race as a species?" Foucault asks. "Or should man be understood to mean human society as the universal element within which different individual reasons join together? Are only some human societies the bearers of these values? Is it a matter of individuals, and if so, what individuals, and so on? The text just says 'man's way out'" (Foucault 2010, p. 28). Critical of Kant's blindness to the birth of political subjects only under certain conditions, Foucault argues that it is essential to be more specific.

According to Foucault, Kant attributes the state of tutelage to "an act, or rather to an attitude, a mode of behavior, a form of will," which result from a number of human frailties (Foucault 2010, p. 29). Among them are cowardice, fear, and laziness, as human beings do not necessarily take responsibility for thinking for themselves without the direction of others. By implication, those who direct others are individuals who take upon themselves the task of guiding fellow citizens out of tutelage. Some of them are genuinely caring, others are conniving and shrewd. Ultimately, though, all of them fail to "carry out this process of transformation" because they subjugate others to their authority, while speaking on behalf of others and impeding in the movement of free individual subjects (Foucault 2010, p. 34). They are false liberators, dangerous counsels, and ingenuous tutors.

---

70 As Macey documents, this self-critical awareness resonates with Foucault's broader concern with the role of intellectuals in critique of conservative resurgence during the early 1980s (1993, p. 459).

Toward the end of the two-hour-long lecture, Foucault calls attention to Kant's famously confusing differentiation between the private use of reason – *Räsonnieren* – and the public one. As Foucault points out, the former applies to the use of the faculty of reason in a particular function for society where individuals are obliged to fulfill certain roles as members of the political body. Individuals think, argue, and probe what they are supposed to do, but ultimately they obey as private individuals. In the public use of reason, individuals do not address others in specific functions; rather, they speak as universal subjects making up "a dimension of the public," which is "at the same time the dimension of the universal" (Foucault 2010, p. 36). Kant addresses readers publicly by publishing his works. Unlike Foucault who gives public lecture within the functional or institutional context of a university, Kant circulates his work through a journal, which counts as a public mode of communication with fellow universal subjects. Consequently, Foucault concludes, *Aufklärung* is opposed to tolerance because the former connotes a rational engagement with others as universal subjects, whereas the latter rules out "reasoning, discussion, and freedom of thought in its public form" (Foucault 2010, p. 37).

Returning to the quintessential question of agency in the present, Foucault criticizes Kant for being tautological and contradictory. Instead of answering where in the transformative process of *Aufklärung* the present is, Kant merely suggests the following in Foucault's paraphrase: "We are in the period, in the *Zeitalter*, in the age of *Aufklärung*" (Foucault 2010, p. 37). Foucault also mentions how Kant identifies fear, laziness, and cowardice as self-inflicted "'obstacles'" to practicing cultural self-realization only after having said that such "'obstacles'" have been overcome in Enlightenment. Furthermore, Foucault adds, Kant introduces Frederick the Great as a princely agent of liberation, someone whose refusal to prescribe religious norms in Prussia creates a clear division between private and public, but this suggestion is in contradiction with Kant's earlier statement regarding authoritative liberators, not to mention the wars that are waged for absolutist states in the last quarter of the nineteenth century.

Paradoxically, then, Kant argues that "the greatest possible growth of this freedom of public thought," which is, "opening this free and autonomous dimension of the universal for the use of the understanding," fosters obedience in civil society (Foucault 2010, p. 38). The more the public is able to engage in free discourse, the more order there exists in the private household of the state. From Foucault's perspective, this analysis, as groundbreaking as it is, negates itself.

In the more formal version of this lecture published as an essay under the title "What Is Enlightenment?", Foucault repeats that Kant's *Aufklärung* connotes "a phenomenon, an ongoing process," as well as "a task and an obligation" (Foucault 1984b, p. 35). Much of the essay resonates with what Foucault says in the lecture, but in print he places a greater emphasis on the interaction between two mutually dependent aspects of cultural self-realization in *Aufklärung*, namely collective labor and individual courage. He writes: "Enlightenment must be considered both as a process in which men participate collectively and as an act of courage to be accomplished personally" (Foucault 1984b, p. 35). The purpose of this dual praxis is to find "a 'way out'" of the state of immaturity such that this "negative" definition of what Enlightenment is offers a solution to the necessity of freedom of religion and freedom of speech in an otherwise rigidly supervised absolutist state (Foucault 1984b, p. 34). As Foucault explains, Kant presents this political structure in a bold effort to sign "a sort of social contract" with Frederick II (Foucault 1984b, p. 37). Despite its ambiguous and contradictory elements, Kant delineates a way out of the political struggle between ruler and ruled without walking at the head, since everyone is capable of using reason legitimately, rightfully, and in public. For Foucault, this ontological study of modernity offers a thoughtful model for caring for oneself and for others.

For the rest of the lecture series between January 12 and March 9, Foucault does not refer to Kant anymore; instead, he examines the ancient Greek notion of *parrhesia* in its "rich, ambiguous, and difficult" sense as "a virtue, a quality," "a duty," and "a technique, a process" (Foucault 2010, p. 43). He describes the parrhesiast as someone who is "responsible for directing others, and particularly for directing them in their effort, their attempt to constitute an appropriate relationship to themselves" (Foucault 2010, p. 43). This obligation or responsibility, he explains, means telling "the whole truth" even at the risk of dying, not to mention the possibility of angering the listener (Foucault 2010, p. 43). In caring about oneself and others, the parrhesiast stands up against the tyrant instead of signing a sort of reconciliatory contract with him. Similar to *Aufklärung*, *parrhesia* is a "spidery" notion, but where they differ from each other is in the way cultural realization via truth-telling – the transformative passage from *Unmündigkeit* to courage – is pursued for oneself and for others regardless of consequences (Foucault 2010, p. 45). Despite the strong resonance between these concepts, Foucault highlights the revolutionary aspect of *parrhesia*, an aspect that is conspicuously absent from Kant's definition of *Aufklärung*. According to Foucault, this explains why Kant revises "the agent of *Aufklärung*" in *The Contest of the Faculties* (*Der Streit der Fakultäten*, 1798) (Foucault 2010, p. 39). Here, Kant tries to resolve the contradictions in his originally cautious conception of *Aufklärung* by replacing Frederick the Great with the kind of revolutionary "spectacle" that mobilizes "spectators". (Foucault 2010, p. 17).

Parrhesia *in International Citizenship*

During the last decade of his life between the late 1970s and early 80s, Foucault was drawn to the idea that living dangerously or being close to death played a central role in resisting modern biopolitical technologies. The kinds of "experiences" he interrogated had marked paradigmatic shifts from biopower, domination, and discipline to biopolitics, courage, and veridiction (Foucault 2010, p. 5). His support for the Iranian Revolution, Poland's *Solidarność*, and Vietnamese boat people exemplified outside of his scholarship the ways in which he imagined potentials for opposing state-sponsored and market-driven productions of truth with money and power, with money *as* power.[71] He argued that governments around the globe practiced rituals in truth-making, that they were constantly engaged in theatrical or lyrical manipulations of "a whole restrictive economy" (Foucault 1990, p. 18). Under such devastating circumstances, he felt that he had a particular responsibility as philosopher not for partaking in revolutions directly since this was insignificant and of lesser value, but for bearing witness to revolutionary passions or what he called "revolutionary enthusiasm." (Foucault 2010, p. 39). Since every revolution, whether it was successful or not, was chaotic, what mattered to him, as Kant had said before him, was the people's ability to exercise its right to shape the political constitution and avoid war (Foucault 2010, p. 18). A revolution was "the completion and continuation of the very process of *Aufklärung*" insofar as it engraved enthusiasm, sympathy, and potential for moving from *Unmündigkeit* to democratic politics in people's memory. Thus, *parrhesia* constituted a public mode of testimony to this transformative process.

According to Laurence McFalls and Mariella Pandolfi, Foucault was aware of the fact that *parrhesia* as a radical exercise in truth-telling did not go so far as to undermine completely the truth of the market in contemporary governance. As

---

71 According to Janet Afary, it is important to differentiate Foucault's intimate spectatorship of the Iranian Revolution – that is, Komeini's Islamic fight against the modern and authoritative Shah – from the other human rights-related events. She writes: "While in no way minimizing the political significance of these interventions over Poland and the Vietnamese boat people, each of which had an impact on French politics, we maintain that they had a character very different from Foucault's writings on Iran." First, she claims, Foucault wrote a lot more about Iran than he did about Poland or Vietnam. Second, his support for the Polish movement and the Vietnamese boat people was in line with others, most notably Jean-Paul Sartre and Raymond Aron, Pierre Bourdieu and Simone Signoret. On Iran, though, he was completely alone. See Afary (2005, p. 8). Macey also illustrates how Foucault's journalistic coverage of events in Iran exposes a deep "dilemma in terms of the duties of the intellectual" (1993, p. 411).

ubiquitous as it was, money influenced how individuals and communities were treated by public officials and in social services. Yet, Foucault presented "only the narrowest of escape routes from therapeutic dystopia," meaning a universal and non-transparent mode of subjecting individual and collective practices of care to economic calculations of efficiency and profit-making in neoliberal managements of governmentality (McFalls and Pandolfi 2014, p. 185). On the surface, these policies appeared to be beneficial and benevolent, but below the surface they ruled out communicative procedures. For Foucault, *parrhesia* was the only possible answer to such *therapeusis*.

Although Foucault teased out contradictions in Kant's groundbreaking definition of *Aufklärung*, the former made clear on numerous occasions – both in the lecture and elsewhere – that he belonged to the latter's critical tradition ranging from Weber and Nietzsche to the Frankfurt School. It was essential that he found his entry into the ancient Greek concept of *parrhesia* through Kant's modern conception of *Aufklärung* as part of his genealogical inquiry into contemporary neoliberal political economy. This did not mean that Foucault dismissed Nietzsche while embracing Kant toward the end of his life. On the contrary. His deliberations on the various technologies of self in modern society built upon Nietzsche's conception of self as the product of a creative, if not aesthetic, work. Furthermore, the notion of *Aufklärung* signaled a transhistorical engagement with or a general tendency toward a theory of governmentality or a culture of self and others.

Michael Hardt has argued that Foucault's intense, yet incomplete inquiry into the notion of *parrhesia* is indicative of "a militant life," "a revolutionary life," which seeks to blur boundaries between the private and the public (Foucault 2010, p. 159). The return to ancient Greek thought provides Foucault with a safe "distance" from which to analyze contemporary political crises and new possibilities for freedom in liberal democracy (Hardt 2010, p. 151). I concur with Hardt's reading insofar as Foucault's understanding of *parrhesia* and *Aufklärung* manifests itself in a firm commitment to cultural self-realization in modern society. He probes particular ways of joining political struggles as a philosopher in the era of liberal governance. This is the reason why at the end of his essay on Enlightenment Foucault calls for a "critical ontology of ourselves," which is not "a theory, a doctrine, nor even a permanent body of knowledge that is accumulating"; rather, it connotes "an attitude, an ethos, a philosophical life in which the critique of what we are is at one and the same time the historical analysis of the limits that are imposed on us and an experiment with the possibility of going beyond them" (Foucault 1984b, p. 50).

Foucault conceived of *parrhesia* as a verbal revolutionary action whereby Kant's contradictory notion of *Aufklärung* could be revitalized in the discursive regime. If *Aufklärung* meant a transformative process in which human beings realized themselves as rational political subjects, *parrhesia* was a concept long forgotten in modern society for insisting upon this cultural realization in radically democratic terms. After his previous scholarship on biopower had forced him to search for a solution to or a way out of the disciplinary formation of politics in biopower, Foucault discovered in *parrhesia* the potential for going a step further and subverting the false claims of governments united by common interests in self-enrichment, power, and oligarchy. Although words and images were always already in circulation within neoliberal political economy, this philosophical framework offered an ancient, yet still modern possibility of consolidating governed citizens around the globe in solidarity.

Bibliography

Afary, Janet (2005): *Foucault and the Iranian Revolution: Gender and the Seductions of Islamism*. Chicago: University of Chicago Press.

Cheah, Pheng (2006): *Inhuman Conditions: On Cosmopolitanism and Human* Rights. Cambridge: Harvard University Press.

Jay, Martin (2008): "Visual *Parrhesia*? Foucault and the Truth of the Gaze." In: *A Time for the Humanities: Futurity and the Limits of Autonomy*. Edited by James J. Bono, Tim Dean, and Ewa Plonowska Ziarek. New York: Fordham University Press, pp. 77–89.

Foucault, Michel (1984a): "Face aux gouvernements, les droits de l'homme." In: *Libération* 967, Juin 30-Juillet 1.

Foucault, Michel (1984b): "What Is Enlightenment?" In: *The Foucault Reader*. Edited by Paul Rabinow. New York: Pantheon Books, pp. 32–50.

Foucault, Michel (1990): *The History of Sexuality: An Introduction*. Vol 1. Translated by Robert Hurley. New York: Vintage Books.

Foucault, Michel (1999): "Structuralism and Poststructuralism." In: *Aesthetics, Method, and Epistemology*, edited by James D. Faubion, vol. 2 of *Essential Works of Foucault, 1954–1984*, edited by Paul Rabinow. New York: New Press.

Foucault, Michel (2010): *The Government of Self and Others: Lectures at the Collège de France 1982–83*. Edited by Frédéric Gros. Translated by Graham Burchell. New York: Palgrave Macmillan.

Hardt, Michael (2010): "Militant Life." In: *New Left Review* 64, pp. 151–160.

Herscher, Andrew (2014): "Surveillant Witnessing: Satellite Imagery and the Visual Politics of Human Rights." In: *Public Culture* 26.3, pp. 469–500.

Kant, Immanuel (1784): "Beantwortung der Frage: Was ist Aufklärung?" In: *Berlinische Monatsschrift*. Dezember-Heft, pp. 481–494.

Keenan, Thomas (2004): "Mobilizing Shame." In: *The South Atlantic Quarterly* 103.2–3, pp. 435–449.

Macey, David (1993): *The Lives of Michel Foucault*. London: Hutchinson.

McFalls, Laurence and Mariella Pandolfi (2014): "Parrhesia and Therapeusis: Foucault on and in the World of Contemporary Neoliberalism." In: *Foucault Now: Current Perspectives in Foucault Studies*. Edited by James D. Faubion. Cambridge: Polity Press, pp. 168–187.

Rancière, Jacques (2010): *Dissensus: On Politics and Aesthetics*. Edited and translated by
    Steven Corcoran. London: Continuum.
Schmitt, Carl (2011): "The Concept of Piracy (1937)." In: *Humanity* 2.1, pp. 27–29.
UNHCR (2011): "Rescue at Sea, Stowaways and Maritime Interception." http://www.unhcr.org/
    cgi-bin/texis/vtx/home/opendocPDFViewer.html?docid=4ee1d32b9&query=rescue%
    20at%20sea, November 13.
    http://www.unhcr.org/450037d34.html
Weber, Max (1919): *Politik als Beruf*. München: Duncker und Humblot.
Wood, Allen W. (1998): "Kant's Project for Perpetual Peace." In: *Cosmopolitics: Thinking and
    Feeling Beyond the Nation*. Edited by Pheng Cheah and Bruce Robbins. Minneapolis:
    University of Minnesota Press, pp. 59–76.

Lora Wildenthal
Imagining Threatened Peoples: The Society for Threatened Peoples (*Gesellschaft für bedrohte Völker*) in 1970s West Germany

The examination of how a human rights organization collectively imagines a wrong, defines its program of work to counteract that wrong, and then sustains that work, is fundamental to writing the history of human rights. Such choices, made in particular contexts, can have long-lasting effects on how people well beyond that organization imagine human rights. This essay concerns the Society's first decade, the 1970s, and the question of how it then constituted the category of threatened peoples for its West German audience. What did the various cases of threatened peoples have in common, and what made threatened peoples a distinctively new focus in West German human rights activism?

The creation of Biafra in 1967 and the ensuing Nigerian Civil War sparked a remarkable movement in West Germany for solidarity with the people of that new country.[72] In 1970, however, the Nigerian Civil War ended with the defeat of secessionist Biafra. At that point, some of those West German activists reorganized. They changed the name of their group from Biafra Aid Campaign (*Aktion Biafrahilfe*) to the Society for Threatened Peoples (*Gesellschaft für bedrohte Völker*) and over the 1970s they developed into one of Germany's most innovative and important human rights nongovernmental organizations.[73] While still concerned about Biafrans in and out of Nigeria, they expanded their focus to a range of cases they identified as "threatened peoples." This process involved several shifts in the West German imagination of human rights during the 1970s: toward group rights, toward a critique of the West German Left, and toward imagining German and non-German victims of human rights violations within the same framework. This last shift was highly unusual in West German human rights activism, and it has since remained controversial, as it seems to relativize the uniqueness of Nazi human rights violations.

---

72 I thank Brianne Rodgers, Yasna Causevic, Iris Castro, and Tilman Zülch for their assistance. On Biafra's impact in West Germany, see Florian Hannig 2014a, Heerten 2011, and Heerten 2014.
73 Beyond the Society's own publications, the main published account is Wüst 1999, pp. 237–271.

Since 1970, the Society for Threatened Peoples has focused on minorities and indigenous groups, in particular with respect to genocide, forced migration, forced cultural change, and discrimination.[74] It has also demanded political change in Germany and in other countries by exposing German state and corporate complicity in abuses of indigenous and minority peoples and by opposing the narrowing of access to political asylum in Germany. The Society has around 6,000 members, making it at least in terms of formal members the second-largest human rights organization in Germany after Amnesty International.[75] It has held special consultative status at the United Nations since 1993, and in 1994 it helped found the main consortium of human rights NGOs in Germany: the Human Rights Forum (*Forum Menschenrechte*). The Society was especially influential in the 1970s and 80s with its work with Indians in the Americas and with Sinti and Roma in Europe.[76] It again gained wide notice in the 1990s for its work with Kurds during the Gulf War and with Bosnians in the Yugoslavian wars (Zülch 1993). Although it is not widely known outside Germany, probably because it has remained a largely Germanophone organization in the age of Internet English, its influence on contemporary human rights discourse is widely recognized by Germans today.

From Biafrans to Threatened Peoples

In 1970, as noted, the Society for Threatened Peoples emerged from its single-issue predecessor, the Biafra Aid Campaign. Yet already before 1970, there had been discussion of adding cases of other threatened peoples to the Biafran case, specifically South Sudanese and Kurds in Syria and Turkey, and Latin American Indians.[77] Indeed, those three cases featured prominently in *Pogrom* in 1970. The new Society for Threatened Peoples chose the word "pogrom," a word often used by the Biafrans themselves, for its periodical to connect atrocities both domestic and international, both past and present, and detailed its mission as follows:

---

74 The Society's current statement of goals is "Aufgaben und Ziele," n.d., n.p.

75 At the end of 2012, it had 5,643 members and 3,359 *Bedrohte Völker – Pogrom* subscribers. See Gesellschaft für bedrohte Völker (2013). See Wüst 1999, pp. 240–244 for older membership statistics.

76 In 1977 and 1978 the Society sponsored U.S. Indians on speaking tours of West Germany that were well attended; see the special issue *Pogrom* 9, no. 54–56 (1978). On Sinti and Roma, see Zülch 1979a and Zülch 1983.

77 See "Bilanz" 1969, on Kurds, *Pogrom* 5, no. 29–30 (1974), and on Indians, Lewis 1969.

Pogrom
– will in the future report regularly on those areas, especially in the Third World, whose population is physically threatened by racism, colonialism, chauvinism ...
– will not shy away from criticizing those responsible in the East, West, and in the so-called Third World, in equal measure;
– will expose the involvement of German state policy and of companies;
– will give representatives of the affected opportunities for stating their position;
– will point out political, educational, and humanitarian ways to help;
– [and] report on campaigns of this type and help coordinate actions and information of German and international groups (*Pogrom* 1, no. 3 [July 1970], n.p.).

This was a program for domestic activism for change, to expose West German official and commercial abuses, to provide information, and to cooperate across state borders directly with the affected groups. It drew connections among cases such as the Biafrans, South Sudanese, Kurds, and Brazilian Indians. They were considered "physically threatened by racism, colonialism, chauvinism." The key elements of "threatened peoples" are italicized here: cases of *peoples* suffering from *physical threats* up to and including *genocide*, whose suffering and indeed existence was in danger of being ignored or *forgotten*. They were "physically threatened." They faced "discrimination and extermination away from the global public eye"[78]; these were "peoples who, forgotten by the world, were threatened by genocide" ("An alle Aktionsgruppen" 1968).

The Society's focus on *peoples* had important ramifications. For the Society, the turn to group rights was a way to define the perpetrators' deeds at least as much as a way to define the peoples themselves. For the Society, a *state* targeted a people for violence; by its abuse, the state determined who was part of a threatened people. In other words, the contours of that people emerged via the harms done by the state. "People" as used in Society materials did not require rigorous international law or anthropological definitions or even to be shown to exist prior to the state's abuse, although ethnic distinctiveness was taken for granted by both members and the public regarding most cases. The case of Biafra had shown this ambiguity in action: while Biafran spokespeople emphasized that Biafra was a multiethnic state, European and American commentators tended to speak of it as an Igbo state. Theoretical or conceptual matters did not trouble the Society; it never tried to define a "people," in ethnic or in international law terms, in any serious way. The absence of discussion of international law concepts throughout *Pogrom* suggests that the Society found such exercises un-

---

78 Untitled flier dated 17 February 1970, in biafrahilfe-all.pdf. This is why the Society did not work on well-known cases such as the Vietnam War or the Israeli-Palestinian conflict.

necessary.[79] Moreover, the use of "people" did not preclude concern for individuals, as individuals suffered because they were in a group or perceived as such.[80] Articles in *Pogrom* often showed that cultural difference was a reason for state violence, but the Society generally did not offer a cultural interpretation of conflicts. It criticized those who labeled conflicts as religious or tribal and it insisted that conflicts should be seen as political struggles.[81] In sum, the Society relied on the concept of a "people," but it did not take on associated meanings of cultural stasis or exotic cultural difference. At least in the 1970s, the manner in which the Society used "people" turned attention not so much to the exotic qualities of that group as to the targeting of that group, as instigated by capitalism, racism or political conflict.

The turn to "peoples" – to group rights – served to widen greatly the kinds of human rights violations and victims imaginable for the Society's audience. Not just censorship, imprisonment and torture appeared in the pages of *Pogrom* – the sorts of human rights violations that tended to affect highly articulate individuals who were well-integrated into their societies. Now forced migration, poverty, colonialism, neocolonialism, war, development, and even capitalism and state power per se also appeared in *Pogrom* as human rights issues. And human rights victims encompassed both articulate activists for whom the Society sought to be a mouthpiece, as well as the inarticulate and radically excluded of all ages. Moreover, the Society was not preoccupied with the question of whether the people it sought to help advocated violence. Threatened peoples sometimes did; for example, Biafrans and the Anya-Nya movement of South Sudan used military force. The Society did not want to fund wars, but it did not want to repudiate peoples simply because they had resorted to violence.[82] State abuse, and not the cultural or other qualities of victimized people, defined the groups that interested the Society. Thus, there was no barrier to including ethnic Germans (such as expellees, or those still living in East Bloc countries) in the Society's mission.[83]

---

79 A rare exception, itself criticizing the idea of clear or homogeneous group identity, is Schultze and Schultze 1974.

80 A late example of such a statement is Duve 1998a.

81 E.g. regarding Bangladesh, *Pogrom* 2, no. 9 (1971), p. 1; regarding South Sudan, *Pogrom* 6, no. 37 (1975), p. 56.

82 See "Editorial I" (1971); "Das Antirassismusprogramm" (1971); "Editorial. Weltkirchenrat" (1973); and *Pogrom* 10, no. 64 (1979), p. 4.

83 On ethnic Germans in the East Bloc, see Rogall 1989, Zülch 1989a, Kotzian 1989. A more recent example of how a "threatened people" need not be culturally different is the 2011 work by the Society for the so-called wolf children (*Wolfskinder*), orphaned and homeless children left behind at the time of the expulsions who had grown up marginalized in Lithuania, and were

The Society's emphasis on *physical threats* was a manifestation of that 1970s antitotalitarian effort to locate criteria for political action beyond politics, ideology and, for the kind of humanitarianism developed by *Doctors Without Borders*, even beyond institutions. Drawing attention to the immediacy of physical suffering was intended as a new radicalism. At the same time, attention to physical suffering could moderate political differences and promote consensus. The Biafra Aid Campaign's fundraising cooperation with the longstanding Catholic charity *Caritas*, for example, gained credibility for the new organization, as the West German public trusted the latter organization.[84] For the Society, the emphasis on physical suffering supported its claim to be anti-ideological.

However, members of the Campaign and Society did not want it to be perceived as "only" humanitarian, but rather as a political human rights organization: "Charitable aid by itself lengthens lives. The suffering of the Biafran population and the mass murder of so far ca. 1 million civilians is due to political causes. That is why our effort starts there."[85] To Tilman Zülch, being political meant daring to attack powerful wrongdoers openly and refusing corporate donations.[86] It also meant offering high-quality information and analysis so that readers could understand complex conflicts and take action.[87] Humanitarian work without solidarity would merely be an "alibi" ("Editorial II" 1971, n.p.). So while it was simply necessary sometimes to give money and time, as when Zülch rented an apartment for Biafran refugees,[88] it was important to the Campaign not to do humanitarian work alone.

For this reason, the Society focused on political violence, especially *genocide*. The Society defined genocide expansively and as an impetus for action in the present, as well as commemoration of past victims.[89] As Nobel Prize-winning writer Heinrich Böll, one of the Society's prominent supporters, put it in a 1970 speech:

---

left out of the welfare provisions offered to refugees and expellees in West and unified Germany. "Letzte Zeitzeugen" 2011. What was important for the Society's work with this group was that they were forgotten, not that they were or were not in some sense German.

84 Tilman Zülch, personal communication, Göttingen, 24 May 2012.
85 "Bilanz" 1969 and untitled flier thanking donors dated April 1969 in biafra-all.pdf.
86 Tilman Zülch, personal communication, Göttingen, 24 May 2012.
87 Untitled flier recruiting new members, n.d., in biafrahilfe-all.pdf.
88 Tilman Zülch, personal communication, Göttingen, 24 May 2012.
89 On the importance of not defining genocide too narrowly, see Zülch and Guercke 1969, p. 158. On not letting one's concern about genocide be restricted to the past, see *Pogrom* 1, no. 3 (July 1970), inside front cover. Regarding Bangladesh, see *Pogrom* 2, no. 9 (1971), p. 5.

Who would have intervened in Hitler's politics of destruction if it had remained domestic politics? Some politicians and diplomats consider it improper for a German who was a contemporary of Auschwitz to intervene in the politics of another country. Should Auschwitz act in this way as a brake on brotherhood, or should it not be a motive for it? ("Heinrich Böll" 1970, p. 14)

Far from restricting what Germans might properly say or do in protest, the Shoah ought to drive Germans to act, in order to show that they had learned from the past. In invoking the Shoah as a spur to Germans to act against genocidal violence in the present, the Society expressed an idea that went back to, for example, the visionary West German peace activist Reimar Lenz, and one that was shared by the West German Third World solidarity movement more generally (Slobodian 2012, p. 147).

To label a situation genocide, then, was to issue a call to action. This context helps us understand what may seem like an inflationary use of the term in the 1970s.[90] Typical headlines in *Pogrom* were "Auschwitz – Biafra – Bangladesh" or "Bangladesh: Auschwitz Every Day" ("Auschwitz" 1971; "Bengalen" 1971). One of the Society's best-known causes in the 1970s was that of the Aché Indians in Paraguay. Mark Münzel, a West German anthropologist, became convinced during his fieldwork with the Aché that the Paraguayan government was knowingly allowing their extinction; after he was expelled from the country he intensified his accusations.[91] Anthropologists and historians have more recently examined the case of the Aché and conclude, without minimizing the dire situation at that time, that it is incorrect to assert that the regime planned genocide. However, they also note that Münzel's and Arens's work helped the Aché gain negotiating power with the Stroessner regime (Horst 2007, pp. 67, 80–99 and Reed and Renshaw 2012). Charges of genocide generally do have political effects – usually, of course, the effect of eliciting denials not only from the perpetrating government, but also from other governments, lest they be compelled to act (Smith 2010). The choice of the term was therefore itself eminently political.

Besides *peoples*, *physical threats*, and *genocide*, being *forgotten* was key to the Society. Being forgotten meant not fitting into dominant political ideologies of the day, and so not having any powerful allies in the outside world, and

---

90 There is no scholarly consensus today on defining genocides, of course. See Bloxham and Moses 2010 and references cited there.

91 Münzel's first report appeared in *Pogrom* 4, no. 18 (1973); see also *Pogrom* 5, no. 28 (1974); *Pogrom* 8, no. 49 (1977); and *Pogrom* 8, no. 50–51 (1977). See also Zülch 1975, pp. 147–161. From 1976 on, Münzel served on *Pogrom*'s editorial board. See also the work of an American scholar making the same claim of genocide: Arens 1976.

perhaps not even being known to the outside world. The first issue of *Pogrom* announced:

> Great power politics, economic interests, blind nationalism and racism threaten whole peoples in various parts of the world (e.g. in Biafra, Iraqi Kurdistan, the South Sudan, Portuguese Guinea and Indian parts of Latin America). Since these peoples are of little or no consequence as power factors, governments, parties, international organizations and the media pass them over or only mention them only marginally. This lack of interest is all the stronger, the less easily conflicts can be made to fit the usual ideological or political clichés (*Pogrom* 1, no. 1 [1970], n.p.).

For the Society, the Cold War obscured victims: both Left and Right helped to create an ideological veil that could only be rent by providing information. An emphasis on information was how the Society strove to translate concern about Biafrans into concern about "threatened peoples" more generally.

The emphasis on information was one of the most striking qualities of the Campaign and Society. They executed major translation projects to create a body of information on threatened peoples for German readers. For instance, Zülch and Campaign co-founder Klaus Guercke published an anthology on Biafra in 1968, and a new edition followed in 1969.[92] This book contained over 250 pages of translated press clippings, interviews, poems, and tables, as well as photos (some taken by Zülch during his visit in Biafra in early 1969). It was bigger, contained more data, and offered more diverse points of view than did any contemporary publications on Biafra in English or French, even though those were the languages in which almost all new information about Biafra was generated. *Pogrom* carried forward this explicit goal of supplying high-quality information. All of its 1970s issues contained foreign press items that Society members had translated into German. The Society also located anthropological, other scholarly, and NGO-commissioned research on cases of state abuse of population groups. These full-length studies were authored in English, Spanish, or Dutch, so again Society members translated them into German for publication. About a third of all *Pogrom* issues of the 1970s carried such articles; one 1977 issue even contained 100 pages of a periodical by and for Colombian Indians that the Society had translated from Spanish into German (*Pogrom* 8, no. 53 [1977]). Longer studies appeared as free-standing books, and yet more information appeared in the Society's pamphlet series *vierte welt aktuell* (e.g. Münzel 1979 and Savvidis 1980). As demand grew for the Society's publications, *Pogrom* occasionally pleaded with

---

92 Zülch and Guercke 1969. I used that second edition. The first edition was entitled *Biafra: Todesurteil für ein Volk? Eine Dokumentation* (Berlin: Lettner-Verlag, 1968).

readers to help with what must have been an overwhelming burden of translation work.[93] Altogether, someone who collected the Society's literature through the 1970s had a sizeable and sophisticated ethnographic and current affairs library in German.

The Society gained wide visibility for some of its research through the influential political affairs paperback series *rororo aktuell*, edited in the 1970s by its strong supporter, the journalist and later Social Democratic politician Freimut Duve. Duve, who had visited South Africa in 1961 and was a vocal critic of apartheid, wanted to bring to West German readers information about Asia, Africa, and Latin America and critical perspectives on development policy.[94] Two books produced by the Society appeared in the *rororo aktuell* series in the 1970s, gaining wide visibility and going into multiple editions: a volume on minorities forgotten in the age of détente, and a volume on the Roma in the Holocaust and after (Zülch 1975 and Zülch 1979a). These books, along with the *rororo aktuell* series generally, were important points of reference for West Germans, especially on the Left. Of course, those on the Left had quite different sources of information on the Third World as well, which led to the Society's lasting and formative confrontation with the Left.

To be sure, the Campaign and Society saw themselves and were seen as part of the Left – as part of the array of movements in 1960s and 1970s West Germany known as the Extra-Parliamentary Opposition (*Ausserparlamentarische Opposition*, APO). But they undertook open, polemical exchanges especially with Marxist-Leninist parts of the Left. The confrontation went back to the Campaign's earliest days, given the fact that to work for the Biafran cause was already to criticize "the Left" and to claim an untheoretical, "humanitarian" standpoint. This was because the Biafran war and the international response to it did not fit the molds of the Cold War or of Third World national liberation movements and decolonization. Both Britain and the Soviet Union supported Nigeria and opposed Biafra; no great powers supported Biafra. Moreover, the Biafran secessionists were not fighting for independence from a European imperial metropole; they were fighting the newly independent postcolonial state of Nigeria. For a certain rigid Left analysis, the Biafrans were reactionaries because they were fighting against newly independent Nigeria, because their only state ally abroad was the authoritarian Portugal of António Salazar, and because their greatest helpers abroad were the Catholic and Protestant churches. If those Leftists knew that expellee

---

93 See "An unsere Leser" 1976, where it is mentioned that the readership increased sharply in 1975.

94 Duve was editor of the series from 1970. See Duve 1998b and "20 Jahre" 1981, p. 243.

politician Herbert Czaja and the lobby organization League of Expellees (*Bund der Vertriebenen*) supported Biafra, that would have only confirmed them in their analysis. The Socialist German Students' League (*Sozialistischer Deutscher Studentenbund*, SDS), the key West German New Left organization, refused to speak out for Biafra (Zülch 1969a, p. 197).

The Campaign and Society were scathing about Leftists who reasoned about Biafra or other cases in those terms. Historian Golo Mann, writing in Zülch and Guercke's anthology on Biafra, exclaimed: "there are situations in which theory is useless, in which all theory is indeed harmful! All twisted artificial thinking must then be thrown out of the window" (Mann 1969, p. 10). The Society pointed out occasions over the course of the 1970s where Left organizations and journalists excused the violence of perpetrator regimes if they were in some sense socialist. Prominent examples concerned violence against the Kurds[95] (because some West German Leftists supported Iraq's Baath Party), Bangladesh[96] (because Maoists supported China's aid to Pakistan in that war), and the Crimean Tatars and Azerbaijanis[97] (who suffered under Stalin and after). As Zülch complained, only causes such as the Black Panthers, FRELIMO of Mozambique, and El Fatah could gain support from the West German Left, at a time when each of those organizations had leading figures committed to Marxism-Leninism (*Pogrom 2*, no. 11 (1971), n.p.). This was tantamount to excusing genocide, as Zülch argued:

> The pro-Soviet German Left is reluctant to confront Stalinist crimes and almost always uncritically accepts neo-Stalinist policies, to which the discrimination against the Crimean Tatars belongs just as much as the invasions of Hungary (1956) and Czechoslovakia (1968), while the Maoist groups see Stalin as an iconic socialist figure. If one follows their arguments, in the end one would have to distinguish between progressive and reactionary genocide and could then only reject the latter (*Pogrom 5*, no. 26 [1974], p. 6.).

This passage shows how the use of the term genocide, however inflationary, helped the Society gain an argumentative footing that purported to be outside ideology. Zülch made clear that the Society had no reservations about cooperating with groups across the political spectrum if they shared concerns about an abused people. To one reader who complained that *Pogrom* had carried a notice appealing for support for Czech dissident Jiří Müller, whose cause had been embraced by conservative Cold Warriors, Zülch replied that the Society worked with a wide political range of organizations without attaching itself to any of them:

---

95 See "Vorbemerkung" 1974 and *Pogrom* 7, no. 41 (1976), p. 4.
96 See "Bengalen" 1971, "Auschwitz" 1971, and *Pogrom* 2, no. 11 (1971), inside back cover.
97 See *Pogrom* 5, no. 26 (1974), p. 6 and "Bruch" 1980.

...to us it seems very useful to drive the process of clarification onward, within the Left too, to the point where a clear gulf develops between those who consider human rights and democracy under the rule of law to be indispensable, and those who sympathize with Stalinist or neo-Stalinist systems (Zülch 1976, n.p.).

The Society strongly criticized Soviet violations of its minorities' human rights over the 1970s.[98]

Meanwhile, some on the Left fought right back. The Society faced criticism from the Left for having denounced the Sandinista regime's Miskito Indian policy in the early 1980s, and for supporting Croatian independence in the early 1990s. In 1991, the Society was forced out of the main Third World solidarity movement umbrella group, the Federal Congress of Development Action Groups (*Bundeskongress entwicklungspolitischer Aktionsgruppen*, BUKO); it was compelled to resign when the other member organizations refused to have any dealings with it (Wüst 1999, pp. 249–50). While the Society has received much positive press coverage between the 1970s and today, it also has a slightly prickly relationship with the left-liberal and progressive press.[99] One evergreen issue for journalists critical of the Society, on the Left and beyond, is Zülch's affiliation with the expellee lobby – and of course the Society is overwhelmingly identified with Zülch's person. This polemic has lasted until today, particularly among self-described Left and antifascist publications; a quick Internet search using the name of the Society and the term *völkisch* yields numerous items.[100] These writers criticize what they see as the Society's resuscitation of nationalist and racist concepts from the Nazi years such as the concept of the *Volksgruppe*, and the Society's

---

98 See, e.g., *Pogrom* 5, no. 26 (1974), Sheehy 1975, and Vollmer and Zülch 1989. Ethnic Germans in the Soviet Union were mentioned briefly in the 1974 *Pogrom* issue and at greater length in Vollmer and Zülch 1989; see below.

99 See, e.g, Schneider and Schenz 1997. Zülch claimed to me that the Society was not always treated well in the pages of Germany's main progressive newspaper, *taz, die tageszeitung*. Tilman Zülch, personal communication, Göttingen, 24 May 2012. He named an example that rankled: journalist Philipp Mausshardt confronted Zülch with the fact that one of the Society's inaugural board members, journalist Peter Grubbe, was in fact the Nazi-era war criminal Claus Peter Volkmann. Grubbe became known after the war as a critical left-leaning journalist well versed in Third World topics. Zülch removed him from the Society's board (Mausshardt 1995). In Zülch's view, the article drew disproportionate attention to the Society among the various organizations where Grubbe/ Volkmann had worked. However, I have not found consistently negative coverage of the Society in the *taz*. The case of Grubbe/Volkmann would seem to have much to do with postwar German society but nothing specifically to do with the Society.

100 See e.g. La Banda Vaga 1999; "Die Gesellschaft kämpft" 2001; Fischer 2004; "Völkische Gesellschaft?" 2008.

attention to Germans' victimization, which they see as relativizing Nazi crimes. *Volksgruppe* (literally, nationality group) is a term stemming from nationalist Weimar- and Nazi-era international law scholarship that was revived by West German scholars associated with the expellee lobby after 1945, and Zülch uses the term and is acquainted with that body of scholarship.[101] However, I find it impossible to discern any influence of that body of work on the actual contents of *Pogrom* and other Society publications and I suspect that the same is true of those journalists. Otherwise, they would have long ago made more specific allegations. Meanwhile, West Germany's Federal Border Guard categorized *Pogrom* as "Left-extremist" literature to be seized upon entry to the country in 1978 ("Grenzschutz" 1978, n.p.).

The Society and the Left disputed, more than the particulars of each case, the role of context and historical development in understanding violence. Zülch irritated with his relentless drawing of equivalences. Meanwhile, his Leftist opponents contextualized, and presumably could not imagine grounding political action any other way. The Biafra Aid Campaign asserted that the cause of a conflict was simply irrelevant once a humanitarian catastrophe was underway, but no self-respecting Old or New Leftist could ever say that (Zülch 1969b, p. 12). How could the cause of a conflict be irrelevant to one's position on it? This struggle played out not only between the Society and the Left, but also inside the Society, where there was discussion of imposing an internal rule that Society members had to commit themselves to condemning all genocides equally (Zülch 1980).

Genocide was central to the Society's confrontation with the Left. As Zülch wrote in 1971, with regard to Bangladesh: "If the Left remains silent about genocide, it loses its real justification for existence, as Sartre said already in 1968 in his appeal on Biafra" ("Auschwitz" 1971, p. 3). The Society sought to reorganize the

---

101 For usage of "Volksgruppe," see, e.g., *Pogrom* 1, no. 1 (1970), inside front cover. On *Volksgruppenrecht*, see Schönwälder 1996 and Wildenthal 2012, pp. 45–62, 101–131. These concepts were discussed at conferences such as those held by the Federal Union of European Nationalities (*Föderalistischer Verein Europäischer Volksgruppen*, FUEV), which Zülch and other Society members attended, and to which the Society formally belonged. Zülch gives a partly critical account of meetings of these European nationality rights activists, mentioning far-Right Sudeten German representatives and a disruption by some West German neo-Nazis, and mentioning with apparent approval the principles of *Volksgruppenrecht* (Zülch 1979b). See also materials on pages following, on the Internationaler Verband zum Schutze bedrohter Sprachen und Kulturen, FUEV, and *Volksgruppenrecht*. Zülch was acquainted with the international law work on *Volksgruppenrecht* by e.g. Theodor Veiter and Rudolf Laun: ibid. and Tilman Zülch, personal communication, Göttingen, 25 May 2012. See also his positive mention of FUEV (Zülch 1989b, p. 278).

Left around opposition to state violence – up to and including genocide – instead of class conflict, or class conflict mapped onto interstate relations.

States and Peoples, Germans and Other Victims

The Society for Threatened Peoples is controversial, as other human rights NGOs in Germany and elsewhere are not, because it is the only West German human rights organization to have gone against a pattern of avoiding comparison of wrongs suffered by Germans with those suffered by non-Germans. From an abstract legal standpoint, there need be no problem with such comparisons, and indeed should not be. Human rights norms are intentionally phrased as universals and therefore do render various kinds of victims comparable. From the standpoint of historical politics, however, such comparisons can be toxic in the eyes of Germans and others.

What kinds of human rights violations affected those Germans who were not targeted by the Nazis? West Germans pointed to expulsions of ethnic Germans from Poland, Czechoslovakia, and elsewhere in the wake of the Second World War, as well as Allied policies of wartime aerial bombardment, unconditional surrender, and the extended retention of prisoners of war (Wildenthal 2012, Douglas 2012). Less controversially, they have pointed to the plight of Germans in the Soviet zone of occupation and later East Germany, and to ethnic Germans living in other East Bloc states, such as Poland, the Soviet Union, or Romania. There is no inherent reason why an organization could not combine activism about Nazi crimes with activism regarding the expulsions. In practice, however, when West German human rights organizations discussed both the crimes of Nazism and the Allies' wrongs, members viewed each other with so much suspicion that cooperation was impossible (Wildenthal 2012).

The Society for Threatened Peoples broke that pattern. While most of its activism has concerned geographically distant non-Germans, the exposure of Nazi crimes, the fate of the expellees, and the fate of ethnic Germans living under Communism have figured as well. It is true that the German refugees and expellees have not been among the Society's cases per se; this is because, for a West German public at least, they have not fit the Society's criterion of being forgotten. However, the expellee cause has never been absent from the Campaign and Society. Zülch frequently condemns the expulsions, and invokes them together with the Holocaust as the basis of his and other Germans' commitment to human rights for people everywhere threatened by state violence. He has been a member from the outset of the advisory board of the planned Center against Expulsions in Berlin (originally named *Zentrum gegen Vertreibungen* and now administered by the *Stiftung Flucht, Vertreibung, Versöhnung*).[102] This project, which will more or less explicitly compare the Nazi genocide of the Jews to the expulsions of Germans, has been controversial since the early 2000s. In 2003, Zülch accepted the Human Rights Prize of the Sudeten German Homeland Association (*Menschenrechtspreis der Sudetendeutschen Landsmannschaft*) – one of those expellee lobby groups that had done little to distance itself from its own questionable leaders. These are the expellee-related snippets of news that have given the Society a whiff of ill repute, and not only among Leftists. The Society's emphasis on peoples, as opposed to their oppressive states, opened up the possibility of placing various groups of Germans among the cases of threatened peoples, a noteworthy development in the overall history of post-1945 German human rights activism.

This essay has provided contexts for the emergence of the Society for Threatened Peoples and some discussion of the implications of its key terms. The Society successfully imagined threatened peoples and thereby transformed the human rights scene for West Germans in the 1970s and since. It did so by setting out fresh criteria for human rights violations and by introducing a great deal of new information to the reading public. This essay has argued that the reason why the Society has been so lastingly controversial is that its analysis of the plight of threatened peoples relies on the idea of great distance between a people and its state. While this is a truism of international human rights work – it is states that commit or permit human rights violations – it is also a controversial proposition in the context of post-Holocaust Germany. The idea of the people's responsibility for their state, before, during and after the Nazi period does not fit well with the idea of (some) Germans as a threatened people. However, human rights norms alone cannot resolve this tension – if they could, they would comprise a universal political language, which they certainly do not.

---

102 See its website http://www.sfvv.de/, visited on 31 July 2014.

Bibliography[103]

"An alle Aktionsgruppen und alle für Biafra tätigen Einzelpersonen" (1968): In biafrahilfe-all.pdf.
23 September.

"An unsere Leser" (1976): In *Pogrom* 7. No. 41, p. 4.

"Das Antirassismusprogramm" (1971): In *Pogrom* 2, no. 9, pp. 5–7.

"Appell Deutscher Intellektueller an die Bundesregierung" (1970): In biafrahilfe-all.pdf.
11 January.

Arens, Richard (1976): *Genocide in Paraguay*. Philadelphia: Temple University Press.

"Aufgaben und Ziele" (n.d.): At www.gfbv.de/gfbv_deutschland_aufgaben.php, visited on
31 July 2014.

"Auschwitz – Biafra – Bengalen" (1971): In *Pogrom* 2. No. 11, p. 2

La Banda Vaga Rätekommunistisch-anarchistische Gruppe (1999): "Volk, Völker, am Völkesten –
Über die irreführende Analyse der "Gesellschaft für bedrohte Völker." 26 October. At
http://labandavaga.org/volk-voelker-am-voelkesten-ueber-die-irrefuehrende-analyse-
der-gesellschaft-fuer-bedrohte-voelker, visited on 31 July 2014.

"Bengalen. Auschwitz wird alltäglich" (1971): In *Pogrom* 2. No. 9, p. 4.

"Eine Bilanz Juni 1968-Mai 1969" (1969): In biafrahilfe-all.pdf.

Bloxham, Donald and A. Dirk Moses (Eds.) (2010): *The Oxford Handbook of Genocide Studies*.
Oxford: Oxford University Press.

"Bruch der Menschenrechte und des internationalen Völkerrechts – und einige Apologeten"
(1980): In *Pogrom* 11. No. 77, pp. 51–52.

Douglas, R. M. (2012): *Orderly and Humane. The Expulsion of the Germans after the Second
World War*. New Haven: Yale University Press.

Duve, Freimut (1998a): "Minderheitenschutz ist Bürgerschutz." In *Pogrom*, No. 200, p. 56.

Duve, Freimut (1998b): *Vom Krieg in der Seele. Rücksichten eines Deutschen*. Reinbek bei
Hamburg: Rowohlt.

"Editorial I" (1971): In *Pogrom* 2, no. 9, inside front cover.

"Editorial II" (1971): In *Pogrom* 2, no. 9, inside front cover.

"Editorial. Weltkirchenrat: Zweierlei Moral?" (1973): In *Pogrom* 4, no. 21, pp. 3–7.

Fischer, Ralf (2004): "NGO: Deutsche Opfer. Die Gesellschaft für bedrohte Völker setzt auf
völkische Ideologie." In *iz3w. informationszentrum 3. welt*, No. 274, pp. 6–7. Reprinted
as "Völkische Gesellschaft für bedrohte Völker?" In *Sozialistische Positionen. Beiträge zu
Politik, Kultur und Gesellschaft* (24 April 2008). At www.sopos.org. Visited on 31 July 2014.

Gesellschaft für bedrohte Völker (2013): "Bericht über die Menschenrechtsarbeit 2012." At
http://www.gfbv.de/arbeitsbericht.php, visited on 31 July 2014.

---

103 A note on citations from "biafrahilfe-all.pdf": Some archival documents from the Society for Threatened Peoples that are cited below were consulted using a scanned collection of Biafra-related documents prepared for internal use by Society staff member Abdul Raffert. I designate this electronic collection as he did, "biafrahilfe-all.pdf." I thank him for providing me a copy. The originals of those scans are held in the Society's archive at its main office in Göttingen, which I visited in May 2012. While at the archive, I also consulted an overlapping set of documents in their original form, which are organized by boxes. If an archival document has a clear author or title, it is cited with its own bibliography entry; if not, details are given in a footnote.

"Die Gesellschaft für bedrohte Völker kämpft, gegen alle aber wofür?" (2001): In *Streitblatt. Kommunistische Monatszeitung* no. 14. April. At http://www.streitblatt.de/streitblatt/sb14/GFBV.HTM, visited on 31 July 2014.

Grass, Günter (1968): "Völkermord vor aller Augen." In *Die Zeit* (11 October 1968). Reprinted in *Bedrohte Völker (ehemals Pogrom)* 39. No. 6 (2008), p. 27.

"Grenzschutz führte Buch über 'Linke'" (1978): In *Süddeutsche Zeitung* (17 May). Located at Society Archive, Göttingen, in box labeled "GfbV Presse 1976–1978."

Hannig, Florian (forthcoming 2014a): "The Biafra Crisis and the Establishment of Humanitarian Aid in West Germany as New Philanthropic Field." In *German Philanthropy in Transatlantic Perspective*. Bauerkämper, Arnd and Gregory Witkowski (Eds.). Bloomington: Indiana University Press.

Hannig, Florian (forthcoming 2014b): "Biafra und die Globalisierung humanitärer Hilfe – eine westdeutsche Perspektive." In *Humanitarianism in Times of War 1914–2012*. Maul, Daniel and Dietmar Süss (Eds.). Göttingen: Wallstein.

Hannig, Florian (forthcoming 2014c): "Mitleid mit Biafranern in Westdeutschland. Eine Historisierung von Empathie." In *WerkstattGeschichte. Themenheft Humanitarismus*.

Heerten, Lasse (2011): "A wie Auschwitz, B wie Biafra. Der Bürgerkrieg in Nigeria (1967–1970) und die Universalisierung des Holocaust." In *Zeithistorische Forschungen/Studies in Contemporary History* 8. No. 3.

Heerten, Lasse (2014): "The Dystopia of Postcolonial Catastrophe: Self-Determination, the Biafran War of Secession, and the 1970s Human Rights Movement." In *The Breakthrough. Human Rights in the 1970s*. Eckel, Jan and Samuel Moyn (Eds.). Philadelphia: University of Pennsylvania Press, pp. 15–32.

"Heinrich Böll – ein Wort zur Woche der Brüderlichkeit" (1970): In *Pogrom* 1. No. 1, p. 14.

Horst, René D. Harder (2007): *The Stroessner Regime and Indigenous Resistance in Paraguay*. Gainesville: University Press of Florida.

Kotzian, Ortfried (1989): "Integriert, aber nicht assimiliert: Die deutschen Vertriebenen und Umsiedler in ihren neuen Heimaten." In: *Aufstand der Opfer. Verratene Völker zwischen Hitler und Stalin*. Vollmer, Johannes and Tilman Zülch (Eds.). Göttingen: Gesellschaft für bedrohten Völker, pp. 269–271.

Kovats, Marlies and Gerle Stammberger (2008): "Wie alles einmal anfing." In *Bedrohte Völker (ehemals Pogrom)* 39. No. 6, pp. 82–83.

"Letzte Zeitzeugen berichten über ihr Schicksal als 'Wolfskinder' nach 1945 (2011): At http://www.gfbv.de/pressemit.php?id=2695, visited on 31 July 2014. 9 May.

Lewis, Norman (1969): "Genocide." In *Sunday Times Magazine*. 23 February, pp. 34–59.

Mann, Golo (1969): "Geleitwort." *Soll Biafra überleben? Dokumente, Berichte, Analysen, Kommentare. Eine Dokumentation*. Zülch, Tilman and Klaus Guercke (Eds.). 2nd, expanded edition. Berlin: Lettner-Verlag, pp. 9–10.

Mausshardt, Philipp (1995): "Es gibt zwei Leben vor dem Tod," *die tageszeitung* (29 September), pp. 12–14.

Münzel, Mark (1979): *Die frohe Botschaft unserer Zivilisation: Evangelikalische Indianermission in Lateinamerika*. Göttingen: Gesellschaft für bedrohten Völker.

"Die politische Problematik des Konfliktes Nigeria/Biafra" (n.d.): In biafrahilfe-all.pdf.

Reed, Richard and John Renshaw (2012): "The Aché and Guaraní: Thirty Years after Maybury-Lewis and Howe's Report on Genocide in Paraguay." *Tipití: Journal of the Society for the Anthropology of Lowland South America* 10. No. 1, pp. 1–18.

Rogall, Joachim (1989): "Diktierte Option: Die 'Umsiedlung' der deutschen Minderheiten." In *Aufstand der Opfer. Verratene Völker zwischen Hitler und Stalin.* Vollmer, Johannes and Tilman Zülch (Eds.). Göttingen: Gesellschaft für bedrohten Völker, pp. 143–148.

Sartre, Jean-Paul (1970): "Der Weltherrschaft der Gangster." In *Peace News.* 30 January. Reprinted (1970) in *Pogrom* 1. No. 1, p. 4.

Savvidis, Tessa (Ed.) (1980): *Der Völkermord an den Armeniern vor Gericht. Der Prozess Talaat Pascha.* Göttingen: Gesellschaft für bedrohten Völker.

Schneider, Jens and Viola Schenz (1997): "Schnell eine Mahnwache vor der Tür." In *Süddeutsche Zeitung.* 12 July.

Schönwälder, Karen (1996): "Minderheitenschutz: Anerkennung kultureller Pluralität oder Ausdruck 'völkischen Denkens'?" In *Antifaschismus.* Deppe, Frank, Georg Fülberth, and Rainer Rilling (Eds.). Heilbronn: Distel, pp. 453–467.

Schultze, Waltraut and Heinz Schultze (1974): "Wer und was ist ein Indio?" In *Pogrom* 5. No. 27, pp. 20–21.

"Schweigemarsch" (1968): In *Die Zeit.* 16 August.

Sheehy, Ann (1973): *The Crimean Tatars, Volga Germans and Meskhetians: Soviet Treatment of Some National Minorities.* London: Minority Rights Group.

Sheehy, Ann (1975): "Die Meschier – Kampf um Land in der Sowjetunion." In *Von denen keiner spricht. Unterdrückte Minderheite – von der Friedenspolitik vergessen.* Zülch, Tilman (Ed.). Reinbek bei Hamburg: Rowohlt, pp. 132–136.

Slobodian, Quinn (2012): *Foreign Front. Third World Politics in Sixties West Germany.* Durham: Duke University Press.

Smith, Karen E. (2010): *Genocide and the Europeans.* New York: Cambridge University Press.

Tenhumberg, Heinrich (1969): "Massenmord trotz Völkerrecht?" In *Soll Biafra überleben? Dokumente, Berichte, Analysen, Kommentare. Eine Dokumentation.* Zülch, Tilman and Klaus Guercke (Eds.). 2nd, expanded edition. Berlin: Lettner-Verlag, pp. 226–230.

Tugendhat, Ernst (2008): "Festrede zum 40-jährigen Bestehen der Gesellschaft für bedrohte Völker." In *Bedrohte Völker (ehemals Pogrom)* 39. No. 6, pp. 12–14.

"Völkische Gesellschaft für bedrohte Völker?" (2008): In blog "Es is mehr daran als mensch glaubt." 24 April. At http://eisberg.blogsport.de/2008/04/24/voelkische-gesellschaft-fuer-bedrohte-voelker/, visited on 31 July 2014.

Vollmer, Johannes and Tilman Zülch (Eds.) (1989): *Aufstand der Opfer. Verratene Völker zwischen Hitler und Stalin.* Göttingen: Gesellschaft für bedrohten Völker.

"Vorbemerkung" (1974): In *Pogrom* 5. No. 29–30, pp. 4–5.

Wildenthal, Lora (2012): *The Language of Human Rights in West Germany.* Philadelphia: University of Pennsylvania Press.

Wüst, Jürgen (1999): *Menschenrechtsarbeit im Zwielicht: Zwischen Staatssicherheit und Antifaschismus.* Bonn: Bouvier.

Zülch, Tilman (1969a): "Biafranische Studenten: Für eine neue Republik," In *Soll Biafra überleben? Dokumente, Berichte, Analysen, Kommentare. Eine Dokumentation.* Zülch, Tilman and Klaus Guercke (Eds.). 2nd, expanded edition. Berlin: Lettner-Verlag, pp. 194–197.

Zülch, Tilman (1969b): "Plädoyer für die Republik Biafra." In *Soll Biafra überleben? Dokumente, Berichte, Analysen, Kommentare. Eine Dokumentation.* Zülch, Tilman and Klaus Guercke (Eds.). 2nd, expanded edition. Berlin: Lettner-Verlag, pp. 11–18.

Zülch, Tilman (1976): Letter to Rudolf Bruder dated 6 September 1976. Located in the Society archive, Göttingen, in box labeled "Biafra allgemein 1968–1978; Biafra Korrespondenz 1972–1982."

Zülch, Tilman (1978): "Kurdistan. Über Schwierigkeiten in der Bundesrepublik objektiv über die Kurden zu berichten, z. B. der 'Berliner Extradienst'." In *Pogrom* 9. No. 54–56, 182.

Zülch, Tilman (Ed.) (1979a): *In Auschwitz vergast, bis heute verfolgt. Zur Situation der Roma (Zigeuner) in Deutschland und Europa*. Reinbek bei Hamburg: Rowohlt.

Zülch, Tilman (1979b): "Von Macht und Ohnmacht Europäischer Minderheiten." In *Pogrom* 10. No. 60, pp. 45–46.

Zülch, Tilman (1980): Letter to Käthe Meentzen dated 10 June 1980. Located in Society Archive, Göttingen, in box labeled "Biafra (1968–1980)."

Zülch, Tilman (1983): *Sinti und Roma in Deutschland. 600 Jahre Geschichte einer verfolgten Minderheit*. Zentralrat deutscher Sinti und Roma (Ed.). Bonn: Bundeszentrale für politische Bildung.

Zülch, Tilman (1989a): "Die Eroberung Nordostpreussens." In *Aufstand der Opfer. Verratene Völker zwischen Hitler und Stalin*. Vollmer, Johannes and Tilman Zülch (Eds.). Göttingen: Gesellschaft für bedrohten Völker, pp. 149–153.

Zülch, Tilman (1989b): "Es gab nicht nur Opfer." In *Aufstand der Opfer. Verratene Völker zwischen Hitler und Stalin*. Vollmer, Johannes and Tilman Zülch (Eds.). Göttingen: Gesellschaft für bedrohten Völker, pp. 275–278.

Zülch, Tilman (1993): *Ethnische Säuberung – Völkermord für Grossserbien. Eine Dokumentation der Gesellschaft für bedrohte Völker*. Hamburg: Luchterhand.

Zülch, Tilman and Klaus Guercke (Eds.) (1968): *Biafra: Todesurteil für ein Volk? Eine Dokumentation*. Berlin: Lettner-Verlag.

Zülch, Tilman and Klaus Guercke (Eds.) (1969): *Soll Biafra überleben? Dokumente, Berichte, Analysen, Kommentare. Eine Dokumentation*. 2nd, expanded edition. Berlin: Lettner-Verlag.

"20 Jahre rororo aktuell" (1981): In Der Spiegel, p. 243. 12 October.

Nina Berman
Neoliberal Charity: German Contraband Humanitarians in Kenya

Human Rights and Humanitarianism

How is the imagination of human rights related to humanitarian practice? More specifically, how is the history of this relationship relevant to understanding present-day forms of humanitarian practice? To answer these questions, this essay offers a brief discussion of approaches to the history of human rights, including its relationship to humanitarian practices and debates over rights that emerged in the context of colonialism. The link to colonial rule, specifically, highlights the conditional nature of humanitarian practices and its connection to the adoption of particular economic orders. Today's humanitarianism is also conditional and intricately defined through its relationship to neoliberalism. A case study on what I call "contraband humanitarians" in Kenya illustrates the ways in which this type of humanitarian work can be tied to central tenets of neoliberalism. My discussion highlights the ways in which contraband charity is distinguished by what Didier Fassin calls "humanitarian reason," a belief system that buttresses contemporary global inequality (Fassin 2012). The conclusion addresses the function of contraband charity in the context of present-day economic globalization, specifically what is becoming known as the Second Scramble for Africa.

Humanitarianism, Human Rights, and Empire

Scholars have located the origin of human rights debates in different historical moments and they have presented this genealogy through both idealist and materialist lenses. In *Inventing Human Rights*, Lynn Hunt ties the birth of the idea of human rights to debates in eighteenth-century North America and Europe, highlighting the relevance of the Enlightenment idea of individual autonomy: "To have human rights, people had to be perceived as separate individuals who were capable of exercising independent moral judgment" (Hunt 2007, p. 27). Her evidence for the origins of a new sensibility that enabled the notion of human rights to take root are "accounts of torture or epistolary novels," the reading of which, Hunt claims, "had physical effects that translated into brain changes and came back out as new concepts about the organization of social and political life." In contrast to materialist explanations according to which the notion of the individual may be tied to the emerging needs of capitalism (for individuals who are divorced from place and social ties and can become movable labor, for example), Hunt's idealist interpretation suggests that "[n]ew kinds of reading (and viewing and listening) created new individual experiences (empathy), which in turn made possible new social and political concepts (human rights)" (Hunt 2007, p. 33–34).

Samuel Moyn, on the other hand, argues that the concept of human rights, as we understand it today, is a much more recent invention, and that it is tied to macro-level political events. Moyn provides ample evidence that the human rights discourse in Western societies gained currency after World War II before becoming popularized in earnest only in the course of the 1970s. Moyn explains the popularity of the concept as being grounded in a need for utopian vision. He cites various factors – among them "the search for a European identity outside Cold War terms" and "the end of formal colonialism and the crisis of the postcolonial state" – and summarizes them by suggesting that "the best general explanation for the origins of this social movement and common discourse around rights remains the collapse of other, prior utopias, both state-based and internationalist" (Moyn 2010, p. 8). While Moyn emphasizes the ideological function of the notion of human rights, he asks us to understand the discourse of human rights in the context of material histories.

Reading Hunt and Moyn side-by-side shows that since its inception the notion of human rights has functioned as a political discourse, one that needs to be explored in terms of its relationship to the material histories it negotiates. Debates about what is human and what consequences the idea of the human has in terms of rights predate eighteenth-century discussions of natural and citizen rights (although the inflation of the term *human rights* is, as Moyn argues, certainly a more recent phenomenon). Neither the notion of rights nor that of the human is owned exclusively by the West, but the discourse of "human rights" is a particularly Western phenomenon, one that is grounded in the longer history of Europe's relationship to non-European, particularly non-Christian, cultures (Barnett). Therefore, colonial and imperial enterprises turn out to be central for debates on ideas of the human. On this issue, Anthony Pagden deserves to be quoted at length:

> It is undeniable that, at present, the "international community" derives its values from a version of a liberal consensus which is, in essence, a secularized transvaluation of the Christian ethic, at least as it applies to the concept of rights. ... The history of rights, of *iura*, and in particular of those rights which were to become "human rights," is doubly embarrassing for their culturally sensitive defendants in that such rights were not only a creation of the Roman legal tradition but were developed in the form we understand it today, in the

context of imperial legislative practices, and have remained closely associated with *imperial* expansion and its consequences until at least the late nineteenth century. Some plausible account of the evolving relationship between rights and the development of the European empires might, perhaps, provide a better position from which to evaluate why we continue to believe that "our" values are necessarily conterminous with those of the human race as a whole, and whether we are justified in so doing (Pagden 2003, p. 173).

Some of the earliest evidence for how ideas of the human and of rights were debated in the context of imperial conquest can be seen in the advocacy of Bartolomé de Las Casas on behalf of Native Americans. The Dominican friar who became an outspoken critic of imperial violence based his activism for American Indians on a concept of universal humanity. Nevertheless, Las Casas's support was ultimately conditional in that it was tied to the desired conversion of American Indians to Christianity. As Daniel Brunstetter has shown, "Las Casas's claims about the humanity of the Indians delimit a tension-laden view of the human that sheds light on the friction between universalism and alterity and thus the place of inequality in the liberal thread of Modernity" (Brunstetter 2010, p. 421; Castro). While acceptance of Christianity was crucial for Las Casas's notion of universal humanity, racism and its dehumanizing practices would ultimately secure the exclusion of non-European others from the framework of rights granted to white Christians. In many ways Las Casas's positions exemplify the tension inherent in the conditional support today's humanitarians (generally speaking) extend to the recipients of their aid – namely, accepting parameters of neoliberal capitalism.

Reading Las Casas alongside Hunt and Moyn emphasizes the ways in which human rights discourses, while clearly playing distinct functions on the national level, negotiate power relations on a global scale. To be sure, human rights discourses are invoked by different agents, and the differential power status of these agents betrays their distinct goals: political, disability, or gay rights activists who lobby for their rights in a specific country are, for example, situated differently from government representatives who evoke human rights in order to justify political and economic policy in order to pursue goals that may in fact lead to a worsening of the human rights situation, most often in countries other than their own. It is useful in this regard to consider the relationship of human rights to humanitarianism.

How is humanitarianism related to the notion of human rights? According to a host of dictionary definitions, *humanitarianism* is a doctrine or a set of beliefs and practices that are based in the intent to promote the "welfare of other people" or "human welfare." Significantly, however, unlike human rights debates and activism, *humanitarianism does not primarily refer to rights*, and even if it does refer to rights, the gesture is mostly rhetorical. For one thing, human rights at this point in time have no institutional teeth: unless they are legislated locally and made part of the citizenship rights of a nation-state, they are not enforceable in our current global legal landscape (Brysk and Shafir 2004). In addition, humanitarianism is intrinsically related to global relations of social inequality, but it masks this relation by emphasizing *affect* rather than rights and ideas of social justice. Humanitarianism, as Didier Fassin has argued, is grounded in "a politics of inequality" and draws on "the mobilization of empathy rather than the recognition of rights" (Fassin 2012, p. 3, p. x).

Humanitarianism is a term with a recent linguistic history. Google Ngram shows no significant use of the term until 1850 (though it shows indications of earlier spikes in usage), with a peak in 1941, then a significant drop and an upward trend again since 1992 (Google Books, Ngram Viewer 1). The chart for the term *humanitarian,* however, shows a steady increase over time, with only a slight drop in the late 1970s and early 1980s (Google Books, Ngram Viewer 2). The graph for the German term *humanitär* displays a similar rise in frequency but it also a drop after the year 2000 (Google Books, Ngram Viewer 3). While humanitarian rhetoric may be a more recent phenomenon – and various forms of charity, philanthropy, or welfare predate Western colonialism and have existed in cultures across time and space – the particular type of humanitarian practice that is tied to global power politics dates back to the beginnings of colonialism. Like the positions of Las Casas (who argues for rights but also makes them conditional), contemporary humanitarianism displays the deep contradictions that are the legacy of the long-standing nexus between imperial power and discussions of the human and nonhuman.

Humanitarianism, as it is pursued mostly in poor nations by international nongovernmental organizations (INGOs), governmental and international supragovernmental organizations, as well as a wide range of individuals is very much structured by the principles of conditional support that emerged in the context of colonialism and continue under the auspices of neoliberal globalization. The extent to which humanitarianism has become an integral part of neoliberal Western identity can be observed in the actions of ordinary citizens who take the humanitarian and developmentalist agenda into their own hands.

German, Swiss, and Austrian Humanitarian Activities in Africa

Over the past few decades, German, Swiss, and – to a lesser extent – Austrian participation in a wide range of humanitarian activities in Africa has become extremely popular. In 2013, the total of all forms of private donations in Germany was estimated to amount to approximately 6.3 billion euro (Deutsches Zentralinstitut für soziale Fragen 2014). More than 75 percent of private philanthropic organizations are active internationally; almost 80 percent of their work is designated as "humanitarian aid"; and the largest percentage of German donations for internationally active organizations supports humanitarian aid to Africa (Ulrich 2009, p 12; betterplace lab 2011, slide 20). During the summer of 2011 appeals to donate in response to the famine in East Africa raised 91 million euro within four weeks (Deutsches Zentralinstitut 2011). In July of that year in Switzerland, one news organization reported that 7.8 million Swiss francs were raised in the course of only a few weeks (Müller 2011). In August, Swiss citizens were reported to have donated 20 million Swiss francs through one particular donating platform for the famine in East Africa (news.ch 2011). In 2013 the volume of private donations in Switzerland was 1.6 billion Swiss francs, thus exceeding the amount of giving per person in Germany (the population of Germany is roughly eighty-two million, while that of Switzerland is about eight million) (swissfundraising 2013). Austria sends less aid to countries of the global south in comparison to the aid provided to those areas by Germany and Switzerland (Fundraising 2013, p. 7). One report states that surveys reveal that Austrians prefer to give to domestic projects (Fundraising 2013, p. 3).

German donors and their money influence events in Africa in substantial ways and German humanitarian organizations that focus on Africa are ubiquitous. (For the sake of convenience and because of their significant cultural similarities, henceforth I refer to German-speaking persons collectively as "Germans"). Annett Heinl and Gabriele Lingelbach have shown that West German giving to organizations that operate abroad emerged in the 1950s in the context of development aid (*Entwicklungshilfe)* activities and discourses (Heinl and Lingelbach 2009, p. 287–312). The economic, political, and social situations of "Third World" countries have attracted growing public attention since that time. Human rights advocacy in particular relates German philanthropic activity in Africa to what historian Lora Wildenthal has identified as one of four usages of the "language of human rights," namely "activism on behalf of foreigners." In former West Germany this activism can be traced back to the Society of Threatened Peoples (*Gesellschaft für bedrohte Völker)*, which, according to Wildenthal, began as the

Biafra Aid Campaign (Aktion Biafra-Hilfe) in 1968 and soon thereafter "broad-ened its scope to any 'people' (Volk)" (Wildenthal 2013, 11). German humanitar-ian impulses, as Glenn Penny argues, are also grounded in the long-standing identification with indigenous peoples (most importantly, American Indians), which sensitized (some) Germans to the plight of indigenous peoples and to the repercussions of colonial conquest (Penny 2013). In addition, as Michael Roth-berg and others have pointed out, critical discussions of the Shoah in Germany (and elsewhere) opened a space for the discussion of genocides of other groups and thus helped generate the human rights framework that was crucial for the emergence of humanitarian initiatives and the development of new legal norms regarding humanitarian responsibilities (Rothberg 2009; Hilpold 2013).

The popular discourse on humanitarianism also plays a role in inspiring humanitarian impulses. The older generation of humanitarians at present are more likely to have been directly inspired by Albert Schweitzer, who represents the key paradigm for today's humanitarianism on both the institutional and the personal level (Berman 2004, 61–97). For the middle-aged and younger genera-tion the USA for Africa song and fund-raiser "We Are the World" in 1985 signals a pivotal moment that popularized humanitarianism. Musical artists such as Madonna and Bono and, in the German context, the late actor Karlheinz Böhm and soccer star Philipp Lahm use their celebrity status to promote the humani-tarian agenda.

In most instances, German humanitarians come to Kenya via tourism. Kenya has been one of the favorite vacation destinations for tourists from German-speak-ing countries, who over the years have constituted between 10 and 20 percent of tourist arrivals in the country (Berman 2004, p 186). In 2009 a total of 940,386 international arrivals were recorded at the two main airports, 395,828 of them cat-egorized as tourists. Among the tourists were 63,592 Germans, 15,810 Swiss, and 5,302 Austrians (Ministry of East African Affairs, Commerce and Tourism 2014). Diani, which is located on the coast south of Mombasa and one of the main centers of beach tourism in Kenya, is particularly popular with Germans. Germans were crucial in developing its tourism infrastructure, and over the past fifty years Ger-man-speaking tourists and residents have contributed to shaping life in the area. In addition to vacationing there as tourists, they have been active as managers of hotels; owners of boutiques, travel agencies, nightclubs, diving businesses, and restaurants; landlords of expensive villas; and employers of Kenyans. Some move to Kenya to retire, and some engage in binational romantic relationships. Over time the development of the tourism and real estate infrastructure and the activ-ities of the tourists and settlers have had a significant impact on the local com-munity, affecting shifts in landownership, commercial infrastructure, population growth, interpersonal relations, and various patterns of social and cultural practices. In addition, postindependence Kenyan governments have neglected the coastal region and have in fact facilitated land grabbing of some of the most precious beachfront plots. The result of these various changes is a shift from a largely self-sustaining community to a much larger population that is overwhelmingly impoverished, with high rates of unemployment, drug abuse, and prostitution. While the local Digo of the area numbered several thousand up until the 1960s, more than 70,000 people live in the larger Diani area today.[104]

Most of the German tourists and residents who engage in humanitarian activity in Diani are unaware of the reasons for the poverty they encounter. Humanitarians tend to lack understanding about the repercussions of tourism development, the inaction of the Kenyan government, misguided development aid policies (affecting Kenya more broadly), structural adjustment policies imposed on Kenya by the World Bank and the International Monetary Fund (which are responsible for the real estate boom in Diani that has led to large-scale gentrification), and the role Westerners play in land grabbing as well as the rise of the drug trade and prostitution in the area. Rather, they interpret what they see along the lines of deeply ingrained notions about Africa's need for assistance.

While some humanitarians pursue their activities in the official institutionalized settings (such as schools, INGOs), not a single German, Swiss, or Austrian INGO is registered in Kwale County (to which Diani belongs). Hundreds of large- and small-scale projects, however, have been funded by individuals from these and other European countries. Some activities occur through locally registered associations or businesses, but much humanitarian activity takes place entirely outside of official channels charged with monitoring development and economic activity. I have chosen the terms *contraband humanitarian* and *contraband charity* to highlight this outsider dimension; in addition, at times contraband charity does indeed involve illegal actions. *Charity*, it should be noted, is the term that is used locally, in Diani and Kenya more broadly, to refer to humanitarian activities of all kinds.

Contraband Humanitarians

Tourism frequently creates the contact zone that leads to humanitarian activity. Once tourists realize that even small sums of money can have a tremendous impact, many of them pursue philanthropic activity with great enthusiasm. Initial

---

104 73,475 according to the Kenya 2009 census. The figures for Diani were provided to me by the Diani Chief's office.

contact is often made in the hotel at which the visitors stay or at a restaurant, a bar, or the beach. In the late 1990s I conducted my first study of German, Swiss, and Austrian repeat visitors who vacationed on the Diani coast and learned about the extent and nature of their interaction with the local population. In all cases there was significant contact between the local population and the tourists; the majority (70–80%) of repeat visitors I interviewed supported Kenyans materially in one way or another. They paid education fees for different types of schools, such as primary and secondary schools, language institutes, and driving schools; bought school supplies and uniforms; took care of hospital bills and paid for other medical needs; brought clothes, household items, and electronic appliances; and even helped people build their own homes (Berman 2004, p. 195–204).

For some of the tourists these kinds of measures of support were the first step toward becoming a committed contraband humanitarian, and often they created donor networks back home that allowed them to pursue projects of significant scale. By founding these donor networks, German contraband humanitarians created the type of organization that journalist Linda Polman calls "MONGO," for "My Own NGO," a term that highlights the subjective and perhaps haphazard dimension of this type of nongovernmental organization (Polman 2010, p. 48–62). Over time, these fundraising efforts have had a visible effect; the larger Diani area is crowded with schools, water tanks, dispensaries, nurseries, houses, toilets, and wells that were built for locals with the funds of contraband humanitarians. There is not a single public or private school in the area that does not have a sponsor, mostly European, whose name is engraved on school desks or acknowledged on the entrance wall of the building.

Let us take a look at two examples of contraband humanitarians who have been active in the area over the last several years. Gustav and Bertha Müller have been traveling to Kenya since 1991.[105] While they first pursued their aid activities alone, they eventually established a support network in Germany (their MONGO) that is raising ever-increasing sums of money. When I initially interviewed Mr. Müller in 2009 he indicated that his network had raised over 25,000 euro and that he expected the sum to rise to 100,000 euro in 2011. As of May 2010, the association, which is also loosely connected to a larger and more visible network, was registered as a nonprofit organization in Germany ("eingetragener Verein"). A core of about twenty active members draws on a constantly growing donor network; overall membership has grown to seventy individuals (March 2014).

---

105 The names of all individuals I interviewed have been changed, and I also altered other aspects of their stories to ensure anonymity. I provide a more detailed discussion of the activities of the Müllers, in the context of historical patterns of aid to Africa, in Berman 2013.

The explicit goal of the organization, as expressed in its constitution, is to "improve the living conditions of human beings in Africa," with a focus on education and health care. The organization emphasizes that it is guided by principles of self-help. Beginning in 2005, the main focus of the Müllers and their association has been Kijiji village, which is located at a significant distance from Diani. About 12,000 individuals live in the area connected to the village. Among the various projects, including some in locations other than this particular village, are replacing defunct water pumps; building toilets and shower stalls in several areas; sponsoring school children (as of 2014, Germans pay fees and supplies for eighty-nine children; in 2011 the organization sponsored forty-eight children); supporting primary and secondary schools, both public and private (funding the building of new structures, building toilets, supplying books, providing a meal program, and erecting water tanks); supporting the Kwale District Eye Centre (through donations of cash and equipment as well as by collecting used eyeglasses and buying and reselling items from the Eye Clinic Charity Shop); supporting orphans (three children from Kijiji village were brought to an orphanage in another location); building water tanks in various locations (to date nine water tanks have been built in Kijiji village alone); providing mosquito nets (in 2008, for example, the initiative distributed over one thousand nets); supporting health dispensaries (the organization provides a significant amount of medications, particularly in support of an epilepsy network); creating employment (through support of seamstresses, wood-carvers, and musicians); and supporting an SOS Children's Village (to date three children have been sponsored).

Funds for the Müllers' organization are raised in Germany. Initially, the couple relied on their private network, and over time their association reached a substantial number of supporters in their hometown and the surrounding areas. While some of their activities, such as the building of toilets, require government approval (in this case from the Ministry of Health), none of the planning occurs in collaboration with state institutions. As a result, almost none of the organization's activities are coordinated with Kenyan government agencies, a situation that would be (as yet) unthinkable if, say, the flow of such activity were reversed. Would Germany, for example, allow Qatari or Chinese humanitarians to fix the dismal situations in its areas of urban poverty?

My second example of a contraband humanitarian operating in the area in recent years is a Swiss woman, Ms. Bäumler, who over time has made significant contributions to infrastructure development in Diani and has also helped select individuals directly. She first came to Kenya in 1988 and slowly got to know people in the area through contacts made with the hotel staff. She initially brought children with her to the hotel and then began to pay for the education of certain ones. But she soon expanded her range of activities, establishing an organization in

Switzerland that served as a fund-raising platform to support projects in Diani. She advertised her initiative in newspapers, on the radio, and on television. Sponsors included individuals from all walks of life as well as faith-based organizations, and some donations were as large as ten thousand Swiss francs. One of her most successful projects dating back to this early phase of her activities is an elementary school that in 2012 provided about seventy scholarships to select students. She also enabled older students who needed funds to attend secondary school and brought disabled children into an orphanage.

In the early 1990s she fell in love with one of the hotel employees and in 2001 left her husband and secure employment as a salesperson in a large department store behind and relocated to Diani. Ms. Bäumler was forty-eight when she made this life-changing decision. Once she moved to Diani, her level of activity increased: she raised funds to dig wells and built three large water tanks that are located in various places across the area; she repaired roofs, built toilets, took drug addicts to the treatment program of the local Catholic church, and adopted the child of a mother who had died of AIDS and who himself is infected with the virus. All of this, Ms. Bäumler said, was done without asking for reciprocity; it was done out of a good heart ("alles ohne Gegenleistung, von gutem Herzen").

What are the implications of contraband charity? For contraband humanitarians proof that their work is meaningful is easily established: providing for education, improving sanitation and health care, and taking care of orphans are actions that correspond to United Nations and other development agencies' goals and accord with widely acknowledged areas of human rights. Financially, all of the projects supported by Mr. Müller and Ms. Bäumler are dependent on funds flowing from Germany and Switzerland. Without this donor support, none of the projects would be able to survive. Yet Mr. Müller's and Ms. Bäumler's investments in education have the potential to produce long-term effects. Those who have received an education through the efforts of these philanthropists may have a greater chance to create sustainable futures for themselves.

Contraband humanitarians achieve their goals with a minimum of bureaucracy and overhead costs, and they are able to track the outcome of their aid through long-term personal contacts. What, then, could be wrong with this kind of aid? In spite of the seemingly obvious beneficial dimensions contained in this kind of aid, there are also long-term repercussions that most contraband humanitarians are not prepared to grasp. Contraband charity, building on the five hundred-year-old tradition that was established by the nexus of colonialism and the Christian mission and continued through various models of modern forms of imperial and capitalistic aid, is part of and contributes to a culture of charity that has detrimental effects on various levels. Contraband charity in Diani, beginning with the actions of individuals in the 1980s and earlier, had an impact on aspects of the larger society that contraband humanitarians rarely consider: on the state, the economy, and, perhaps most important, local culture.

Relationship to the Kenyan state. Mr. Müller and his organization operate almost entirely outside of the official political and administrative framework and, through their activities, release the state from its responsibilities, thereby fueling the potential for corruption. Mr. Müller's organization is not registered in Kenya (and only recently became registered in Germany), and Mr. Müller has never been to the offices of the county commissioner, education officer, or development officer. At some point Mr. Müller considered registering as a local organization but felt that such a move would inevitably lead to conflict with the Germany-based organization: "Because then we have two organizations with different goals," he explained. In only a few cases Mr. Müller went through official channels – such as when a sanitary unit attached to a dispensary had to be approved – and most of the time these interactions were initiated and carried out by his local contacts. Ms. Bäumler's Swiss donor network is also not registered in Kenya. After relocating to Kenya, she went through official channels more often – for example, when she established the primary school – even if most of that work was done by others for her. Most of Ms. Bäumler's other projects, however, have also been conducted without any connection to official development plans.

More important, however, the large amount of informal aid flowing into the coastal area may in fact encourage inaction by government officials. If their work is being done by someone else, they face less pressure to create and maintain a functioning infrastructure. State funds can disappear without anyone noticing their absence – after all, schools, dispensaries, toilets, and wells were built. INGOs in Africa and other areas of the world developed out of the frustrations resulting from severe shortcomings of state-controlled services, including corruption, mismanagement, graft, and political oppression. But the initiatives led by non-state actors produce their own problematic outcomes and, in some cases, undermine the potential for governmental institutions to be effective. In part, my research on contraband humanitarians confirms the finding of other critics who have illustrated the negative repercussions of INGOs and NGOs in Kenya. As with other forms of aid, contraband charity "props up corrupt governments" (Moyo 2009, p. 49; also, among others, Wrong 2009; Easterly 2006; Lancaster 1999; Ayittey 1998; Kabou 1991; Erler 1985).[106] Funds directly provided by humanitarians to schools may end up in the pockets of corrupt principals. The principal of one of the schools that receive substantial aid through Mr. Müller's organization

---

106 Jeffrey Sachs is one of the most prominent supporters of development aid. For a summary of his main points, see Sachs 2014.

was locally known for being corrupt and pocketing donor money. In this regard contraband charity not only feeds graft and corruption; it is also a dimension of the "NGOization" of Kenyan society, whereby mostly foreign-based organizations complement, but more often interfere with, the responsibilities of the state and local communities (Mutua 2009; Amutabi 2006; Igoe and Kelsall 2005; Hearn 1998). Overall this type of charity leads to further erosion of the state and thus facilitates basic neoliberal principles.

Impact on the Kenyan economy. Mr. Müller and Ms. Bäumler both feed and impede the growth of local industries. Their activities employ those who construct building structures, and many items used for the projects are bought locally. But the cargo that their organizations bring from Europe is problematic. In spite of prohibitions by the Ministry of Health, contraband humanitarians import and hand out medications free of charge, a practice that interferes with the local pharmaceutical market. As medications are delivered to government dispensaries without any official mechanism controlling the volume and nature of the donations, the reselling of these materials has become a widespread phenomenon (Bate, Hess, and Mooney 2010; Siringi 2004). Donors are usually unaware of the black market for drugs and medical supplies and cannot fathom that a medical doctor would be involved in illegal activities. Interestingly, several airlines transport goods for approved charitable organizations for free (such as Air Berlin and Condor), which facilitates the import of often-defunct items. Cargo is inspected at Kenyan airports, but much of what is deemed useless by, for example, a district health commissioner passes customs. In Kwale an official of the Ministry of Health showed me a defunct surgery bed, a defunct radiology machine, and hundreds of useless AIDS prevention kits that were rotting away in storage. What results in convenient tax write-offs for German and Swiss companies and individuals litters the Kenyan landscape. Again, contraband charity corresponds with neoliberal strategies of controlling markets of the global south.

Effect on local culture. Humanitarians are dependent on their local confidants and usually do not suspect them of being complicit in illegal schemes or of simply betraying their trust. It is certainly true that a much higher percentage of their funds arrive in Kenya than is the case, for example, with systematic development aid, in which a substantial portion of the resources remain in the donor country and large sums disappear into the pockets of government officials. But there are questions around the allocation of funds, such as donations made to unregistered schools or those given directly to corrupt principals. How exactly is the money being spent? What is the mechanism for establishing that a child is indeed an orphan? Mr. Müller, for example, blindly trusted local confidants who, as I was able to establish, clearly betrayed him but in measured ways so as to not raise suspicion. Given that it is often based on whim and lacks a system of checks and balances, contraband charity ultimately encourages a culture of betrayal and graft. Neither Mr. Müller nor Ms. Bäumler have sufficient knowledge of local language, culture, and customs. Even after two decades of travel to and living in the area, they do not speak any of the local languages, and their English skills are also not on a level that would allow them to communicate in adequate ways. Mr. Müller often comes across as rude and bossy, although he is unaware of it. In this regard both individuals perpetuate the colonial paradigm of settlers who interact with the indigenous population in reductive and reduced language that is devoid of the nuances intelligent conversation requires and allows (Nyada 2014).

The most consequential dimension regarding the impact of neoliberal charity on local culture is the fact it has contributed significantly to the destruction of local systems of solidarity and self-help. In the past the Digo of the Diani area and beyond made use of, among others, two institutions their societies had created through which individuals benefited from communal action and the community benefited from the collective actions of individuals. One of them, *utsi*, involved the entire village or a large part of it; the other, *mweria*, was designed to address the needs of smaller groups of people.[107] The time for an *utsi* was determined by the village elders, and people collaborated on a variety of activities carried out under the umbrella of *utsi*. Some *utsi* involved the entire village, some would draw on all able-bodied men, and others involved able-bodied women.[108] *Utsi* were announced for the purpose of harvesting coconuts (*kubwaga nasi pamoja*), hunting (*kuwinda*), fishing (*kuvua*), cleaning the beach or areas of the village (*kusafisha*, *kuosha*), planting (*kulima*), harvesting on communal land (*kuvuna*), and weddings and funerals (*harusi, mazishi*). *Utsi* involving women specifically were aimed, for example, at guarding against wild animals (*wanyama porrini*). There was also collective action again thieves (*wezi*). *Mweria*, the word for the system of communal self-help involving smaller groups of individuals, means: "Today for me, tomorrow for you, it goes around." Ten people might get together to fix their roofs, one after another, or they might harvest or plant together on their individuals plots, renovate their houses, or dig holes for pit toilets.

Today both institutions, *utsi* and *mweria* (and other communal practices), are more or less extinct. Some forms of *utsi* are simply no longer possible today: hunting, for example, has basically died out as much of the forest has been

---

107 I was unable to find scholarly literature about these two institutions. My discussion is based on extended conversations with villagers in the Diani area during 2009 and 2014 and on observations made since I first visited Diani in the early 1980s.
108 The term *able-bodied* was used by villagers I interviewed.

reduced and what is left of it is protected as a *kaya*, a sacred forest (such as Kaya Diani, Kaya Ukunda, and Kaya Kinondo). *Utsi* for the purpose of raising funds for a wedding or funeral still exist, but examples of collective action carried out in the form of these two practices are rare. One villager from Mvumoni said that he remembered an *utsi* that led to the building of a primary school around 1970: in Mwaroni a number of villagers with adjacent land all agreed to give up a slice of their property, and in the middle of that land they built the school. The last *utsi* that the assistant chief of Bongwe (a sublocation of Diani) recalled occurred in 1997, a year that had brought a terrible drought. At that time the council of elders decided to call for a rainmaking *utsi* (*kuomba mvua*). The last *mweria* he remembered occurred more recently: in 2012 a group of people decided that they wanted to built traditional toilets in the village of Vukani, and they dug holes for all members of the *mweria* group. Remnants of both institutions are thus occasionally still visible, but overall these forms of communal solidarity have disappeared over the course of the past fifty years. It seems that the disappearance was gradual, but the most significant changes occurred in the 1970s, when the emerging tourism industry began to have an impact on the local community. At that time villagers began to work for salaries in the hotels, and tourists began their charitable missions.

Utsi and *mweria* are centrally defined through the idea of reciprocity – that is, all members of the community have to invest in the collective action in order to receive something for themselves. This aspect, as historian Steven Feierman explains, was also inherent in precolonial forms of sub-Saharan forms of philanthropy more broadly (Feierman 1998, p. 4). After reviewing various forms of philanthropy in precolonial Africa, Feierman stresses that "after colonial conquest, every one of the philanthropic institutions [he discusses] ... was transformed" (Feierman 1998, p. 21). The vanishing of *utsi* and *mweria* is another case in point.

The disappearance of communal forms of support created a vacuum because both the Kenyan state and the capitalist economy – which in the narrative of modernization should have taken over those areas of social and economic activity that had been traditionally self-organized by local communities – showed only rudimentary interest in the Diani community. While the tourism infrastructure initially brought welcome change through salaried job opportunities, neither the state nor the capitalist institutions of the area were prepared to deal with the repercussions produced by the development of the Diani area (population growth, unemployment, and illegal activities and with them increased poverty and need). Over the course of fifty years Diani went from a self-sustaining community to one in need of outside help. Or was the outside help that arrived in the area beginning in the 1980s another factor engendering the loss of self-supporting institutions? Neoliberal charity, with its lack of reciprocity and paternalistic structures, was certainly a significant chapter in fostering a culture of charity, in which communities abandoned their age-old forms of communal help in favor of handouts from charity workers, including contraband humanitarians.

Neoliberal Charity

Charity is an intrinsic feature of nondemocratic societies and is integral to capitalism in its neoliberal version. Overwhelmingly, charity ameliorates conditions of inequality and compensates for some failures of the state. In our contemporary period the growing relevance of charity in all areas of economic, political, and social activity points to the fact that charity is seen as the best avenue to address various forms of inequality and injustice. But its effect is to the contrary: it erodes democratic institutions of solidarity, be they traditional in origin (such as *utsi* and *mweria*) or modern in design (the welfare state). In this sense contraband charity does not mitigate the negative effects of neoliberal development; rather, by sabotaging state institutions and local economies, it is integral to the neoliberal economy itself. Contraband humanitarians do not connect the dots and thus are not aware of the detrimental role they play. The prevalence of contraband charity efforts demonstrates how widespread the belief in neoliberal charity is, even though it actually results in the further erosion of states and enhances the informal economy. Contraband charity does not address systemic dimensions of injustice and inequality; indeed, it ultimately makes those structures more formidable and unyielding. Contraband charity perpetuates and reinforces inequality and sustains political and economic neoliberal policies. The notion of "philanthropic colonialism," as Peter Buffet put it in his 2013 *New York Times* op-ed piece on "The Charitable-Industrial Complex," comes to mind (Buffett 2013). Ultimately, today's humanitarianism, while drawing on the language of human rights, contributes to the erosion of rights. In her study of welfare and citizenship in Italy, Andrea Muehlebach traces the disappearance of the twentieth century welfare state ethos of social contract and the rise, instead, of a new ethos of charity. This charity, she argues, creates "wounds woven into the very fabric of a society that has placed the unrequited gift at its moral center at a moment of intense neoliberalization." Muehlebach's study confirms central insights of my analysis of humanitarian activity in Kenya; I agree with her that "morals do pulsate at the heart of the market; that the gospel of laissez-faire is always already accompanied by hypermoralization ... markets and morals [are] indissolubly linked and ... the contemporary neoliberal order works to produce more than rational, utilitarian, instrumentalist subject" (Muehlebach 2012, p. viii, p. 6, p. 8).

These larger systemic dimensions tie contraband charity in Africa more broadly to the most recent phase of economic activity on the continent. German philanthropic activities in Kenya increased around the same time that neoliberal economic and political practices were introduced, and the evidence strongly suggests that these practices have impoverished many Kenyans over the past thirty years (Index mundi 2011; *UNICEF* 2013).

Whether the present push for globalization, which is occurring in Kenya and across the continent as part of a Second Scramble for Africa, leads to the improvement of the livelihoods of poor Kenyans remains doubtful. While the debate surrounding "aid" in all its various forms is controversial, my study highlights evidence that challenges assumptions about the positive impact of aid. Thus far, so-called aid has been unable to counteract the widening gap between rich and poor in most African countries, including Kenya and visible in the Diani area. The ideological and material functions of philanthropy, especially in its contraband form, are significant in the context of these larger economic and political developments.

Bibliography

Amutabi, Maurice Nyamanga (2006): *The NGO Factor in Africa: The Case of Arrested Development in Kenya*. New York: Routledge.

Ayittey, George B. N. (1998): *Africa in Chaos*. New York: St. Martin's Press.

Barnett, Michael (2011): *Empire of Humanity: A History of Humanitarianism*. Ithaca: Cornell University Press.

Bate, Roger, Kimberly Hess, Lorraine Mooney (2010): "Antimalarial Medicine Diversion: Stock-outs and Other Public Health Problems". In: *Research and Reports in Tropical Medicine* 1, pp. 19–24.

Berman, Nina (2004): *Impossible Missions? German Economic, Military, and Humanitarian Efforts in Africa*. Lincoln: University of Nebraska Press.

Berman, Nina (2013): "Contraband Charity: German Humanitarianism in Contemporary Kenya". In Bronwen Everill and Josiah Kaplan (Eds.): *The History and Practice of Humanitarian Intervention and Aid in Africa*. London: Palgrave, pp. 67–92.

betterplace lab, "Spenden in Deutschland: Zahlen und Fakten zu den privaten Spenden in Deutschland, Stand: Juni 2011," http://www.betterplace-lab.org/projects/german-donor-market, visited on November 14, 2014).

Brunstetter, Daniel R. (2010): "Sepúlveda, Las Casas, and the Other: Exploring the Tension between Moral Universalism and Alterity". In *The Review of Politics* 72, pp 409–35.

Brysk, Alison and Gershon Shafir (Eds.) (2004): *People Out of Place: Globalization, Human Rights, and the Citizenship Gap*. New York: Routledge.

Buffett, Peter (July 26, 2013): "The Charitable Industrial Complex". In: *The New York Times*.

Castro, Daniel (2007): *Another Face of Empire: Bartolomé de Las Casas, Indigenous Rights, and Ecclesiastical Imperialism*. Durham: Duke University Press.

Deutsches Zentralinstitut für soziale Fragen (2014): "Spendenbilanz 2013: Katastrophenspenden bringen Wachstum". http://www.dzi.de/dzi-institut/das-dzi/presse/presse-detailansicht/?10933, visited on November 14, 2014.

Deutsches Zentralinstitut für soziale Fragen (2011): "Deutschland: Schon 91 Mio. Euro Spenden für die Hungernden in Ostafrika". http://www.dzi.de/dzi-institut/das-dzi/presse/presse-detailansicht/?9040, visited on November 14, 2014.

Easterly, William (2006): *The White Man's Burden: Why the West's Efforts to Aid the Rest Have Done So Much Ill and So Little Good*. New York: Penguin.

Erler, Brigitte (1985): *Tödliche Hilfe: Bericht von meiner letzten Dienstreise in Sachen* Entwicklungshilfe. Freiburg: Dreisam.

Fassin, Didier (2012): *Humanitarian Reason: A Moral History of the Present*, trans. Rachel Gomme. Berkeley: University of California Press.

Feierman, Steven (1998): "Reciprocity and Assistance in Precolonial Africa." In: Warren F. Ilchman, Stanley N. Katz, and Edward L. Queen II (Eds.)*: Philanthropy in the World's Traditions*. Bloomington: Indiana University Press, pp. 3–24.

Fundraising Verband Austria (2014): "Spendenbericht 2013". http://www.fundraising.at/FACTSFIGURES/SPENDENAUFKOMMEN/Spendenberichte/tabid/421/language/de-DE/Default.aspx#2013, visited on November 14, 2014.

Google Books, Ngram Viewer, 1, https://books.google.com/ngrams/graph?content=humanitarianism&year_start=1500&year_end=2014&corpus=15&smoothing=3&share=&direct_url=t1%3B%2Chumanitarianism%3B%2Cc0, visited on November 14, 2014.

Google Books, Ngram Viewer, 2, https://books.google.com/ngrams/graph?content=humanitarian&year_start=1500&year_end=2008&corpus=15&smoothing=3&share=&direct_url=t1%3B%2Chumanitarian%3B%2Cc0, visited on November 14, 2014.

Google Books, Ngram Viewer, 3, https://books.google.com/ngrams/graph?content=humanitär&year_start=1500&year_end=2008&corpus=20&smoothing=3&share=&direct_url=t1%3B%2Chumanitär%3B%2Cc0, visited on November 14, 2014.

Hearn, Julie (1998): "The 'NGO-isation' of Kenyan Society: USAID and the Restructuring of Health Care." In: *Review of African Political Economy* 25.75, pp. 89–100.

Heinl, Annett and Gabriele Lingelbach (2009): "Spendenfinanzierte private Entwicklungshilfe in der Bundesrepublik Deutschland" In: Thomas Adam, Simone Lässig, and Gabriele Lingelbach (Eds.): *Stifter, Spender und Mäzene: USA und Deutschland im historischen Vergleich*. Stuttgart: Franz Steiner, pp. 287–312.

Hilpold, Peter (Ed.) (2013): *Die Schutzverantwortung (R2P): Ein Paradigmenwechsel in der Entwicklung des Internationalen Rechts?* Leiden: Nijhoff.

Hunt, Lynn (2007): *Inventing Human Rights: A History*. New York: Norton.

Igoe, Jim and Tim Kelsall (Eds.) (2005): *Between a Rock and a Hard Place: African NGOs, Donors and the State*. Durham: Carolina Academic Press.

Index mundi (2011): "Kenya: Population below Poverty Line," http://www.indexmundi.com/g/g.aspx?c=ke&v=69; visited November 14, 2014.

Kabou, Axelle (1991): *Et si l'Afrique refusait le développement?* Paris: L'Harmattan.

Kenya Census 2009 (2010): http://www.knbs.or.ke/index.php?option=com_content&view=article&id=149&Itemid=635, visited November 14, 2014.

Lancaster, Carol (1999): *Aid to Africa: So Much to Do, So Little Done*. Chicago: University of Chicago Press.

Ministry of East African Affairs, Commerce and Tourism, Kenya (2014): "Tourism Performance Overview 2010," http://www.tourism.go.ke/ministry.nsf/pages/facts_figures, visited November 14, 2014.

Moyn, Samuel (2010): *The Last Utopia: Human Rights in History*. Cambridge: Belknap.

Moyo, Dambisa (2009): *Dead Aid: Why Aid Is Not Working and How There Is a Better Way for Africa*. New York: Farrar, Straus and Giroux.

Muehlebach, Andrea (2012): *The Moral Neoliberal: Welfare and Citizenship in Italy*. Chicago: The University of Chicago Press.

Müller, Adrian (2011): "Schweizer spenden Millionen, *20 minuten*. http://www.20min.ch/news/dossier/hornvonafrika/story/Schweizer-spenden--Millionen-14721839, visited on November 14, 2014.

Mutua, Makau (Ed.) (2009): *Human Rights NGOs in East Africa: Political and Normative Tensions*. Kampala, Uganda: Fountain Publishers.

news.ch (2011): "Schweizer spenden fleissig für Ostafrika," http://www.news.ch/Schweizer+spenden+fleissig+fuer+Ostafrika/503884/detail.htm, visited on November 14, 2014.

Nyada, Germain (2014)."'The Germans Cannot Master Our Language!' German Colonial Rulers and the Beto in the Cameroonian Hinterlands". Trans. Amber Suggitt. In: Nina Berman, Klaus Mühlhahn, and Patrice Nganang (Eds.): *German Colonialism Revisited: African, Asian, and Oceanic Experiences*. Ann Arbor: University of Michigan Press, pp. 50–70.

Pagden, Anthony (2003): "Human Rights, Natural Rights, and Europe's Imperial Legacy". In: *Political Theory* 31.2, pp 171–99.

Penny, H. Glenn (2013): *Kindred by Choice: Germans and American Indians since 1800*. Chapel Hill: The University of North Carolina Press.

Polman, Linda (2010): *The Crisis Caravan: What's Wrong with Humanitarian Aid*, trans. Liz Waters. New York: Picador.

Rothberg, Michael (2009): *Multidirectional Memory: Remembering the Holocaust in the Age of Decolonization* Stanford: Stanford University Press.

Sachs, Jeffrey (2014): "The Case for Aid". In: *ForeignPolicy.com*, http://www.foreignpolicy.com/articles/2014/01/21/the_case_for_aid, visited on November 14, 2014.

Siringi, Samuel (2004): "AIDS Drugs Being Sold Illegally on Market Stalls in Kenya". In: *The Lancet* 363, p. 377.

swissfundraising, der berufsverband der FundraiserInnen (2013): "Spendenvolumen in der Schweiz wieder gestiegen: Über 1,6 Mrd," http://www.swissfundraising.org/index_de.php?TPL=26010&x26000_ID=596, visited on November 14, 2014.

Ulrich, Angela (2009): "Wohin fließen die Spenden? Eine Analyse zur Verwendung von Spenden in Deutschland". http://www.betterplace-lab.org/media/spendenmarktstudie.pdf, visited on November 14, 2014.

UNICEF (2013): "Kenya at a Glance," http://www.unicef.org/kenya/overview_4616.html, visited November 14, 2014.

Wildenthal, Lora (2013): *The Language of Human Rights in West Germany*. Philadelphia: University of Pennsylvania Press.

Wrong, Michaela (2009): *It's Our Turn to Eat: The Story of a Kenyan Whistle-Blower* (New York: HarperCollins.

Section Two: **Human Rights In Imagination**

Sebastian Wogenstein

Poetic Anarchy and Human Rights: Dissensus in Georg Büchner's *Danton's Death* and Peter Weiss's *Marat/Sade*

In his seminal work *Making Sense of Human Rights*, James W. Nickel argues that, "human rights, as we know them today, are the rights of the lawyers, not the rights of the philosophers" (Nickel 2007, p. 7). Nickel, a professor of law and philosophy, points to the specificity of the rights found in the declarations, conventions, and other treaties that make up today's international human rights framework, as opposed to the broad and abstract concepts that dominated the philosophical discourse on human rights in the 18th and 19th centuries. Moreover, our present-day human rights as legal concepts do not depend on the acceptance of a particular philosophical foundation and are realized through institutions.

This chapter considers the place of literature, and more specifically the theater, in relation to today's human rights discourse, which is dominated by institutional orientations. One path toward addressing this question would be to discuss literary works that involve specific human rights issues and raise awareness of rights violations. My approach takes a different direction and focuses on what I will describe as the "an-archic" leaning of many literary texts. I will argue that such texts raise questions about the institutional framework itself and the ideas on which institutions are built. Instead of presenting *institutional praxis* as a solution to the problem of the ideas' abstraction, such literary texts instead reveal the realities of power that are all too often eclipsed by the institutional focus of much human rights discourse.

The two literary examples provided here, Georg Büchner's *Danton's Death* and Peter Weiss's *Marat/Sade*, dissect the institutional implementation of human rights ideas in the context and legacy of the French Revolution. Although today's human rights are different from the *Droits de l'homme* of 1789 both in scope and applicability, they share an underlying assumption about the equality of humans and the possibility of reform, however these ideas of equality and progress might be framed. It is precisely the plays' commentary on institution-based realization of equality and progress that speaks to human rights discourse today. At the same time, a look at the authors' commitments to social justice reveals that the critical perspective of a text does not necessarily imply resigned acquiescence in the face of perceived social injustice. Rather, these literary texts – in the imagination that produced them and the imagination they might spark in the observer or reader – are both more radical and more realistic than the political leanings of their authors. *Danton's Death* and *Marat/Sade* challenge us to critically review our preconceived narratives or ideas and, by opening up a "dispute about what is given," speak to us in a voice that Jacques Rancière calls "dissensus" (Rancière 2004, p. 304).

The Anarchic Origins of Equality

When Hannah Arendt decried the plight of the stateless refugees during the Second World War as a fundamental rightlessness in a well-known passage of *The Origins of Totalitarianism* (1951), it was precisely the *absence* of effective institutions beyond the state that revealed the idea of human rights to be a grand illusion. Without the protection of a supra-national institution, she argued, the elementary rights that should have applied to everyone proved worthless: "The Rights of Man, after all, had been defined as 'inalienable' because they were supposed to be independent of all governments; but it turned out that the moment human beings lacked their own government and had to fall back upon their minimum rights, no authority was left to protect them and no institution was willing to guarantee them" (Arendt 1966, p. 293 f.). As Étienne Balibar has pointed out, Arendt's argumentation reflects an "extreme form of *institutionalism*" (Balibar 2007, p. 729). Stateless people were not only deprived of the one (and, in Arendt's thinking, only) human right, the "right to have rights" (Arendt 1966, p. 296), but she also makes clear that this condition separated the stateless from the very world that Arendt understands as comprising political life. Cast out of the institution of political life, they were also cast out of the communal world in which one's voice is heard and counts. Not only were they deprived of particular rights, but their situation was in fact much more severe: they became "worldless." For the stateless person, no longer belonging to the political sphere amounted to a loss of one's place in the world: "the loss of a polity itself expels him from humanity" (Arendt 1966, p. 297). As Balibar makes clear, Arendt's "idea of rights is indistinguishable from the construction of the human, which is the immanent result of the historical invention of (political) institutions" (Balibar 2007, p. 733 f.).

Political life is fundamental in Arendt's thinking because only through the institution of the communal world, the polity, can we become equals. This institution creates fellow humans, and in so doing, the "natural" inequality of the human *physis*, or "mere givenness" (Arendt 1966, p. 301), is overcome. Whoever is expelled from this communal world is thrown back into pre-political insignificance, bare life, a condition in which being human means nothing other than being "some specimen of an animal species called man" (Arendt 1966, p. 302).

Balibar calls this a "tragic contingency" in Arendt's philosophy – that for her being truly human (as opposed to a mere designation of species) hinges on one's recognition as a member of the polity (Balibar 2007, p. 734). The same institutions that let human subjects emerge through mutual recognition destroy them when this recognition is withdrawn.

At the heart of Arendt's ideal institutionalism, however, is also a fundamental an-archic principle in the sense of an ideal *nicht-herrschaftliche*, or "no-rule," organization of political life. In her treatise *On Revolution*, Arendt explains that in the prime example of the polity, the Greek *polis*, equality and freedom were guaranteed through *isonomy:* a form of political organization, "in which the citizens lived together under conditions of no-rule, without a division between rulers and ruled" (Arendt 2006, p. 20). It is clear to Arendt that this isonomy depends on a mutual agreement among peers that is observed and enacted and, as such, was not to be confused with democracy, the rule of the many. In isonomy, the "outstanding characteristic among the forms of government, as the ancients had enumerated them, was that the notion of rule (the 'archy' from *archein* in monarchy and oligarchy, or the 'cracy' from *kratein* in democracy) was entirely absent from it" (Arendt 2006, p. 20). To Arendt such isonomy is only possible within the "artificial institution" of the *polis*.

As Balibar observes, however, this assumption of a "no-rule" condition within the *polis* is contrary to Aristotle's and other Greek philosophers' insistence on an *arché*, on the principle of rulership. In Aristotle's opinion, the ideal citizen is "the one who successively knows how to give orders and take orders from others (*archein te kai archesthai dunasthai*)" (Balibar 2007, p. 735). Arendt, by contrast, takes the notion of isonomy from a story told by Herodotus about the Persian prince Otanes who neither wanted to rule nor be ruled. Arendt's decision to follow this understanding of an "an-archic" equality instead of Aristotle's give-and-take orders is indeed remarkable and leads Balibar to suggest that in a very concrete sense, Arendt's institutionalism is built on the notion of a concerted "civil disobedience."[109] Such disobedience "suppresses the 'vertical' form of authority and creates a 'horizontal' form of association in order to recreate the conditions of a 'free consent' to the law" (Balibar 2007, p. 736). Although Arendt's concept of the person – or even the human itself, as noted above – is often criticized as being predicated on the condition of having a voice in the political realm, the notion of a concerted collective disobedience, and thereby the creation of a new "place in the world," seems to suggest at least the possibility of newly emergent spheres of the political within the framework of her thinking.

---

[109] Balibar bases his argument on reading Arendt's essay "On Civil Disobedience."

In responding to Arendt's institutionalism and what he calls her "archipolitical position," Jacques Rancière rejects the notion that speaking as a human subject depends on an institutional framework, that reciprocal recognition is a precondition for politics (Rancière 2004, p. 299). For Rancière, politics refers to a process of emancipation in which those who are marginalized within, or excluded from, the polity contest their marginalization or exclusion. This contestation does not necessarily involve formally claiming certain rights, such as one's human rights. Instead, it may appear when those who are marginalized or excluded speak or act when they are expected to remain silent or unseen. Rather than accepting their exclusion or marginalization, those who are considered unqualified to participate in the polity (the "uncounted") *act* as if they were qualified to do so (Rancière 2004, p. 305). In contrast to what Rancière calls "police," i.e. a "way of counting" that makes it commonsensical to distinguish between those who are considered qualified and those who are not, "politics" involves the questioning of this division. Politics for Rancière does not refer to political life in which the citizen engages, in juxtaposition with the private sphere or the "worldless" bare life in which being human amounts to little more than a species designation. Instead, politics is the process in which dissensus is enacted. This dissensus, he makes clear, "is not a conflict of interest, opinions, or values; it is a division put in 'common sense': a dispute about what is given, about the frame within which we see something as given" (Rancière 2004, p. 304).

Rather than defining the political subject as the one who is qualified to participate in political life, Rancière insists that the subject emerges in the process of "political subjectivization" (Rancière 2004, p. 304). "Political subjects are not definite collectivities," Rancière claims, contrary to Arendt's institutionalism, "they are surplus names, names that set out a question or a dispute (*litige*) about who is included in their count" (Rancière 2004, p. 303). Political subjects, in Rancière's understanding, emerge only through dissensus. Dissensus, correspondingly, also involves questioning the common use and applicability of the claims that are the most fundamental to human rights, freedom and equality: "*freedom* and *equality* are not predicates belonging to definite subjects. Political predicates are open predicates: they open up a dispute about what they exactly entail and whom they concern in which cases" (Rancière 2004, p. 303). In terms of human rights in specific, Rancière suggests paradoxically that, "the Rights of Man are the rights of those who have not the rights that they have and have the rights that they have not" (Rancière 2004, p. 302). This claim entails a number of assumptions. First, rather than rejecting the notion of human rights as mere deception, Rancière sees value in what he calls the "inscription" of these rights, i.e. their dissemination as a written set of rights that portray the community as "free and equal." The resulting portrayal of an imagined community of free and equal members clashes with the experience of those who are marginalized or excluded. Second, this form of "inscription" is not only a contradiction; it also envisions a community in which these rights are actualized.

For Rancière, political subjects "verify" the extension of those rights by putting this imagined freedom and equality to the test. By "stag[ing] a scene of dissensus," they erase the distinction between two worlds that allows for the exclusion of groups of people: "They not only confront the inscriptions of rights to situations of denial; they put together the world where those rights are valid and the world where they are not" (304). At the heart of this merger of worlds is a process of thinking, or imagining, the extension of rights to those who are excluded.

French revolutionary and playwright Olympe de Gouges serves Rancière as an example. Rejecting the exclusion of women from political rights, de Gouges proclaimed in her *Declaration of the Rights of Woman and the Female Citizen* (1791) that, "if woman has the right to mount the scaffold; she must equally have the right to mount the rostrum" (Gouges 1979, p. 91). The dissensus she staged did not only involve protest against women's exclusion from the community of men, who are envisioned by the *Declaration of the Rights of Man and Citizen* (1789) as "born free and equal in rights" ("Declaration" 1990, p. 118). She also rejected the division between the political sphere and the private or domestic sphere to which women were relegated. If women could be sent to the scaffold, she argued, this act in itself implied a public, or political, form of equality that contradicted their exclusion from other functions. For Rancière this is a clear example of politics, in the sense of making "the uncounted" visible and disputing their exclusion: "If they could lose their 'bare life' out of a public judgment based on political reasons, this meant that even their bare life – their life doomed to death – was political" (Rancière 2004, p. 303). But de Gouges's protest was also an *act* of defiance, an *enactment* of the rights she was denied, even though, as Rancière points out, her "deduction could not be endorsed – it could not even be *heard* – by the lawmakers" (Rancière 2004, p. 304). She emerged as a political subject not by belonging to a collectivity, but precisely by disputing who could be included in their count and acting accordingly.

Ironically, another powerful example of Rancière's notion of dissensus is Hannah Arendt herself. Given the centrality of Rancière's rejection of Arendt's division between political and private life to his argument – between the citizens who count and the "worldless" stateless refugees whose "bare life" doesn't – this choice may surprise. When Arendt first expressed her thoughts on the situation of stateless refugees in a 1943 essay titled "We Refugees," she wrote precisely from her personal experience as a stateless refugee: "If we should start telling the truth that we are nothing but Jews it would mean we expose ourselves to the fate of human beings who, unprotected by any specific law or political convention, are nothing but human beings" (Arendt 1978, 65). As Andrew Schaap points out, Rancière misconstrues Arendt's tone in her remarks on the calamity of the stateless people as contemptuous. If Arendt mentions in *Origins of Totalitarianism* that they were thought to be so unimportant that their lives weren't even considered worth oppressing, she was not expressing contempt for the refugees,[110] but rather speaking in a tone of "bitter irony" (Schaap 2011, p. 33).

Arendt's actions in writing about the exclusion of stateless refugees, and her activism in movements to assist them, involved the enactment of precisely the rights that she lacked. She did not resign herself to the invisibility of private life, to which she may have appeared destined in the eyes of many of her contemporaries in the 1940s, both as a stateless person and as a female academic. Instead, she made her voice heard. Although Rancière criticizes her for what he considers her "archipolitical position," Arendt is a prime example of a political subject whose act of dissensus, enacted in her writing and her activism, confronts precisely the exclusionary institutionalism about which she wrote.

Georg Büchner's *Danton's Death* and Peter Weiss's *Marat/Sade* enact dissensus in a number of different registers. Both reveal dimensions of open or concealed violence in institutions and assumptions that are fundamental constituents of today's human rights discourse. Written in 1835 and 1963/64 respectively, the plays confront us with ideas of equality and justice as well as convictions and doubts regarding the characters' plans to reform society. Often, such discussions take place in settings that are traditionally excluded from public speech: the private sphere, the prison, the asylum. They engage the political in precisely the sense that Rancière calls dissensus: as a questioning of fundamental, commonsensical assumptions and the "back-and-forth movement between the first inscription of the right and the dissensual stage on which it is put to test" (Rancière 2004, p. 305). Indeed, by putting what is assumed as "given" to the test on the stage and initiating dispute over it – including "inscriptions" of freedom, equality, and progress – these plays speak anarchically today as they did when they were first performed.

---

110 Rancière speaks of the "plainly contemptuous tone" in Arendt's statement that "nobody wants to oppress" the stateless refugees: "It is as if these people were guilty of not even being able to be oppressed, not even worthy of being oppressed" (Rancière 2004, p. 299).

Georg Büchner: *Danton's Death*

In March 1834, a little more than half a year after completing two years of study at the University of Strasbourg, Georg Büchner, a twenty-year-old medical student and emerging writer, founded a secret "Gesellschaft der Menschenrechte" (Society of Human Rights) in the university town of Gießen, and just a month later a second chapter of the society in nearby Darmstadt. Modeled on the French "Société des Droits de l'homme," this was Büchner's response to the abject social conditions he witnessed in his home state of Hesse, in particular the dire situation of the peasants. Described by his friends as an "idolâtre de la révolution française," Büchner and his comrades printed an eight-page revolutionary pamphlet, *Der Hessische Landbote (Hessian Courier)*, that declares in its programmatic heading: "Peace to cottages! War to palaces!" Contrasting the lives of the rich with the lives of the peasants, Büchner describes the latter as severe exploitation:

> The life of the rich is one long Sunday. They live in fine houses, they wear elegant clothes. They have well-fed faces and speak a language of their own. But the people lie before them like dung on the fields. The peasant walks behind the plough; but the rich man walks behind peasant and plough, driving both him and his oxen, taking the grain and leaving the stubble. The peasant's life is one long working day. Strangers devour the fruit of his fields before his very eyes. His whole body is a sore; his sweat is the salt on the rich man's table. (Büchner 2008, p. ix)

Büchner's revolutionary activities did not remain unnoticed by the authorities. An arrest warrant was issued in 1835, and as late as 1842, five years after Büchner's untimely death, a probe into illegal political movements conducted by the Federal Assembly in Frankfurt mentions Büchner's founding of the "Society of Human Rights" in 1834 as an example of high treason and lists his co-conspirators. Whereas several of his comrades were arrested and imprisoned, Büchner himself was able to flee. The 1842 document charges that Büchner, as the head of the conspiracy, saw the "material hardship of the people as a revolutionary lever" and attempted to "influence the people's lower classes" to participate in a mass uprising that would lead to the establishment of a republic, the "only constitution that would adequately respect human dignity" ("Protokolle" 2013, p. 330). The *Hessian Messenger* is cited as the pamphlet with which Büchner, "taking as a medium of persuasion the religion of the people, tried to declare the sacred human rights through simple imagery and phrases from the New Testament" ("Protokolle" 2013, p. 330). From the confessions of the arrested co-conspirators, the report purports that the initiation of new members simply consisted of a reading of the French Declaration of the Rights of Man and Citizen, voicing one's agreement that preventing anyone from actualizing these rights amounted to oppression, and a vow to use all of one's abilities to remove such oppression." The report also mentions that the central aim of the Society was the "absolute equality of all" ("Protokolle" 2013, p. 331). The report reflects some of the positions Büchner argues in his extant correspondence. In a letter to his parents from Strasbourg, dated April 5, 1833, he explains the reasons why, at this point, he does not entirely reject violence as a means:

> My opinion is this: if something can help in our time, then it is *violence*. [...] Our youth is accused of using violence. But don't we live in a permanent state of violence? Because we are born and raised in a dungeon, we don't realize that we're stuck in a hole with chained hands and feet and a gag in our mouths. What do you call rule of law? A *law* that turns the great majority of citizens into exploited animals in order to satisfy the unnatural needs of an insignificant and spoiled minority? And this law, upheld by raw military violence and the dimwitted diligence of its agents, this law is an *eternal, raw violence* against the right and sound reason, and I will fight against it with *mouth* and *deed* wherever I can. (Büchner 1993, p. 190 f.)

In a similar vein, he writes to his friend August Stöber on December 9, 1833: "The political conditions could drive me mad. The poor people tamely haul the cart on which the princes and liberals act out their ludicrous comedy. I say a prayer every evening to ropes and street-lights" (Büchner 1993, p. 192). In contrast to his revolutionary attitude and activism, however, Büchner's influential revolutionary drama *Danton's Death* is far from unambiguous. Contrary to what one might expect from an "idolâtre de la révolution française," it provides a sharply critical perspective on the French Revolution and some of its protagonists. Büchner indeed stages dissensus in two directions. One is aimed at the social conditions that appear intolerable, which he and his comrades aim to overthrow with the goal of radical equality not unlike the isonomy Arendt describes. The other direction of dissensus, however, involves his dissection of the institutional praxis of the French Revolution not simply as a failed application of a "good idea," but as inherently paradoxical in its trust in rulership, a disposition that in Rancière's terms could be called archipolitical.

Danton's Death relates a brief but important episode from the revolution's Terror phase: the arrest, public trial, and execution of French revolutionary Georges Danton under the rule of the Committee of Public Safety, a committee Danton had initially chaired. Although Büchner relied heavily on historical sources, Danton is portrayed in the final days of his life – contrary to these sources – as a doubtful and decadent moderate while Robespierre, his antagonist, appears as the cold and ascetic demagogue whose obsession is his own virtue, a lustful excess that plays out openly in his elaborate self-stylizations and speeches. Among the play's many fascinating scenes, two stand out, both night scenes at a window. In the first, Robespierre is shown by himself after a heated conversation with Danton, who demands a halt to the killings and accuses Robespierre of hypocrisy. Talking to himself, Robespierre fiercely tries to justify his position at first but then admits, "Why can't I be rid of that thought? He keeps pointing a bloody finger at the same place; no matter how much wadding I put round it the blood still seeps through. Some part of me, I don't know which, contradicts the rest" (I,6, Büchner 2008, p. 23). In a later parallel night scene at a window, Danton is shown with his wife Julie, who rushes to his side when she hears him groan the word "September." When Julie suggests that he was dreaming, Danton replies:

> Dreaming? Yes, I was dreaming, but there was something else. [...] I was riding the earth like a wild horse; it was careering breathlessly along and I, with gigantic limbs, clung to its mane and flanks. My head was thrown back and my hair streamed out into the void; thus it dragged me along. Then I screamed out in terror and woke up. I ran to the window – and then I heard it, Julie. – What does the word want? And among all possible words, why that one? What concern is it of mine? Why does it hold out its bloody hands to me? I never hurt it. Help me, Julie, my brain is numb. Wasn't it in September, Julie? (II,5, Büchner 2008, p. 37)

The reference here is to the September Massacres of 1792, the large-scale murder of prisoners accused of being loyalists, at a time when Danton was Minister of Justice. Although Danton's exact role in the massacres is unclear, Büchner portrays him as accepting personal responsibility and suffering the pangs of conscience. Both scenes discuss personal responsibility for involvement in institutional violence, a responsibility that is first rejected and then, in these most private situations, admitted. In a sense, the private sphere in these instances becomes the most political, if by political we mean an unsettling of the commonsensical and the counting of those whose "bare lives" seemed expendable in the pursuit of an ostensibly justified violent struggle, whether for equality or the survival of the revolutionary republic.

It is interesting that both scenes show the two dominating revolutionary characters of the play, despite their differences, in parallel situations, both confronted with an uncontrollable "something" they can only describe with images of violence. More than half a century before Freud, this "something" in *Danton's Death* is markedly the German word "es." And what are we to make of the windows at night, when a window-pane with some light in the back can darkly mirror the self? Deconstructing the various meanings and functions of windows in architecture, film, and other arts, Thomas Keenan grapples with the notion of a window as a threshold between the public and the private. Both the window in relation to a subject's public or private persona and the window's capacity to function as a membrane speak to the questions at stake in Büchner's play:

> The window implies a theory of the human subject as a theory of politics, and the subject's variable status as public or private individual is defined by its position relative to this window. Behind it, in the privacy of home or office, the subject observes that public framed for it by the window's rectangle, looks out and understands prior to passing across the line it marks – the window is this possibility of permeability – into the public. Behind it, the individual is a knowing – that is, seeing, theorizing – subject. In front of it, on the street for instance, the subject assumes public rights and responsibilities, appears, acts, intervenes in the sphere it shares with other subjects. (Keenan 1993, p. 132)

At first glance, Büchner's scenes may appear removed from today's human rights questions. Unlike the main characters in most of what is considered human rights literature today, Büchner's characters are not victims of systemic violence, genocide, discrimination, or military occupation. And yet, whether political actors like Robespierre, who might under other circumstances speak of the rationales of lesser evil or collateral damage, or those who feel guilt for complicity in exploitation or silence in the face of human rights violations, Büchner's characters show in dramatic fashion not only the tensions and contradictions between a rights-inflected rhetoric and their politics, but also imagine – and, through this imaginative act, dissect – the subjective economies of power that usually remain invisible in abstract political discourse and concealed in historical research. *Danton's Death*, as a play, is in itself a window that subjects the observer or reader to questions about her or his own views on rights and violence or the struggle between radical freedom and equality.

Despite Büchner's admiration for the revolution, to which his own revolutionary activities in Hesse attest, he finds himself compelled to show the revolutionaries "as they were: bloody, messy, aggressive, and cynical," as he writes in a letter to his parents dated May 5, 1835 (Büchner 1993, p. 199). Yet he also makes clear that his drama is no lesson in ethics, but rather the virtual creation of a (past) world that has no particular purpose. Commenting on *Danton's Death* again in a letter to his parents from July 28, 1835, and defending his play against accusations of immoral language, he explains: "The writer is no preacher of morality, he invents and creates characters, he makes past ages live again, and people can then learn just as well from that as from the study of history and from their observation of what happens around them in real life" (Büchner 1993, p. 202). According to Büchner, then, the virtual reality comes to life precisely in the audience's (or readers') engagement with the artwork. In other words, Büchner throws the separation of art from history or "real life" radically into question. The creative and transformative power of art lies in its potential to stage a dissensus, but this dissensus is not a command or a moral judgment. Rather, dissensus occurs in the "undoing" of a consensus that would treat an artwork as an object separate from any engagement in the changing political sphere and instead locked in the immediate cultural-historical context of its production.

In a poignant formulation, Theodor Adorno addresses this question in his *Aesthetic Theory*: "It is from within, in the movement of the immanent form of artworks and the dynamic of their relation to the concept of art, that it ultimately becomes manifest how much art – in spite of, and because of, its monadological essence – is an element in the movement of spirit and social reality." The artwork is the point where the "movement of spirit" and the "movement of social reality" meet, and it is in this meeting that the relevance of literature for human rights lies. An artwork can do all sorts of things, many of which are contradictory: for example, it can evoke, reinforce, or disseminate hope and indignation – or it can do the opposite. Unlike the law and other social institutions, it is in principle an-archic in its autonomy, but this autonomy does not mean it is separate from the political. To the contrary, its dissensual activity consists in presenting the spectator or reader with the possibility of continuously crossing the divide between its virtual world and social reality (Adorno 1997, p. 194).

Peter Weiss: *Marat/Sade*

A play that provokes dissensus, in many ways akin to *Danton's Death*, is Peter Weiss's play *Marat/Sade*, or, in its full title, *The Persecution and Assassination of Jean-Paul Marat as Performed by the Inmates of the Asylum of Charenton under the Direction of the Marquis de Sade*.[111] Like Bertolt Brecht's "epic" or "dialectical theater," Weiss's play minimizes plot development on the stage in favor of engaging the audience in social critique: commentary is part of the performance, and irritating moments prevent the audience from identifying with the characters on stage or being drawn into the illusion of drama. The long title of this play, written in 1963/64, already provides a synopsis of its plot. With explicit reference to Jacques-Louis David's famous painting *La mort de Marat*, the play-within-the-play, the assassination of Jean-Paul Marat, is a kind of tableau vivant, showing Marat in his bathtub immediately before and during his murder. Action on the

---

111 The English translation by Geoffrey Skelton, adapted into verse by Adrian Mitchell, was commissioned by Peter Brook for his famous 1964 production by the Royal Shakespeare Company. Anne Beggs mentions Brook's interest in Antonin Artaud's "theater of cruelty" and notes that, "the English version was crafted with the aim of putting into dialogue the Artaudian aesthetics of non-verbal affect and a Brechtian dialectic of reason and human action inherent in Weiss's drama" (Beggs 2013, p. 61).

stage consists mostly of speeches, dialogues, and declamations, but also occasional physical violence among the patient-actors, the playwright and patient-director Marquis de Sade, and the director of the asylum, Coulmier. There are three distinct and yet permeable timeframes in this play: first, portrayed by de Sade's play, the historical murder of Marat in the context of the French Revolution in 1793, second, the primary timeframe of *Marat/Sade* with the performance of the play by the asylum's inmates under the direction of de Sade in the year 1808, and third, the performance of Weiss's play wherever and whenever it may be staged.

The audience watching the play in the present becomes part of the play; audience members are addressed by the asylum's director directly as though they were the audience of 1808, for example when Coulmier explains his rationale in permitting the production to take place: "We're modern enlightened and we don't agree / with locking up patients We prefer therapy / through education and especially art / so that our hospital may play its part / faithfully following according to our lights / the Declaration of Human Rights" (Weiss 1965, p. 8). Despite this "enlightened" stance, it soon becomes clear that Coulmier tries to silence any voice that doubts social progress or could offend the donors on whose financial support the clinic depends. In a scene titled "Death's Triumph," Marat justifies the bloody revolution while some actors enact a beheading, then play ball with the head. Coulmier intervenes: "Monsieur de Sade / we can't allow this / you really cannot call this education / It isn't making my patients any better ..." Anticipating Coulmier's intervention, de Sade has the Herald, one of the characters, reply: "We only show these people massacred / because this indisputably occurred / Please calmly watch these barbarous displays / which could *not* happen *nowadays*" (Weiss 1965, p. 27).

The bitter irony of the Herald's remark must be acutely palpable to anyone watching the play since it premiered in 1964. With the 20th-century and contemporary genocides and wars in mind, perhaps the most chilling point in the play is when a patient addresses the clinical director face to face:

> A mad animal / Man's a mad animal / I'm a thousand years old and in my time / I've helped commit a million murders / The earth is spread / The earth is spread thick / with squashed human guts / We few survivors / We few survivors / walk over a quaking bog of corpses / always under our feet / every step we take / rotted bones ashes matted hair / under our feet / broken teeth skulls split open / A mad animal / I'm a mad animal / Prisons don't help / Chains don't help / I escape / through all the walls / through all the shit and the splintered bones / You'll see it all one day / I'm not through yet / *I have plans*. (Weiss 1965, p. 37)

In one of the anachronistic conversations between Marat and de Sade, Marat accuses de Sade of lacking compassion, to which de Sade replies: "Compassion / Now Marat you are talking like an aristocrat / Compassion is the property of the privileged classes ... No Marat / no small emotions please / Your feelings were never petty." In response, Marat, the fierce revolutionary, justifies his actions with what we might call a humanitarian stance: "I don't watch unmoved I intervene / and say that this and this are wrong / and I work to alter them and improve them." But then his proclamation trails off: "The important thing / is to pull yourself up by your own hair / to turn yourself inside out / and see the whole world with fresh eyes" (Weiss 1965, p. 31). Like Büchner's revolutionaries, Marat eventually reaches a point of self-doubt shortly before his murder: "Why is everything so confused now / Everything I wrote or spoke / was considered and true / each argument was sound / And now / doubt / Why does everything sound false?"

When at the end the asylum director inquires about the meaning of the play, de Sade gives an answer that appears to sum up not only the play-within-the-play but also, self-reflexively, Weiss's drama: "Our play's chief aim has been – to take to bits / great propositions and their opposites, / see how they work, then let them fight it out / The point? Some light on our eternal doubt / I have twisted and turned them every way / and find no ending to our play ... So for me the last word cannot ever be spoken / I am left with a question that's always open" (Weiss 1965, p. 110)

Yet while de Sade's comment and a brief reply by the clinic director asking the audience to "close the history books" end the battle of words and ideas, the play itself does not end with words, and in this final way once again brings out the shadows of the Enlightenment as it turns from the utopian word to the physical and corporeal. The play ends with the asylum's patients singing and dancing themselves into trance to rhythmic shouts of "Charenton Charenton / Napoleon Napoleon / Nation Nation / Revolution Revolution / Copulation Copulation," prompting Coulmier, who just prior to this incident had declared in a messianic vision "that mankind soon will cease / to fear the storms of war," to incite his armed male nurses to "extreme violence" (Weiss 1965, p. 112). This incitement to violence comes from the same asylum director who welcomes the audience, in his introductory remarks, with a reference to the "Declaration of Human Rights" – notably a term that is closer to the 1948 Universal Declaration of Human Rights than the 1789 Declaration of the Rights of Man and Citizen.

In his study on the aesthetics of violence in the 20th century, Robert Buch reports that Peter Weiss initially considered letting the play end with an attack on the audience (Buch 2010, p. 92). Such a violent breaking down of the fourth wall would certainly have been fitting in the context of the Royal Shakespeare Company's "Theatre of Cruelty" season, in which the English-language version of the play premiered in 1964. It could have enacted in a visceral way a dissensual rejection of art as mere entertainment and illusion. It could also have driven home in a physical way not only the inherent violence of institutions as a reaction to deviation, but also the violence of the social order as an "order of rule" itself. Yet even without the attack on the audience, the dissensus enacted in the play belies the asylum director's introductory remarks that history, in this case the French Revolution, is re-enacted before the audience "for your delectation and for our patients' rehabilitation" (Weiss 1965, p. 8).

The confrontation between de Sade and Marat, which Weiss describes in his notes on the play as "a conflict, carried to the extreme, between individualism and the idea of a political and social revolution," resulted in a heated debate when the play was first performed in 1964 and 1965 ("Anmerkungen zum geschichtlichen Hintergrund" 1967, p. 8). It premiered in West Berlin in April 1964 and less than a year later, in February 1965, was put on the stage in the East German town of Rostock. Weiss saw both productions, in addition to the one Peter Brook directed in London in August 1964. After witnessing the performance in Rostock, in which Marat – claimed in the GDR as a precursor of socialism – clearly dominates in the confrontation with de Sade, Weiss publically took sides. In an interview he declared that he saw "the principle of Marat as the right and superior one. A production of my piece which does not in the end show Marat as the moral victor is misguided" ("Gespräch mit Peter Weiss, Frühjahr 1965" 1967, p. 101). Comparing the three interpretations of his play, he described the Berlin performance as primarily interested in the "beauty of form and appearance," while the one in London brought out the cruelty of the historical events. The performance in Rostock, however, Weiss called an "analytical performance, in which the political message of the piece is in the foreground" ("Gespräch mit Peter Weiss, Frühjahr 1965" 1967, p. 101).[112]

Eventually, Weiss relativized this one-sided interpretation again and explained that he could accept the "black-and-white picture" of the performance in Rostock as an "alternative to the numerous western performances in which Sade was depicted as superior and Marat as insane and errant" ("Peter Weiss über die Inszenierung" 1967, p. 113). Perhaps it should not surprise that the controversy Weiss sparked, and in which he engaged with seemingly contradictory statements, mirrors the confrontation between his characters de Sade and Marat: as a politically engaged writer in a "divided world," Weiss accuses the West of fraudulently claiming to represent "humanity and democracy," yet he also rejects

---

112 In a passionate reply to this partiality, literary critic Hans Mayer expresses his disappointment that Weiss appears willing to give up the play's openness, a key characteristic of the play: "If Peter Weiss, as interpreter of his own play, decides retroactively and without reservation in favor of Marat, then his play becomes meaningless" ("Peter Weiss über die Inszenierung" 1967, p. 112).

the East's imperiousness in demanding a clear political allegiance ("10 Arbeits-punkte" 1967, p. 117). In many ways akin to Büchner, Weiss declares on the one hand that "art must have the power to change the life, or else it has missed its mark," while simultaneously admitting to approaching the act of writing without a preconceived stance: "I write to find out where I stand, and that's why I must always bring in all my doubts" ("Gespräch mit Peter Weiss, 1965" 1967, p. 98 f.)

Conclusion

What then is the place of literature, broadly conceived, in relation to today's human rights debates? Beyond the hope that literary texts can generate empathy and have an educational function, as perhaps most famously argued by Richard Rorty and Lynn Hunt, literary texts also have the potential to provoke dissensus and disrupt archipolitical practices of exclusion, whether the exclusion of the "un-counted" or the exclusion of violence in orders of "rule." We live in an era in which human rights have been described as the "last utopia" (Moyn 2007, p. 10), the "central principle of order" (Opitz 2002, p. 11), or "the *doxa* of our time," in the sense that they "define the space of the conceivable and utterable" (Hoffmann 2011, p. 1). At the same time, and despite the growth of international treaties, institutions, and organizations whose aim is the protection of human rights, Arendt's denouncement of human rights as mere deception has not lost its power, considering for example the large parts of the globe's population whose lives remain largely invisible and whose deaths do not appear to count. In addition to drawing attention to their precarious condition, literary texts can question the premises that underlie the archipolitical institutionalism that decides who counts, and who rules.

Literary texts are neither philosophical treatises nor political programs that try to answer the big questions and provide solutions. Rancière speaks about dissensus as a dispute "about the frame within which we see something as given," suggesting that it involves questioning the common use and applicability of the claims that are fundamental to human rights, freedom and equality. In this sense, *Danton's Death* and *Marat/Sade* can be said to enact dissensus by creating specific characters in specific scenarios from which, as Büchner says, "people can then learn just as well [...] as from the study of history and from their observation of what happens around them in real life" (Büchner 1993, p. 202). Both *Danton's Death* and *Marat/Sade* show the messiness of the struggle over ideas and the violence that may – or, perhaps, must inevitably – accompany their institutional implementation. Literature certainly will not provide us with a path to social or political isonomy, but if we engage with plays like *Danton's Death* and *Marat/ Sade* as facilitators of thinking, they can help us recognize the complex economy of power, the violence, and the threats that lurk within the beliefs we so readily accept.

Bibliography

"10 Arbeitspunkte eines Autors in der geteilten Welt." (1967). In: Karlheinz Braun (Ed.):
     Materialien zu Peter Weiss' 'Marat/Sade'. Frankfurt am Main: Suhrkamp, pp. 114–119.
Adorno, Theodor (1997): *Aesthetic Theory*. London: Bloomsbury.
"Anmerkungen zum geschichtlichen Hintergrund unseres Stückes." (1967). In: Karlheinz
     Braun (Ed.): *Materialien zu Peter Weiss' 'Marat/Sade'*. Frankfurt am Main: Suhrkamp,
     pp. 7–11.
Arendt, Hannah (1966): *The Origins of Totalitarianism*. New York: Harcourt.
Arendt, Hannah (1978): "We Refugees." In: Hannah Arendt: *The Jew as Pariah: Jewish Identity
     and Politics in the Modern Age*. Ed. by Ron H. Feldman. New York: Grove Press, pp. 55–66.
Arendt, Hannah (2006): *On Revolution*. New York: Penguin.
Balibar, Étienne (2007): "(De)Constructing the Human as Human Institution: A Reflection
     on the Coherence of Hannah Arendt's Practical Philosophy." In: *Social Research* 74.3,
     pp. 727–738.
Beggs, Anne (2013): "Revisiting Marat/Sade: Philosophy in the Asylum, Asylum in the Theatre."
     In: *Modern Drama* 56:1, pp. 60–79.
Buch, Robert (2010): *The Pathos of the Real: On the Aesthetics of Violence in the Twentieth
     Century*. Baltimore: Johns Hopkins University Press.
Büchner, Georg (1993): *Complete Plays, Lenz and Other Writings*. Trans. by John Reddick.
     London: Penguin.
Büchner, Georg (2008): *Danton's Death, Leonce and Lena, and Woyzeck*. Trans. by Victor Price.
     Oxford: Oxford University Press.
"Declaration of the Rights of Man and Citizen (1789)" (1990). In: Walter Laqueur and Barry
     Rubin (Eds.): *The Human Rights Reader*. New York: Meridian.
"Gespräch mit Peter Weiss, 1965." (1967). In: Karlheinz Braun (Ed.): *Materialien zu Peter Weiss'
     'Marat/Sade'*. Frankfurt am Main: Suhrkamp, pp. 96–100.
"Gespräch mit Peter Weiss, Frühjahr 1965." (1967). In: Karlheinz Braun (Ed.): *Materialien zu
     Peter Weiss' 'Marat/Sade'*. Frankfurt am Main: Suhrkamp, pp. 101–102.
Gouges, Olympe de (1979): "The Declaration of the Rights of Woman." In: Darline Gay Levy et
     al. (Eds.): *Women in Revolutionary Paris 1798–1795*. Urbana: University of Illinois Press,
     pp. 87–96.
Hoffmann, Stefan-Ludwig (2011): "Genealogies of Human Rights." In: *Human Rights in the
     Twentieth Century*. Stefan-Ludwig Hoffmann (Ed.). Cambridge: Cambridge University
     Press.
Hunt, Lynn (2007). *Inventing Human Rights: A History*. New York: W. W. Norton.
Keenan, Thomas (1993): "Windows: of vulnerability." In: *The Phantom of the Public Sphere*.
     Bruce Robbins (Ed.). Minneapolis: University of Minnesota Press, pp. 121–141.
Moyn, Samuel (2010). *The Last Utopia: Human Rights in History*. Cambridge, MA: Belknap.

Nickel, James (2007). *Making Sense of Human Rights*. Malden: Blackwell.

Opitz, Peter J. (2002). *Menschenrechte und internationaler Menschenrechtsschutz im 20. Jahrhundert: Geschichte und Dokumente*. München: Fink.

"Peter Weiss über die Inszenierung das 'Marat/Sade'" (1967). In: Karlheinz Braun (Ed.): *Materialien zu Peter Weiss' 'Marat/Sade'*. Frankfurt am Main: Suhrkamp, pp. 111–114.

"Protokolle der Deutschen Bundesversammlung vom Jahre 1842, 23. Sitzung, 25. August 1842, Beilage 6 zu § 254; Frankfurt a. M. Bericht vom 31. Januar 1842" (2013). In: Georg Büchner: *Sämtliche Werke und Schriften. Historisch-kritische Ausgabe* (Marburger Ausgabe). Vol. II.2. Burghard Dedner (Ed.). Darmstadt: Wissenschaftliche Buchgesellschaft, pp. 328–332.

Rancière, Jacques (2004): "Who Is the Subject of the Rights of Man?" In: *The South Atlantic Quarterly* 103.2/3, pp. 297–310.

Rorty, Richard (1994): "Human Rights, Rationality, and Sentimentality." In: Stephen Shute and Susan Hurley (Eds): *On Human Rights: The Oxford Amnesty Lectures 1993*. New York: Basic Books, pp. 111–134.

Schaap, Andrew (2011): "Enacting the right to have rights: Jacques Rancière's critique of Hannah Arendt." *European Journal of Political Theory* 10.1, pp. 22–45.

Weiss, Peter (1965): *The Persecution and Assassination of Jean-Paul Marat as Performed by the Inmates of the Asylum of Charenton under the Direction of the Marquis de Sade*. Translated by Geoffrey Skelton, verse adaptation by Adrian Mitchell. Woodstock, IL: Dramatic Publishing.

Oliver Kohns

The Aesthetics of Human Rights in Franz Werfel's *The Forty Days of Musa Dagh*

Franz Werfel's novel *The Forty Days of Musa Dagh*, originally published in German in 1933, is not just as a novel about systematic violations of human rights, but above all as a political intervention, in the form of a novel, on behalf of the fundamental rights of a certain group of human beings – in this case, the Armenians. The genocide of the Armenians at the hands of the fading Ottoman Empire during the First World War forms the historical backdrop to the novel. According to estimates by the historian Michael Mann, between 1.2 and 1.4 million Armenians were killed in 1915 and 1916 – that is, probably two thirds of the Armenians living in the Ottoman Empire at the time (see Mann 2005, p. 140).[113] Ideological rationales included the Turkish rulers' widespread fear that the Armenian population might collaborate with Russia, Turkey's wartime enemy (Mann 2005, p. 143). Economic motives also played a role; for example, the expropriation of the (partly prosperous) Armenians served to create a Muslim economic elite loyal to the Young Turks (see Adanir and Kaiser 2000, p. 283). Finally, the quest for a "unifying patriotism" was seen as essential for holding together the remains of the crumbling multiethnic Ottoman Empire (Anderson 2008). The Armenian genocide was not only "successful" in that there are almost no Armenians left in Turkey today; its "success" has been underscored by the fact that the mass murder has been consistently denied by all Turkish governments from 1919 to this day and only received little attention abroad. "As time passed, it became the 'forgotten genocide'," sums up Edward Minasian (Minasian 2007, p. xxx).

According to accounts of what inspired the novel, Werfel came across the story of the Armenians in 1929 while traveling in Syria. During a visit to a carpet factory, he and his wife saw "emaciated children with El Greco faces and enormous eyes" who, they were told, were "the children of Armenians killed off by the Turks" (Mahler Werfel 1958, p. 220). In a note prefacing *The Forty Days of Musa Dagh*, Werfel states that it was the "miserable sight of some maimed and famished-looking refugee children" that gave him "the final impulse to snatch from the Hades of all that was, this incomprehensible destiny of the Armenian nation" (Werfel 1934, p. v). For Werfel, the task of the literary text – following a tradition that dates back to classical antiquity – derives from its ability to preserve

---

113 Other estimates put the death toll at between 800,000 up to 1.5 million; see Adanir and Kaiser (2000), p. 282.

the memory and the sufferings of the dead against "time's destructive force" (Assmann 1996, p. 124). Literature is able to do so by transforming one medium into another: The literary text converts the "miserable sight" seen by the author into writing, and, in the eyes of the readers, back into an imaginary visualization of an otherwise forgotten "that was." That the recollection of the Armenian killings is capable of eliciting major political fears and backlashes can be seen by looking at the reception of Werfel's novel – and the history of its failed filming in the 1930s (see Welky 2006).

In this essay, I will attempt to interpret Werfel's novel as a draft to an aesthetics of human rights. I would like to argue in the following steps: First (II.), I'll try to show how the issue of human rights can be understood as an aesthetic problem, and in the strictest sense as a problem of imagination. Based on Hannah Arendt's and Joseph Slaughter's critique of human rights, my thesis will be that the aesthetic of human rights can be interpreted as the installation of a normative imagination of a specific image of "man" – the "citizen", which is always male, "white", and bourgeois. Second (III. and IV.), a reading of *The Forty Days of Musa Dagh* will lead to the thesis that Werfel's novel is structured by an aesthetics of human rights. This means that the Armenians are represented here not only as victims of a genocide, but at the same time as subjects of a "Bildungsroman" in which they develop into "citizens" and thus to legitimate holder of human rights. Werfel's text, thus, performs an inversion – or, more precisely, an expansion – of the preference of the human rights (and of the "Bildungsroman") towards "bourgeois, white male citizen", since the Armenians are depicted as a non-European and non-bourgeois group.

"Men are born and remain free and equal in rights." Thus reads the first sentence of the 1789 Declaration of the Rights of Man and of the Citizen.[114] In fact, it reads like a reply to the opening statement of Rousseau's *Social Contract* of 1762: "Man is born free; and everywhere he is in chains" (Rousseau 1782). It is only through a cursory reading, however, that Rousseau's sentence can be understood as a call to return to natural freedom. On the contrary, by emphasizing that man is in chains "everywhere," Rousseau rather stresses a fundamental difference between the sphere of the "state of nature" and the sphere of political order (see Fetscher 1993, p. 102–103). In contrast, the Declaration of the Rights of Man and of the Citizen grounds political freedom in "bare natural life – which is to say,

---

114 An English translation of the Declaration can be found, for example, at http://avalon.law. yale.edu/18th_century/rightsof.asp. The first article of the Universal Declaration of Human Rights of 1948 – "All human beings are born free and equal in dignity and rights" – is an almost verbatim quote of this sentence; see http://www.un.org/en/documents/udhr/.

the pure fact of birth," negating any difference between "nature" and "politics" (Agamben 1998, p. 75). The political life is thus determined by his "nature" – with nature, in the tradition of the natural law, referring both to "man's" existence prior to civilization and to "man's" timeless essence, the core of his being (see Hamacher 2004, p. 346). Insofar as these two dimensions of "man's" "nature" inevitably fail to describe empirical human beings – who, in 1789 just as today, are liable to find out that they are *not* born free and equal in rights – the Declaration of the Rights of Man and of the Citizen, in the figure of "man," established a political fiction: namely that of "Man" as "a completely emancipated, completely isolated being" – who, as Hannah Arendt has noted critically, "seemed to exist nowhere" prior to his invention in the Declaration (Arendt 1962, p. 291). Postulating this fiction laid the foundations for a key political strength of human rights, as the obvious gap that exists between a freedom posited as "natural" and the empirical lack of freedom can be taken as a perennial call to political action. As a "utopian program," human rights generate a political imagination that forces us (or, at least, should have the power to force us) to make political reality conform to a fictional *image* – even though this image may never have accorded with any reality in the first place (see Moyn 2010, p. 1).

Hannah Arendt, in her *Origins of Totalitarianism*, has shown that this political fiction produces a number of logically related paradoxes – which she calls "aporias of human rights." First of all, there is the relationship between "nature" and "history." By referring not to "history," but to a "nature" thought to be unalterable, human rights claim to be fundamentally different from "privileges which history had accorded certain strata of society" – even though their formulation came out of the specific historical situation of the French Revolution. "Historical rights," writes Arendt, "were replaced by natural rights" (Arendt 1962, p. 298). From this paradox follows the aporetic relationship between human rights and civil rights. Ever since 1789, when "the French Revolution combined the declaration of the Rights of Man with the demand for national sovereignty," both have seemed to be inextricably intertwined: Apparently universal and valid for *all*, human rights are at the same time proclaimed to be the rights of the citizens of a specific nation-state, which is why Arendt states that "human rights were protected and enforced only as national rights" (Arendt 1962, p. 230). The association between human rights and the creation of national sovereignty is therefore more than an accident of history. By emphasizing that it takes national rights for human rights to be acknowledged and guaranteed – that is, to be more than ineffective proclamations of pure humanity – Arendt underlines the importance of institutional structures that defend and protect human rights, even though these institutions enter into an inevitable conflict with human rights (see Gündoğdu 2011, p. 9).

Following Arendt, a number of authors have criticized the linkage between universal human rights and nationally defined civil rights. Joseph Slaughter writes that "[h]uman rights are not yet the rights of humanity in general; they are the rights of incorporated citizens" (Slaughter 2007, p. 89). Arendt has described the disastrous historical consequences of this linkage: stateless people, whose numbers burgeoned after the First World War, not only lost their affiliation with a political community, but hence also their human rights: "The mere fact of being human did no longer confer any rights."[115] Without the protection and recognition of human rights by the nation-state, all that remains is the "abstract nakedness of being human" (Arendt 1962, p. 299). Arendt's analysis of human rights therefore boils down to an aporia: human rights are in actual fact civil rights, the rights guaranteed to citizens of a particular nation, or else they are the rights of those who have no rights and therefore nothing but empty words (see Rancière 2004a, p. 302).

Linking human and civil rights enormously enhanced the status of the nation as sole guarantor of political rights; the question of the nation thus became a key political problem of modernity. Arendt accordingly emphasizes that the creation of human rights indirectly enabled modern nationalism: since the state alone guaranteed the human rights of its citizens, it lost "its legal, rational appearance and could be interpreted by the romantics as the nebulous representative of a 'national soul'" (Arendt 1962, p. 231). By surrounding the reified state with a "pseudomystical aura of lawless arbitrariness," the nation itself is increasingly conceived as a natural – as opposed to an historical, or contingent – entity (Arendt 1962, p. 231). In his commentary on the problem of human rights, which closely follows Arendt's argument, Giorgio Agamben emphasizes that linking human rights to the civil rights guaranteed by the nation state has made the question of "which *man* was a *citizen* and which one not" a key problem of modern biopolitics (Agamben 1998, p. 76). With the state becoming first the guarantor of the life of its citizens and then an organic *corpus mysticum*, an individual's participation in this collective body becomes *the* political issue that drives all forms of racism and fascism in modern times (see Koschorke, Lüdemann, Frank and Matala de Mazza 2007). The Declaration of the Rights of Man enormously exacerbates the problem of political exclusion, which is why Arendt demands that the "right to have rights" – that is, an individual's right to belong to a political community – should be a basic right (Arendt 1962, p. 298).

---

115 "... entsprach dem bloßen Menschsein keinerlei Recht mehr"; see Arendt (2006), p. 619. The passage in which this phrase appears in the German version is missing in the English version.

Human rights thus formulate a yet unsolved problem of participation in political life that, since 1789, has been circumscribed by the borders of the nation-state and the possession of citizenship (see Joas 2013, p. 18). If one assumes, as Rancière does, that aesthetics is at the core of politics, this problem is an *aesthetic* issue – that is, a problem of the visibility (and perceptibility) of certain human beings or groups in political discourses (see Rancière 2004b, p. 13 and Rancière 1999, p. 58). It is, however, not only at this abstract level – at which every negotiation of political participation and perception can be called an aesthetic issue – that we can compare the implementation of human rights with aesthetic practices. A special role has been ascribed to the capacity for imagination. Rooted in aesthetic discourses since the Renaissance, imagination has been described again and again as a key prerequisite for the development of empathy (see Schulte-Sasse 2001 and Kaveny 2009, p. 110–111). Against this background, Lynn Hunt, in her book *Inventing Human Rights*, describes the development of the novel (in particular, the epistolary novel) in the second half of the eighteenth century – which was both predicated on and encouraged a new technique of imaginative and identificatory reading (see Kleinschmidt 1979, p. 50–51) – as the central cultural foundation for the emergence of human rights (Hunt 2007, p. 50–51). "In the eighteenth century," Hunt writes, "readers of novels learned to extend their purview of empathy. In reading, they empathized across traditional social boundaries between nobles and commoners, masters and servants, men and women, perhaps even adults and children" (Hunt 2007: 40). It may be doubted, however, whether a reading-inspired extension of empathy is a sufficient explanation for the development of human rights (see Joas 2013, p. 59). Empathy, it might be said, does not function universally but selectively. Since suffering in "real life" is not always structured in an aesthetic way – simply because reality is ultimately not structured in an aesthetic way –, fictions may be regarded as being able to produce a more universal empathy than suffering in real life does. Fictional texts may be able to promote empathy with human beings, but due to their aesthetical structure they set the conditions under which a suffering human being can be given sympathy and empathy. In this sense, Rousseau had already been critical of imagination-fueled sympathy, arguing that melodramatic suffering here all too easily upstaged real suffering (see Kohns 2007, p. 47).

This problem is taken into account by Slaughter who analyzes the connection between aesthetic imagination and the formulation of human rights. In his *Human Rights, Inc.*, Slaughter argues that human rights and the narrative genre of the *Bildungsroman* are closely related. He defines the genre rather conventionally as a narrative elaboration of the protagonist's socialization in the form of an eventually harmonious relationship between individual self-determination and social determinism (see Slaughter 2007, p. 100). Insofar as both human rights and the

Bildungsroman are predicated on, and produce, the same norms and forms for an individual's socialization, Slaughter sees their relationship as one of "codependency" (Slaughter 2007, p. 52). For Slaughter, who takes his cues from Arendt's critique of human rights, these norms and forms undergo an ideologically driven elevation from the particular to the universal by nominating the "bourgeois white male citizen to universal subject" (Slaughter 2007, p. 4). The hero of the novel is not universal "Man," but a specific representative of a cultural and political constellation that the novel is capable of turning into a universal norm. Though the novel as an aesthetic form is able to produce sympathy and empathy with its heroes, and it can be seen as an invitation for sympathy with human beings in general, this process includes a normative imagination of what a human being should look like.

According to Slaughter, human rights and the *Bildungsroman* are "mutually enabling fictions: each projects an image of the human personality that ratifies the other's idealistic visions of the proper relations between the individual and society and the normative career of free and full human personality development" (Slaughter 2007, p. 4). These two dimensions – the idealistic notion of the relationship between individual and society, and the normative notion of free and full personality development – are mutually dependent on each other. Slaughter refers to Étienne Balibar's term of the "citizen subject," which, as the latter argues, has taken the place of the "subject" since the French Revolution. While the "subject" is conditioned to obey rulers and other authorities, the "citizen subject" is subject only to laws; however, he has to obey them more unconditionally than any subject has ever had to obey a prince (see Balibar 1991, p. 48–49). For Slaughter this transition is made possible because of the power of education that makes citizens internalize respect for the law. As a fictional articulation of this process in its ideal form, the *Bildungsroman* produces, in Slaughter's words, "a narrative pattern for participation in the egalitarian imaginary of the new bourgeois nation-state"; the *Bildungsroman* tells the story of men's transformation into law-abiding, loyal, and thus free "citizens" (Slaughter 2006, p. 1410). Seen from this perspective, the novel, including the *Bildungsroman*, appears as a key cultural form that, by presenting an eventually harmonious order between the individual and the state, makes it possible to "imagine" both human and civil rights (see Slaughter 2007, p. 4).

Thus, to imagine human rights is to imagine the figure of the citizen, which is why the *Bildungsroman*, as a narrative of becoming a citizen, seems to be a form particularly suited to imagining human rights. Imagining human rights in an aesthetic medium – such as, for example, the novel, particularly the *Bildungsroman* – thus has a specific function: It makes available a cognitive model both of an individual's development into a citizen and of a person's legitimate legal status and thus mediates between the proclamations of human rights and empirical reality (analogous to the schema of imagination in Kant's *Critique of Pure Reason* [see Kant 1922, p. 114–115]). As vehicle for imagining human rights, fictions gain political importance while remaining ideologically unstable. Fictions can adopt a normative perspective (by positing the "bourgeois, white male citizen" as social norm), but they can also make visible and audible formerly negated or repressed demands for human and civil rights – and thus draw attention to what Rancière has called "scenes of dissensus" (Rancière 2004a, p. 304). Or, to quote Slaughter, "the projection of a normative egalitarian imaginary not only sets the terms and limits of universality's constituency, it makes possible nonhegemonic rearticulations of universality's compass" (Slaughter 2007, p. 5).

That Werfel's novel *The Forty Days of Musa Dagh* aims to be something other than a sentimental portrayal of human suffering is shown by the political discourses that are inserted into the text, especially the two "Interlude of the Gods" chapters set in Constantinople. Clearly taking his cues from Johannes Lepsius' 1916 *Bericht über die Lage des Armenischen Volkes in der Türkei* (Report on the Situation of the Armenian People in Turkey) as well as his 1930 account, *Der Todesgang des Armenischen Volkes* (The Way to Death of the Armenian People), Werfel actually grants Lepsius an appearance in the novel.[116] The conversation between Lepsius and Enver Pasha in the first "Interlude" in particular shows that Werfel was interested in the ideological motivation behind the genocide. Confronted by Lepsius with the "Armenian question," Enver Pasha, in Werfel's account, marshals every argument he can think of in favor of ethnic nationalism (Werfel 1934, p. 132). Not without contradicting himself, Lepsius first refers to the Armenians as Enver's "fellow-countrymen" and immediately afterwards as "another race [*Nation*], with the conclusion being in both cases that the Ottoman army has no right to annihilate the Armenians" (Werfel 1934, p. 136). Enver rejects both arguments, calling the Armenians, in a paradoxical turn of phrase, "internal enemies": an enemy within the state that not only stands in the way of the enforcement of the "national will," but, by hindering the nation's unity, even prevents the formation of this will (Werfel 1934, p. 135–136). Taking the metaphor of the nation as an organic body literally, Enver sees the Armenians – who for him are only a nui-

---

116 The conversation between Lepsius and Enver Pasha and the account of the deportation of the inhabitants of Zeitun are in parts taken verbatim from Lepsius' report; see Lepsius (1930), p. xii–xviii, and 4–11. As for the events on Musa Dagh, Werfel based his account on the priest Dikran Andreasian's report about "Zeitun and Suedije," which was published in German translation in 1919 in an anthology edited by Lepsius; see Kugler (2000), p. 124.

sance in the formation of a "natural [*sic*] empire" (Werfel 1934, p. 138)[117] – not as human beings but as pathogens in the body of the Turkish people. "There can be no peace … between human beings and plague germs," postulates Werfel's Enver, anticipating the rhetoric of the Nazis (Werfel 1934, p. 139). Through the perspective of Johannes Lepsius, Werfel's analysis of the genocide transcends the clichés of "Asiatic barbarous backwardness" and presents it as the consequence of the "narcotic of nationalism," that is, as a product of the country's modernization (Werfel 1934, p. 139).

The second "Interlude of the Gods" then plays out the conflict that continues to be central to human rights discourse to this day – that is, the conflict between the imperative of universal human rights on the one hand and the insistence on national sovereignty on the other hand. There, Lepsius tells a nameless German privy councilor: "This isn't by any means a mere matter of domestic policy, for the Turks to settle as they see fit. Not even the complete extermination of a tribe of pygmies can be considered as entirely a matter between exterminators and victims" (Werfel 1934, p. 532). It is only consistent that the fight for human rights thus shifts away from the question of national sovereignty towards a "*Weltinnenpolitik*" (global domestic politics) that also includes the colonialist regimes of Africa. By focusing the main story on the fate of the Armenians, Werfel's novel clearly sides with Lepsius' arguments, resisting the German privy councilor's desire to avert his eyes from what is happening. The novel tries to refute Enver Pasha's ideology and to present the Armenians as human beings – which, in the era of human rights, means: as potential citizens.

That Werfel decided to act on his allegedly galvanizing encounter in Syria by writing a historical *novel* – and not a political or documentary treatise – is not a matter of course (see Buch 1987, p. 113). We therefore need to ask what it is that fiction in particular can do on behalf of political intervention – in this case, to demand human rights or lament their massive violation. The answer undeniably is to be found in the specific form of imagination conveyed by the novel. The fictional character of *The Forty Days of Musa Dagh* becomes evident in those elements of the novel that Werfel could not have taken from any of his sources – because he made them up. Among these elements are changes in the historical chronology that serve to heighten the symbolism. The eponymous "forty days" are a case in point: While the historical flight of the Armenians to Musa Dagh lasted forty-six days (Minasian 2007, p. 21–22), Werfel's "forty days" not only refer to the forty days that Moses spent on Mount Sinai – "Musa Dagh" means "Mountain of Moses" (Werfel 1934, p. 295) – but also to the "forty-year crossing of the

---

117 The German original reads "nationales Reich"; see Werfel (1990), p. 164.

desert of the children of Israel" mentioned in the novel.[118] The most significant deviation from the historical record, however, is the introduction of the Bagradian family for which there is no historical evidence.

The main focus is on Gabriel Bagradian, the novel's protagonist and the leader of the Armenians on Musa Dagh. The parallels to the mythical figure of Moses are striking (see Eke 1997, p. 712). Like Moses in the Exodus story, Gabriel – who had lived in "complete assimilation" in Paris for the past twenty-three years and, since his marriage to Juliette, a Frenchwoman, had been "more French than ever" and "Armenian ... only in a sense – academically" (Werfel 1934, p. 5–6) – assumes his leadership role as a complete outsider and stranger among the Armenians. It might be argued that Werfel, by inserting Gabriel Bagradian into the story and thus creating the impression that the Armenians were capable of survival only because of a "Westernized" leader, does not do justice to the actual, historical resistance of the Armenians at Musa Dagh. As Ritchie Robertson has noted, however, the figure of Gabriel fulfills a narrative function: As a "Europeanized" Armenian, Gabriel mediates between the "Oriental," foreign Armenians and the (implied) 'Western' readers of the German-language novel and is thus able to encourage the development of empathy with the fate of the Armenians (see Robertson 1992, p. 253). It needs to be noted, however, that Gabriel's perspective on the differences between the "European" and the "Oriental" way of life is undergoing a fundamental transformation in the course of the story, as the development of the fictional character is defined by his increasing "re-nationalization" – that is, a return to his Armenian "roots" and his progressive identification with the Armenians.

At the beginning of the story, Gabriel is introduced as "a scholar, a *bel esprit*," a philosophizing cosmopolitan who does not care much about nationalities: "He was a thinker, an abstract man [*ein Mensch an sich*]" (Werfel 1934, p. 6–7). Like Arendt's study of totalitarianism several years later, Werfel's novel, too, sets out to prove the impossibility and barrenness of being an "abstract man." The "new direction to fate" that brings Gabriel, together with his family, first to Stambul and eventually to Musa Dagh is therefore the first step towards his taking leave of his identity as a "*Mensch an sich*" (Werfel 1934, p. 7). Intuiting the coming calamity, Gabriel explains to his wife: "My ancestors in me, who suffered incredible things, can feel it. ... Nobody could understand who hasn't been hated because of his race" (Werfel 1934, p. 63). He was, he now realizes, "Armenian! In him an ancient blood-stream, an ancient people" (Werfel 1934, p. 28). Gabriel is "re-

---

118 "... vierzigjährige Wüstenwanderung der Kinder Israels"; see Werfel (1990), p. 780. This passage has been left out in the (abridged) 1934 translation.

nationalized" by recognizing his biological and psychological roots and by becoming aware of the "ancestors in [him]" and their – and thus also his own – collective, ethnic history of persecution.

Whereas Gabriel initially sees himself as a "bad speaker," concluding that he could never be a "leader of the people," he realizes, at the moment of greatest danger, that he has the ability to become the military and political leader of the fugitive Armenians (Werfel 1934, p. 59). The moment when Gabriel speaks to the "people" [*Volk*] of the Armenian villages at the foot of Musa Dagh to incite and encourage it to flee to the mountain, seems to be a critical turning point in his life:

> He knew with his whole being: 'For this one second it's worth while to have lived.' Always, when talking to these villagers, his Armenian had seemed laboured and embarrassed. But now it was not he who spoke to them – and this knowledge brought him complete peace – it was the force which had brought him here, down the long, winding road of centuries, the short, twisted path of his own life. He listened in amazement to this power, as it found the words in him so naturally. (Werfel 1934, p. 206)

The passage is about self-discovery, which paradoxically comes through this being seized from outside: As "the force which had brought him here," Gabriel's "ancestors in [him]" speak through him, and it is then and there, as it were, that his process of becoming aware of his Armenian origins is completed. By speaking in a foreign voice, Gabriel finds himself and regains access to his native tongue which had become foreign to him after spending more than two decades in France. Following the logic of the topos of inspiration, this becoming aware happens effortlessly, transforming Gabriel's previously "laboured [*gekünstelte*]" relationship to his own language into a natural one. Given this transformation, it is possible to read Gabriel's stay on Musa Dagh as a process of subjectivation that can be described, by using Slaughter's categories, as *acculturation*, *apprenticeship*, and *socialization* (Slaughter 2007, p. 100). Werfel's novel can thus be understood as a *Bildungsroman*.

The Forty Days of Musa Dagh unfolds a structure of the "double subject" – double subject, double topic.[119] Gabriel Bagradian, who first sees himself as a universal, "abstract man" – as a pure individual – learns at the outset of the novel what it means to be an "Ottoman subject" of Armenian background (Werfel 1934, p. 7). The crimes committed by the government in Constantinople render it impossible

---

119 According to Slaughter, the genre of the *Bildungsroman* has "double subjects": "it imagines a relational individualism – a harmonious concordance of the person's universalist predispositions and the interpellative force of social formations and relations, of which the human personality is a part and an effect" (Slaughter 2007, p. 100).

to have a "harmonious concordance" of an Ottoman subject and the "social formations and relations" of his nation, but Werfel's text nevertheless adheres to the genre rules of the *Bildungsroman* by proposing a second collective subject: the Armenian people on Musa Dagh. By becoming increasingly aware of his Armenian roots, that is, his ethnic, biological and cultural background, Gabriel is able to experience, in a completely harmonious way, the formation of his new but at the same time 'real' self as part, and as consequence, of his relationship with the Armenians as a collective people. It is only in the course of the novel, however, that this collective group (whose existence is necessary to render the relationship between the two subjects completely harmonious) comes into being as a political subject – primarily because Gabriel's enthusiasm and commitment offer his fellow Armenians the option of self-determination and survival on the mountain as an alternative to certain death in deportation.

In this sense, the unity of the Armenian "people" [*Volk*] is established only when it assembles in front of Gabriel and when he speaks to it. The "people" here for the first time appears as a grammatical subject and an active protagonist:

> By one o'clock the people had begun to arrive. ... The people massed on the wide empty space in front of the house. About three thousand men and women. ... Gabriel Bagradian stayed as long as possible in his room, the windows of which were turned away from the crowd. ... He came out of the house only when Ter Haigasun sent for him. Sallow, despondent faces stared up at his, not three thousand, but one face only. It was the helpless face of exile, here as in hundreds of other places at this hour. (Werfel 1934, p. 201–2)

The "people" receives its unity – literally its "one face" – only at the moment when it is seen and addressed by Gabriel as one. As Gabriel finds his (Armenian) voice, he is at the same time capable of conferring upon the "people" the unity of a face and a voice. The term of the "people" is marked by an ambivalence: While the gathered "crowd" is in the process of becoming a political subject (the Armenian "people"), it is (still) a "people" in the pejorative sense of the word, the common people [*das bloße Volk*], that is, the suppressed, exiled, and hopeless masses.[120] It is only after Gabriel's speech that the two terms – the "people" as a potentially independent political body and the "people" as the humiliated, expelled and per-

---

[120] This fundamental ambivalence inherent in the notion of the "people" has been described by Agamben: "It is as if, in other words, what we call people was actually not a unitary subject but rather a dialectical oscillation between two opposite poles: on the one hand, the *People* as a whole and as an integral body politic and, on the other hand, the *people* as a subset and as fragmentary multiplicity of needy and excluded bodies; on the one hand, an inclusive concept that pretends to be without remainder while, on the other hand, an exclusive concept known to afford no hope"; see Agamben (2000), p. 30.

secuted dregs of the Ottoman state – can be differentiated. In Werfel's novel, this split happens via the Armenians' different responses to Gabriel's proposal. As the narrator comments rather subjectively, "the Armenian, too, could not rid himself of his doglike fear and servility towards this benevolent state."[121] This explains why one group of Armenians stands by Pastor Nokhudian and obeys the deportation order, while the bigger group follows Gabriel to defy the authorities and to organize itself politically on Musa Dagh. While the group headed by Nokhudian marches towards its death, the remaining Armenians retreat to the mountain to no longer live as subjects of the Sultan, but under their own government. "Musa Dagh! Mountain of Moses! At its summit, in the grey dawn-light, a whole population [*das ganze Volk*] set up its camp," the beginning of the second book notes triumphantly (Werfel 1934, p. 295). The "whole population" [*das ganze Volk*] has now become the subject of its own history.

From this moment on, there are two separate embodiments of the Armenian "people" in Werfel's novel. This split, which is enacted through the separation of the two groups following Gabriel's speech, makes it possible to juxtapose accounts of the oppression and annihilation of the Armenians with a positive counter-image. Through this doubling, Werfel's novel is able to present the Armenians as a group of rightless outcasts and *at the same time* as a self-governed (albeit small and threatened) nation composed of a people with human and civil rights. By means of this contrast – which is heightened by the fact that the story of the Armenians on Musa Dagh is interrupted again and again by reports of what happened to the deported Armenians – Werfel's account of the horrible events becomes more than a humanistic plea for empathy with the victims; it becomes a political demand for human and civil rights. The discrepancy between the rightless and killed Armenians and their politically organized counterparts on Musa Dagh is – to use Rancière's terms – an *enactment* of a *dissensus*, that is, of a "division … in the 'common sense'" as to the question of who is entitled to rights and who is not (Rancière 2004a, p. 304). This also explains Werfel's decision to present the genocide "by means of an atypical episode" (Kugler 2000, p. 122) instead of focusing on the deportations and killings. This contrasting technique transforms a potential discourse of empathy into a discourse of rights – and thus forms the core of the political aesthetics in Werfel's novel: his imagination of human rights.

---

121 "… das hündische Gefühl der Angst und Ergebenheit gegen diesen wohlwollenden Staat wurde auch der Armeniersohn nicht los"; see Werfel (1990), p. 247. This sentence has been left out in the (abridged) English translation.

The two embodiments of the Armenian "people" in Werfel's novel thus stage two different ideas of political organization. The decision to remain subjects of the Ottoman state has made veritable martyrs of the Armenians led by Nokhudian. In contrast, the Armenians who have decided to escape to Musa Dagh immediately start to "choose representatives" [*Führer*], form a "council of leaders," and appoint the priest Ter Haigasun "Supreme Head of the People" (Werfel 1934, p. 217–19). Given this vocabulary – and the novel's pro-Armenian stance – Werfel has occasionally been accused of having been infected by the language and logic of a totalitarian regime (that is, that of the National Socialists, which gained power just around the time when he wrote *The Forty Days on Musa Dagh*).[122] In the eyes of these critics, Werfel has sketched a totalitarian vision of a political community that is predicated on an almost "Manichean" opposition between Christians/Armenians on the one hand and Muslims/Turks on the other hand (see Heizer 1996, p. 76). They overlook, however, that the political organization of the Armenians on Musa Dagh described by Werfel is anything but the utopian organic community envisioned by fascist ideology. The political organization of the Armenians on Musa Dagh is based not on a belief in a mythically reified "leader" or on the ideology of a "*Volksgemeinschaft*," but on the casting of votes, elections and, again and again, arguments and discussions about important decisions. The Armenians transform themselves from subjects of the Ottoman state to Balibarian "citizen subjects" – that is, not subject to a ruler, but subject only to the law. Reading the novel, thus, tells something about the relation on the imagination of human rights in a novel: Since *The Forty Days of Musa Dagh* develops an imagination of the human rights, it is necessarily related to its ideology, the installation of the imagination of the "male bourgeois white citizen" as normative image. In this process, Werfel's novel performs an expansion of the ideology of human rights to include the explicitly non-European and non-bourgeois Armenians.

Translated by Manuela Thurner

---

122 See Heizer (1996), p. 87–88; Buch (1987), p. 114–115; Eke (1997): 715; and Kugler (2000), p. 144–145.

Bibliography

Adanir, Fikret, and Hilmar Kaiser (2000): "Migration, Deportation, and Nation Building: The Case of the Ottoman Empire," in *Migrations et migrants dans une perspective historique: Permanences et innovations/Migrations and Migrants in Historical Perspective: Permanencies and Innovations*, ed. René Leboutte. Brussels: P.I.E.-Peter Lang, pp. 273–292.

Agamben, Giorgio (1998): *Homo Sacer: Sovereign Power and Bare Life*, trans. Daniel Heller-Roazen. Stanford: Stanford University Press.

Agamben, Giorgio (2000): "What Is a People?" in *Means without End: Notes on Politics*, trans. Vincenzo Binetti and Cesare Casarino. Minneapolis: University of Minnesota Press, pp. 28–34.

Anderson, Perry (2008): "Kemalism," *London Review of Books* 30, no. 17 (September 11), pp. 3–12, http://www.lrb.co.uk/v30/n17/perry-anderson/kemalism.

Arendt, Hannah (1962): *The Origins of Totalitarianism*, 7th printing. Cleveland: Meridian Books.

Arendt, Hannah (2006): *Elemente und Ursprünge totaler Herrschaft: Antisemitismus, Imperialismus, Totalitarismus.* Munich: Piper.

Assmann, Aleida (1996): "Texts, Traces, Trash: The Changing Media of Cultural Memory," *Representations* 56, pp. 123–134.

Balibar, Etienne (1991): "Citizen Subject," trans. James B. Swenson, Jr., in *Who Comes after the Subject?*, ed. Eduardo Cadava, Peter Connor, and Jean-Luc Nancy. New York & London: Routledge, pp. 33–57.

Bartl, Andrea (2011): "Roman der Unmöglichkeiten: Franz Werfels *Die vierzig Tage des Musa Dagh*," in *Judentum in Leben und Werk von Franz Werfel*, ed. Hans Wagener and Wilhelm Hemecker. Berlin: Walter de Gruyter, pp. 79–93.

Buch, Hans Christoph (1987): "Ein Genozid, der offiziell nie stattgefunden hat: Über Franz Werfels Roman *Die vierzig Tage des Musa Dagh*," in *Waldspaziergang: Unpolitische Betrachtungen zu Literatur und Politik.* Frankfurt am Main: Suhrkamp, pp. 107–117.

Eke, Norbert Otto (1997): "Planziel Vernichtung. Zwei Versuche über das Unfaßbare des Völkermords: Franz Werfels *Die vierzig Tage des Musa Dagh* (1933) und Edgar Hilsenraths *Das Märchen vom letzten Gedanken* (1989)," *Deutsche Vierteljahrsschrift für Literatur-wissenschaft und Geistesgeschichte* 71, pp. 701–723.

Fetscher, Iring (1993): *Rousseaus politische Philosophie: Zur Geschichte des demokratischen Freiheitsbegriffs*, 7th ed. Frankfurt am Main: Suhrkamp.

Gündoğdu, Ayten (2011): "'Perplexities of the Rights of Man': Arendt on the Aporias of Human Rights," *European Journal of Political Theory* 11, no. 1, pp. 4–24.

Hamacher, Werner (2004): "The Right to Have Rights (Four-and-a-Half Remarks)," *The South Atlantic Quarterly* 103, nos. 2–3, pp. 343–356.

Heizer, Donna K. (1996): *Jewish-German Identity in the Orientalist Literature of Else Lasker-Schüler, Friedrich Wolf, and Franz Werfel.* Columbia, SC: Camden House.

Hunt, Lynn (2007): *Inventing Human Rights: A History.* New York: W. W. Norton & Company.

Joas, Hans (2013): *The Sacredness of the Person: A New Genealogy of Human Rights*, trans. Alex Skinner. Washington, DC: Georgetown University Press.

Kant, Immanuel (1922): *Critique of Pure Reason*, trans. F. Max Müller, rev. 2nd ed. New York: The Macmillan Company.

Kaveny, M. Cathleen (2009): "Imagination, Virtue, and Human Rights: Lessons from Australian and U.S. Law," *Theological Studies* 70, pp. 109–139.

Kleinschmidt, Erich (1979): "Fiktion und Identifikation: Zur Ästhetik der Leserrolle im deutschen Roman zwischen 1750 und 1780," *Deutsche Vierteljahrsschrift für Literaturwissenschaft und Geistesgeschichte* 53, pp. 49–73.

Kohns, Oliver (2007): *Die Verrücktheit des Sinns: Wahnsinn und Zeichen bei Kant, E. T. A. Hoffmann und Thomas Carlyle.* Bielefeld: Transcript Verlag.

Koschorke, Albrecht, Susanne Lüdemann, Thomas Frank, and Ethel Matala de Mazza (2007): *Der fiktive Staat: Konstruktionen des politischen Körpers in der Geschichte Europas.* Frankfurt am Main: S. Fischer.

Kugler, Stefani (2000): "Kultur und Geschlecht in Franz Werfels Armenierroman *Die vierzig Tage des Musa Dagh*," in *Beschreiben und Erfinden: Figuren des Fremden vom 18. bis zum 20. Jahrhundert*, ed. Karl Hölz, Viktoria Schmidt-Linsenhoff, and Herbert Uerlings. Frankfurt am Main: Peter Lang, pp. 119–146.

Lepsius, Johannes (1930): *Der Todesgang des Armenischen Volkes: Bericht über das Schicksal des Armenischen Volkes in der Türkei während des Weltkrieges.* Potsdam: Tempelverlag.

Mahler Werfel, Alma (1958): *And the Bridge Is Love.* New York: Harcourt, Brace.

Mann, Michael (2005): *The Dark Side of Democracy: Explaining Ethnic Cleansing.* Cambridge: Cambridge University Press.

Minasian, Edward (2007): *Musa Dagh: A Chronicle of the Armenian Genocide Factor in the Subsequent Suppression, by the Intervention of the United States Government, of the Movie Based on Franz Werfel's* The Forty Days of Musa Dagh. Nashville, TN: Cold Tree Press.

Moyn, Samuel (2010): *The Last Utopia: Human Rights in History.* Cambridge, MA: Harvard University Press.

Rancière, Jacques (1999): *Disagreement: Politics and Philosophy*, trans. Julie Rose. Minneapolis: University of Minnesota Press.

Rancière, Jacques (2004a): "Who Is the Subject of the Rights of Man?," *The South Atlantic Quarterly* 103, nos. 2–3, pp. 297–310.

Rancière, Jacques (2004b): *The Politics of Aesthetics: The Distribution of the Sensible*, trans. Gabriel Rockhill. London: Continuum.

Robertson, Ritchie (1992): "Leadership and Community in Werfel's 'Die vierzig Tage des Musa Dagh,'" in *Unser Fahrplan geht von Stern zu Stern: Zu Franz Werfels Stellung und Werk*, ed. Joseph P. Strelka. Berne: Peter Lang, pp. 249–269.

Rousseau, Jean-Jacques (1782): *The Social Contract, or Principles of Political Right*, trans. G. D. H. Cole, http://www.constitution.org/jjr/socon.htm.

Schulte-Sasse, Jochen (2001): "Einbildungskraft/Imagination," in *Ästhetische Grundbegriffe: Historisches Wörterbuch in sieben Bänden*, Vol. 2, ed. Karlheinz Barck et al. Stuttgart: J. B. Metzler, pp. 88–120.

Slaughter, Joseph (2006): "Enabling Fictions and Novel Subjects: The 'Bildungsroman' and International Human Rights Law," *PMLA* 121, no. 5, pp. 1405–1423.

Slaughter, Joseph R. (2007): *Human Rights, Inc.: The World Novel, Narrative Form, and International Law.* New York: Fordham University Press.

Weissenberger. Klaus (2005): "Franz Werfels Prosa – ihre Entwicklung vom sozialkritischen Pathos zum gemeinschaftsstiftenden Ethos," in *Die Alchemie des Exils: Exil als schöpferischer Impuls*, ed. Helga Schreckenberg. Vienna: Praesens, pp. 191–215.

Welky, David (2006): "Global Hollywood versus National Pride: The Battle to Film *The Forty Days of Musa Dagh*," *Film Quarterly* 59, no. 3, pp. 35–43.

Werfel, Franz (1934): *The Forty Days of Musa Dagh*, trans. Geoffrey Dunlop. New York: The Viking Press.

Werfel, Franz (1990): *Die vierzig Tage des Musa Dagh*. Frankfurt am Main: Fischer.

Michael Bösch and Susanne Kaul

The Right To Tell That It Hurt: Fiction and Political Performance of Human Rights in South Africa

This essay examines the political impact of the ways in which human rights are "staged" by the South African Truth and Reconciliation Commission. The committee for human rights violations collected stories of the victims and presented them during the public hearing. As such, telling of the truth was meant to contribute to restoring the dignity of victims and reconciling the nation after apartheid. By "staging", then, we mean the theatrical performance of these hearings. The aim of this essay is to examine that policy of commemorative juridical culture in the following South African literatures and their filmic adaptations: Gillian Slovo's novel *Red Dust* (2000) and its adaptation by Tom Hooper (2004), and Antjie Krog's book *Country of My Skull* (1998) and John Boorman's adaptation (2004). In these examples, we argue, fiction enforces the victims' voices because of its power to mobilize empathy and contribute to the development of human rights.

The Political Performance of Human Rights in South Africa

The Truth and Reconciliation Commission was set up in the mid-1990s by the Government of National Unity in South Africa and its goal was to help work through the human rights violations under apartheid and to pave the path for a more hopeful future in which human rights would be respected. After the policy of racial segregation had been abolished under the presidency of F. W. de Klerk, Nelson Mandela became president of the new republic. The old rulers called for a general amnesty, while the resistance movements were demanding a prosecution of human rights violations. The result of the negotiations was the *Promotion of National Unity and Reconciliation Act* of 1995, which gave a mandate to the commission to unearth the truth about the human rights violations, in order to comfort the victims and reconcile the nation. The objects of investigation were gross human rights violations (such as murder and torture) between 1960 (Sharpeville massacre) and 1994 (Mandela's inauguration). While the systematic injustice of apartheid had been excluded, the crimes of resistance movements were included. The commission was divided into three committees: the Human Rights Violations Committee collected stories of victims and partially brought them into public hearings, the Amnesty Committee decided (or made considerations) on amnesty applications, and the Reparation and Rehabilitation Committee was charged with restoring the victims' dignity and submitted proposals for the rehabilitation of the victims to the government.

Chairman of the Commission was the Peace Prize Laureate and Anglican Archbishop Desmond Tutu. The work of the Truth and Reconciliation Commission attracted worldwide attention as a juridical form of collective remembrance. It was borne by the public staging of the hearings and supported by a wide media coverage. However, it was also controversial because of the amnesty program, which was considered synonymous with sacrificing retributive justice for reconciliation. South Africa has opted for the public policy of the Truth and Reconciliation Commission to make the work of remembrance shape the culture of the country. Consequently, the hearings were staged for the public and the victims had to tell their stories under such conditions. On the one hand, then, the Truth and Reconciliation Commission was charged with the publication of traumatic experiences, authentic narratives; on the other hand, the outer frame was designed like a theater performance.

This theatricality began with the selection of locations and commissioners who should represent the various groups of society. Not only were the locations were selected on behalf of the local proximity to past injustice, but also public buildings in city-centers, were preferred to those in townships. The South African writer Antjie Krog emphasized the symbolic importance of this decision:

> By choosing the city hall in the centre of town and not a community centre in the township, the Truth Commission wants to portray a symbolic break with the institutional frameworks of the past. This city hall is no longer the official domain of whites and perpetrators: it now belong to all of us [...]. (Krog 1998, pp. 38–39)

In permitting or supporting all African languages in the hearings, the Truth and Reconciliation Commission made a symbolic statement in opposition to the marginalization of black people under the apartheid system. Moreover, the selection of the victims represented different types of human rights violations in order to convey a wide picture of the gross misdeeds of the past, and in regard to the white victims and crimes of the resistance it was about the staging of impartiality in the restitution of human rights. Critics, however, complained a preference of well-known personalities and lurid stories for the sake of media effectiveness.

Desmond Tutu finally shaped the course of the hearings by religious rites: The religious character of the "staging" was particularly evident in the attempt to restore the victims' dignity: Instead of taking them as witnesses in a criminal trial for cross-examination, they thanked the victims for their willingness and courage to tell their stories. The victims had time to cry and they received emotional support. Thus, the emphasis was drawn more to the suffering of the victims than to the factual report because of the healing effect and the expected promotion of public willingness for reconciliation. With the help of this theatrical manner of dealing with the past a path should be prepared, a path for a future, in which human rights would be respected. The collective memory should then be the basis for the new society. In sum, the Truth and Reconciliation Commission was less about the reconstruction of the apartheid crimes than about the project of nation-building because the telling of human rights violations was tied to the purpose of reconciliation. From the perspective of historical science, this is an object of criticism (Posel 2002).

The idea of the Truth and Reconciliation Commission was to come to terms with the past while providing a foundation for a future where human rights would be recognized and protected. The moral difficulty here was that the detection of the torments and killings should be performed in the service of reconciliation, which was incompatible with the prosecution of the crimes demanded in the name of justice. Proponents of the Truth and Reconciliation Commission declared the peaceful future for the country as a higher goal and believed that the policy of reconciliation had made a significant contribution to the reformation of South Africa, which would not have been possible on the legal or institutional way alone. Reconciliation achieved by story telling was regarded as a higher value than that of criminal law and the traditional court process. On the one hand, the necessary inquiry of the human rights violations made the demands for prosecution and penalty understandable and justifiable, indeed, because the governmental penal power was ethically legitimized by the preservation of basic human rights. On the other hand, the waiving of retributive justice in transitional societies was supposed to pave the way to reconciliation. The emphasis here lay on "retributive" justice since there was no sacrifice of justice in general. Maybe there was no sacrifice of justice at all:

> The question, rather, is whether punitive justice has simply been sacrificed to some or other conception of an overridingly important social goal or whether some respect for justice might still be thought to be embodied in this institutionalized encounter. (Allen 1999, p. 326)

Desmond Tutu asserted that the restoration of dignity and human rights via reconciliation had to be regarded as a higher form of justice. He interpreted the healing mission of the Truth and Reconciliation Commission as the realization of justice in a more integrative sense, which corresponded to the African conception of justice called *ubuntu*:

> Here the central concern is not retribution or punishment but, in the spirit of *ubuntu*, the healing of breaches, the redressing of imbalances, the restoration of broken relationships. This kind of justice seeks to rehabilitate both, the victim and the perpetrator, who should be given the opportunity to be reintegrated into the community he or she has injured by his or her offence. This is a far more personal approach, which sees the offence as something that has happened to people and whose consequence is a rupture in relationships. Thus we would claim that justice, restorative justice, is being served when efforts are being made to work for healing, for forgiveness and for reconciliation. (Tutu 1999, pp. 51–52)

Considering the social recommencement, as it was intended by the idea of reconciliation, many people had principal concerns about its religious scope because it was doubtful that political consolidation could emerge from such an imaginary form of policy. But on the other hand, the work of the Truth and Reconciliation Commission could also be legitimized by the idea of political justice in terms of an ethical legitimation of state power. This included the establishment of a democratic culture and a rule of law, which provided basic rights. Especially in transitional societies prosecution was not always the best way to achieve a more just legal system.

The special focus of the Truth and Reconciliation Commission was on the symbolic restoration of the dignity of the victims. After a long period of disregard of basic rights, the restoration of the victims' dignity was an equally important concern as was the institutional enforcement of law. Symbolic policy was part of a fundamental redefinition of the political identity of a society. Human rights were of particular importance to this development because historically they had been established and further developed especially in political transition processes. They included a continuous transitional dynamics which, within the historical context of political experiences of injustice, could also lead to the reformulation of the legal claims. This was illustrated by the fact that the victims were granted a "Right to the truth" which the Truth and Reconciliation Commission sought to meet both by the victim hearings and the ascertainment of personal responsibility for crimes within the amnesty process.

The Truth and Reconciliation Commission's concentration on restorative justice involved a central reference to human rights and even included some aspects of retributive justice like the assignment of guilt. This required both the political imagination of new forms of transition from injustice to a legal system in a peaceful society and the continuous factual work on the "restoration of dignity". To this end, the Truth and Reconciliation Commission made an important contribution, but it could be burdened with the whole responsibility for the political and social integration of the New South Africa.

The previous development of South Africa had revealed how many political problems the young state had to combat. The limits of the Truth and Reconciliation Commission's mandate were partly responsible for this development
because due to the insufficient implementation of the compensation obligation
the idea of restorative justice had been restricted to mere symbolic action. (For the
discussion about reparation see Doxtader/Villa-Vicencio 2001.)

Lucy Allais distinguished between a forward-looking and a past-oriented
justice. The former served social justice and the needs of the victims, the latter
was based on compensation, and only this form of restorative justice was compatible with the basic intention of retributive justice:

> Here, the aim is not to meet victims' needs merely because they are needs, but rather as a
> way of condemning wrongdoing, which means that the ground of obligation with we are
> concerned is the same as that with witch the retributivist is concerned, as opposed to the
> promotion of welfare. In this case, it is essential that reparations are paid by the perpetrator
> [...] Retributivists may accept restorative justice processes in cases where there is an uncon-
> troversial admission of guilt, and with the criminal justice system operating as a backup,
> if it is reasonable to think that these processes will enable us to express condemnation for
> wrongdoing more effectively in these kinds of cases. [...] On this alternative model, restora-
> tive justice is not seen as a new paradigm of justice, but as an alternative to criminal prose-
> cutions situated within the framework of retributive justice. (Allais 2008, pp. 133–134)

The basic intention of retributive justice was to clarify the question of guilt
which was not necessarily attended with a sentencing procedure. To name the
culprit and to discover the truth about their deeds was at least partly doing justice
to the victims. On the other hand, the expectations that the perpetrators do the
reparations were dissapointed by the Truth and Reconciliation Commission.

In retrospect, it has become clear that the work on the imaginary (symbolic
restitution, restoration of dignity, policy of remembrance and reconciliation, etc.)
makes an important contribution to the realization of human rights. In transitional societies the initiation and protection of human rights cannot be achieved
by a juridical process alone; they rather require an appropriate formation of
public awareness and political culture. The establishment of truth commissions
is recognized as a third way between amnesty and prosecution, and with regard
to this, especially the South African Truth and Reconciliation Commission raised
worldwide attention. The OHCHR resolution 'Right to the Truth' gives evidence to
the international recognition of this path.

The Truth and Reconciliation Commission in Fiction

The Truth and Reconciliation Commission politically performed a restoration of human rights by giving the victims a chance to tell their stories during public hearings that were ritualized like a mixture of trial and mass. The stories were recorded and transmitted via media reports, radio and film documentaries. In fiction, the performance of the hearings is presented on a meta level because it is a staging of a staging. There are not many novels and movies about the Truth and Reconciliation Commission. The best-known films are probably *Red Dust* by Tom Hooper and *Country of My Skull* by John Boorman. Both films were produced in England and South Africa, and released in 2004. *Red Dust* is the adaptation of the novel by Gillian Slovo which has the same title and focuses on a single case of an amnesty hearing. The novel by the South African author, who is the daughter of two white anti-apartheid activists and now lives in London, was published in 2000. The film *Country of My Skull* is based on the homonymous book by Antjie Krog (1998) who, like Gillian Slovo, was born in 1952 in South Africa and is now a writer. This book is not a novel, but a nonfictional collection of direct quotes from hearings, journalistic commentary and biographical narrative. The script transforms these records into a story in which the Washington Post reporter Langston is sent to South Africa in order to attend the hearings and to track down Colonel De Jager, the most infamous wrongdoer in the South African Police, and meets Afrikaans poet and journalist Anna who is covering the hearings for radio. They fall in love and have an affair though at first they are at odd's with each other because of their very different attitudes. She is a white South African and believes in reconciliation and in the work of the commission while he is a black American and claims the punishment of the perpetrators. Thus, the political impact of the story is brought to a personal level. The film is largely based on historical material and provides obvious references to famous and infamous characters such as Archbishop Tutu and Colonel de Kock, nicknamed 'Prime Evil', head of the so-called death squads.

Red Dust tells the story about Sarah Barcant, a human rights lawyer who lives in New York and returns to her hometown Smitsrivier in South Africa in order to represent the black South African politician Alex Mpondo in the Truth and Reconciliation Commission because ex-police officer Dirk Hendricks who had tortured him 18 years ago during the apartheid regime has made an application for amnesty. Sarah is there because of her friendship with Ben Hoffman, an old white lawyer who believes in the commission's work and whose words have validity since the novel and the movie present him as a very good character. During the hearings Alex remembers and tells more and more about what has happened to him and his comrade Steve Sizela while they were captured and tortured by Hendricks and his boss Piet Muller. As the truth comes out that Muller killed Sizela, he, who scorned the commission all the time before, finally and ironically applies for amnesty himself. *Red Dust* sheds light on the situation in South Africa outside the Truth and Reconciliation Commission as well, where apartheid is still effective: on the one side views of townships, on the other side the rich neighborhoods of the whites. The privileges of the whites still exist, even in jail: Dirk Hendricks is to be seen alone in a cell, while in the cell next door many blacks are squeezed together like sardines. While the film works a lot with contrasts, Slovo's novel works out the parallelism of the different perspectives: The narrative point of view changes with almost every chapter, and includes the offenders. For example, Piet Muller's caring thoughts about his wife make him seem more human, more differentiated, and more sympathetic. In doing so, the novel does not legitimize the crimes of the former chief of the Security Police but it shows him as a man who can also claim human dignity and human rights, and who applies for amnesty despite the outrage of the victims.

In *Country of My Skull*, the Truth and Reconciliation Commission is also displayed differentiated and ambivalent: On the one hand the sentencing of Colonel de Jager (de Kock) shows that there is no blind general amnesty for murderers. So, justice does not fall by the wayside. On the other hand, the final episode creates the impression of vain endeavor: After the final party of the Truth and Reconciliation Commission all people are in high spirits but Langston's and Anna's kindhearted friend Menzi, on his way home, is killed by guys he allegedly once cheated. The Truth and Reconciliation Commission thus seemingly fails to provide comprehensive peace, when it leaves many people who still seek revenge. This very impressive scene overshadows the success of the Truth and Reconciliation Commission.

The emotional impact in literature is different from that in film. Since the filmic presentation of the Truth and Reconciliation Commission makes the (verbal) stories of the victims and perpetrators visible and audible in flashbacks, it doubles the story and its emotional intensity. *Red Dust* begins with a flashback of Alex Mpondo's memory. Alex appears before the commission in order to find out what happened to his friend Steve who unexplainedly disappeared after being captured. His memory runs as a leitmotif through the entire film: Somebody drags a bleeding body along the ground through blood soaked red dust. Later we learn: It is Steve Sizela, Alex's friend and ANC comrade and fellow prisoner, who was tortured to death and pulled out of the room. The horror of this repeatedly shown take is a constant companion of the film. The increasing temporal extent of the flashback symbolizes the process of bringing back suppressed memories, and the memories receive a stronger evidence by being shown than by merely being told. This process is configured as out-breaking truth, not as subjective memory. The mission of the remembrance work of the Truth and Reconciliation Commission is presented here in its ideal fulfillment.

In one remarkable scene, however, it is drawn into doubt: Truth and Reconciliation Commission opponent Piet Muller is convicted of having murdered Sizela, and without a filmic cut which marks a temporal break or omission, Muller's lawyer announces that his client will apply for amnesty. This is an effective dramatization because it creates the impression that everybody is being granted amnesty at the push of a button. The impulsive outrage of the audience thus appears as an entirely justified reaction, and the whole mission of the Truth and Reconciliation Commission is questioned, maybe not with regard to truth, but with regard to justice and reconciliation.

The movie presents the work of the Truth and Reconciliation Commission in its staged character and in its authenticity at the same time. The stage-like features are obvious. The red curtain of the commission's stage in *Red Dust* is drawn, while the seats of the audience are being folded down and provided with headphones. In *Country of My Skull*, the protest song "Senzenina" is sung by the Zulu at the opening of the hearing.

On the other hand, there are scenes in which the non-staged is staged, which is to say, authentic expressions of emotions are displayed. The sudden flare of anger and the effervescence of memory are non-staged components within the real Truth and Reconciliation Commission hearings. In the movies, these moments of uncontrolled authenticity are arranged effectively. In one scene of *Country of My Skull*, the writer Anna has a nervous breakdown. She laughs hysterically as a reaction to a story about the flying body parts of his child after a mine explosion. Such cinematic stagings of the non-staged indicate that the stories in their awfulness go beyond the ritual procedures of the hearings. These are demonstrations of the effectiveness of individual stories.

The Political Surplus of Fictional Storytelling

The effectiveness of the Truth and Reconciliation Commission is controversial. For example, it has been criticized for implicitly legitimizing the systematic injustice of apartheid, as it focuses on gross human rights violation while failing to shame it as a crime against humanity (Mahmood 2000, pp. 179–180). However, the films draw attention to the social contrast between townships and white neighborhoods, the privilege of whites (even in prison), and the differences between black and white. They conceptualize crimes as acts that are politically encouraged by the apartheid system, and they individualize responsibility for human rights violations.

Another point of criticism concerns the pressure for reconciliation exerted by the commissioners. In asking manipulative questions, they take away and denounce the victim's right to hate. *Red Dust*, however, shows a slow change in Alex's attitude that goes from initial disgust at the confrontation with the tormentor, over exhaustion, into a final settling of hatred. And *Country of My Skull* represents even the astonishing reconciliation of a little boy with the repentant murderer of his parents. This scene seems implausible or has a rousing effect. Director Boorman emphasized that this scene was authentic, while the other hearings in his film, mostly of black women who lost their husbands and sons, had a more representative character. According to Boorman, there had actually been amazing cases of reconciliation. Even if these were somewhat isolated cases, it was significant that the film selected them for its story because it staged the success of the Truth and Reconciliation Commission. And by staging the commission's success cinematically, it made a political contribution for their real effectiveness.

The main criticism that hits the nerve of the Truth and Reconciliation Commission, is the fact that it is often used as a mere instrument of amnesty without arousing repentance and reconciliation. Although repentance is not a requirement for amnesty, is it necessary for reconciliation. If it is merely faked, the staging of the Truth and Reconciliation Commission becomes a farce. The repentance of Dirk Hendricks in *Red Dust* is displayed ambivalent. On the one hand Hendricks appears in the perspective of Alex and Sarah as a hypocrite who pretends to be a dutiful policemen and actually himself a victim, on the other hand, he seems to repent the acts of torture. In the novel, he explains that he was taught to fight communism and his terrorists, and that he believed to act for the benefit of South Africa. By showing remorse he works strategically on his amnesty. The novel which represents Hendricks's interior perspective in some chapters, characterizes him as a man, not a monster: He is worried about his children who left him and about how far he can go with his loyalty to Muller. He does not really show remorse here but rather the desire to leave the past and the captivity behind.

One last important point of criticism, which is related to the question of repentance, is that justice falls by the wayside when the offenders would only have to say the truth in order to be granted amnesty, without remorse and without the requirement to change their attitudes. This is brought into play at the end of *Red Dust* by Muller's opportunistic amnesty application. On the other hand, the film shows how the victims slowly come to terms with their past. The Sizelas wanted to learn the truth about their son, so that they could finally bury him. They have also reconciled with Alex, who seems jointly responsible for Steve's death.

If there is such a thing as a recapitulatory statement of *Red Dust* with regard to the Truth and Reconciliation Commission, then it is put in the mouth of the lawyer Ben who had brought back Sarah to South Africa. He is her mentor and explains to her the meaning and merit of the commission because to her mind it would have failed as long as Hendricks and Muller escape being penalized. Here are his arguments, which remain unrefuted in the movie: "It's not about putting bad guys away. It's about bringing communities together." In Sarah's eyes offenders deserve life imprisonment. Ben, however, believes that the future coexistence is more important than nemesis. Another argument is: "How do you ever restore what they have lost?" In Sarah's perspective, the release of the offenders fails to do justice to the victim's suffering. Ben argues that the punishment does not bring the murdered son back to live. And his third main argument is: "Let them carry their own load." The guilty will not be spared, Ben believes, because they have to make up their guilt in their conscience.

Alex, who regarded the Truth and Reconciliation Commission at the beginning only as a reenactment of torment, finally comes to terms with what he has done and what they have done to him. He is the one who has the final say in the film: "We have the right to say that it hurt." The telling of injustice and suffering thus does not appear as a final stroke mentality but as a dialogical developed liberation from the shackles of the past. And it is appreciated as a political innovation that now everybody has a right to talk about the suffering and injustice that has befallen him/her, which is accompanied by a restoration of human dignity and human rights.

What did the Symbolic Policy of the Truth and Reconciliation Commission and its Fictional Screenings effect?

Theoretically, it is possible that the Truth and Reconciliation Commission with its policy of commemorative culture has had a healing effect on the common future of South Africa. In practice, however, the healing effect is controversial because of the restrictions that have been imposed on the commission's work (e. g. the exclusion of the systematic injustice of apartheid from investigation and the insufficient implementation of the compensation obligation).

The obituaries for Nelson Mandela, who died on 12/05/2013, repeatedly stressed how important his policy of reconciliation had been for the improvement of the situation in South Africa. Mandela and F. W. de Klerk saved the country from a blood bath that was almost caused by the right-wing Afrikaans and the nationalist Zulus during the transitional period. For ending apartheid and leading South Africa into a new area of freedom and peace they received the Nobel Peace Prize. Nevertheless, since the end of apartheid, millions of blacks have continued to live in slums, the crime rate remains very high, and the corruption of the current ruling elite is rampant. Many people accuse Mandela of having "sold out the liberation struggle to white interests", and on having "focused on the cosmetics of reconciliation, while nothing materially changed" in the lives of the black people in South Africa (Mda 2013). Though the majority of South Africans looks favorably on the commission's work and Mandela's policy of reconciliation, they are still pessimistic about racial reconciliation. If things are getting better, they do it very slowly. The South African journalist Mark Gevisser writes:

> The overriding legacy of the Mandela presidency – of the years 1994 to 1999 – is a country where the rule of law was entrenched in an unassailable Bill of Rights, and where the predictions of racial and ethnic conflict did not come true. These feats, alone, guarantee Mandela his sanctity. But he was a far better liberator and nation-builder than he was a governor. (Gevisser quoted after Keller 2013)

There is no quick and economically proven success of the Truth and Reconciliation Commission and the Mandela regime to be recorded; their political effects will still take years to unravel. Reconciliation between victims and perpetrators rarely occurred. The direct impact of the Truth and Reconciliation Commission on the political everyday life is hardly measurable and can hardly be expected: How can political reconciliation of a nation, including the end of racial oppression and the realization of human rights, be an effect of such a short-term commission alone? Maybe it served more as a vehicle for communication and political collaboration than as an effective instrument of reconciliation in a deeper sense. Van der Merve and Chapman assert that "the Truth and Reconciliation Commission cannot be credited with facilitating political reconciliation" because it rather "increased existing tensions by bringing uncomfortable issues back on the agenda" (van der Merve/ Chapman 2008, pp. 258–259). Nevertheless, it is only with the help of a symbolic policy of human rights that the country can be ushered into a new regime where human rights are accepted and realized, because without a change in the people's minds there will be no stable economic improvement.

What now is the significance of these movies as cultural memory media for the effectiveness of the Truth and Reconciliation Commission? First of all, they reach a much larger audience than the radio broadcasts, documentaries and written reports. Having watched *Country of My Skull*, both Mandela and Tutu emphasized that the film will not only strengthen the effectiveness of the Truth and Reconciliation Commission in South Africa, but also make the people all around the world familiar with the essential questions of the policy of reconciliation. The movies reach many more people not only internationally, but also in a deeper and more insistent manner. With the help of the movies many people understand better what is at stake. One of the producers of *Country of My Skull*, Robert Chartoff, admits that he had read regularly about the Truth and Reconciliation Commission in the New York Times, but had not fully understood the idea of forgiveness until he had watched the film. (He says so in an interview on the DVD *Country of My Skull*. The following statements are documented on the DVD, too.) Something similar reports the co-producer Mike Medavoy: An ANC member had said at a screening of *Country of My Skull* in Los Angeles that he could not understand the concept of forgiveness until now. The reactions in South Africa were very intense: The film was regarded to be authentic and created dismay. The Americans, however, considered it as at times exaggerated and unauthentic. Lynn Hendee, who was also a producer of *Country of My Skull*, explains that this was up to the South African culture and the people's mentality: If, for example, in the judgment scene the audience spontaneously begins to sing, this was quite authentically re-enacted and not artificially staged. Of course, a feature film includes several means of manipulation and emotional reinforcement. He controls and directs the sympathy with the characters and their views, and thus he can illuminate the work of the Truth and Reconciliation Commission in either its strengths or weaknesses. On the one hand, flashbacks that show what is told with added music, are manipulative; on the other hand, they bring back the emotional impressiveness of the hearings in which the victims tell their stories, and thus re-enact an authentic situation, which loses its vibrations by the distance of the documentary recording media. All in all, the effect of the feature films is that they reach more viewers all around the world and do so in a more sustainable manner.

The importance of the emotional response of fiction for the recognition of human rights has already been pointed out by Lynn Hunt. While it cannot be proven, as Hunt claims, whether the reading of Rousseau's and Richardson's letter novels actually had a positive influence on the development of human rights, it cannot be denied that novels promote empathy and show that even women, servants and non-French people are similar to the readers. Letter novels demonstrate that others feel like we do and have their own valuable body, which is also worth protecting (Hunt 2007, p. 29). More specifically, Hunt refers to the 'torrents of emotions' which Rousseau's *Julie* has aroused in the readers: Women and men would identify with Julie, so that an empathy "across class, sex, and national lines" came about (Hunt 2007, p. 38). Leaving aside the question what the influence of empathy on real policy is, psychologically speaking it is compelling to assume that reading promotes philanthropy, provided that the novels pay tribute to equality and dignity. This idea, which has arisen in the 18th century and was formulated by Friedrich Schiller as ethical and poetic postulate, can only be affirmed in light of today's audiovisual media, as these have additional communication channels to convey empathy and to encourage people to recognize human rights. True, fiction is no foundation for political decisions. Paul Slovic and Daniel Västfjäll are right in arguing that this is precisely the problem: that people can indeed be moved by individual fates, but are emotionally paralyzed in the face of mass murder (see their contribution "The More Who Die, the Less We Care: Psychic Numbing and Genocide" in this volume). Political thought, of course, has to be rational and based on structural considerations. But without the stories of individual people and their suffering, the value of the individual does not become visible, and therefore it would also not become clear why we would need human rights.

Bibliography

Allais, Lucy (2008): "Social justice and retributive justice". In: *Social Dynamics* 34, pp. 128–139.

Allen, Jonathan (1999): "Balancing Justice and Social Unity: Political Theory and the Idea of Truth and Reconciliation Commission". In: *University of Toronto Law Journal* 49, pp. 315–353.

Doxtader, Eric/Villa-Vicencio, Charles (Ed.) (2006): *To Repair the Irreparable. Reparation and Reconstruction in South Africa*, Claremont: David Philip Publishers.

Hunt, Lynn (2007): *Inventing Human Rights. A History*. New York/London: W. W. Norton & Company.

Keller, Bill (2013): "Nelson Mandela, South Africa's Liberator as Prisoner and President, Dies at 95", In: *The New York Times*, December 5.

Krog, Antjie (1998): *Country of my Skull*. London: Random House.

Mamdani, Mahmood (2000): "The Truth According to the Truth and Reconciliation Commission". In: Amadiume, Ifi/An-Na'im, Abdullahi (Eds.): *The Politics of Memory: Truth, Healing and Social Justice*. London/New York: Zed Books Ltd., pp. 176–183.

Mda, Zakes (2013): "The Contradictions of Mandela". In: *The New York Times*, December 5.

Posel, Deborah (2002): "The Truth and Reconciliation Commission Report: What Kind of History? What Kind of Truth?". In: Posel, Deborah/Simpson, Graeme (Eds.): *Commissioning the Past. Understanding South Africa's Truth and Reconciliation Commission*. Witwatersrand University Press, pp. 147–172.

Slovo, Gillian (2000): *Red Dust*. New York/London: W.W. Norton&Company.

Tutu, Desmond (1999): *No Future without Forgiveness*. New York/Sydney/Auckland/Johannesburg: Rider.

Van der Merve, Hugo/Chapman, Audrey R. (2008) „Did the Truth and Reconciliation Commission Deliver?" In: van der Merve, Hugo/Chapman, Audrey R. (Eds): *Truth and Reconciliation in South Africa*. University of Pennsilvania Press, pp. 241–271.

Filmography

Red Dust (2004), directed by Tom Hooper. UK/South Africa
Country of My Skull (2004), directed by John Boorman. UK/Ireland/South Africa

Elizabeth S. Anker
Embodiment and Immigrant Rights in Alejandro González Iñárritu's *Biutiful*

Perhaps because of their immense, near universal promise, human rights discourses and norms have since their inception been fraught with paradox. Especially with reference to their more contemporary instantiations in the Universal Declaration of Human Rights and other related agreements, critics have widely decried the many contradictions that trouble human rights and the mechanisms of their globalization. Some of these paradoxes ensue from the many legal and practical challenges of rights enforcement, or the need to lend force and actuality to the visionary scope and reach of human rights. Yet structural tensions and inconsistencies also comprise the philosophical architecture of human rights norms and the definition of the human that organizes them.

This essay in particular addresses two of the many paradoxes that have accompanied the internationalization and other achievements of human rights. First, it contends with the plight of stateless persons, or peoples who lack the backing and protections of a sovereign state committed to the principle of human rights. This is a conundrum that Hannah Arendt famously wrestled with in *The Origins of Totalitarianism*, when she lamented how "the loss of citizenship deprived people not only of protection, but also of all clearly established, officially recognized identity" (287). As Arendt observed, this has entailed the reality that "[t]he Rights of Man, supposedly inalienable, proved to be unenforceable – even in countries whose constitutions were based upon them – whenever people appeared who were no longer citizens of any sovereign state" (293). Whereas World War II witnessed the explosion of groups of refugees and other displaced persons, Arendt's prescient insights continue to apply to vast classes of migrants today. It is equally true that unauthorized, or undocumented, immigrants practically speaking cannot make recourse to legal channels of enforcement, lest they risk deportation or other forms of expulsion, and this outlaw status is only compounded by the conditions of abuse and exploitation that often characterize black market and other forms of illicit immigrant labor. No doubt, this paradox is all the more striking in light of the sheer number of combined refugees and unauthorized migrants in the world today.

In addition to the many exclusions of citizenship, this essay examines another paradox that haunts the philosophical design of human rights norms. As I'll argue, liberal accounts of human rights are riddled by a deep ambivalence about the realities of embodiment. It goes without saying that human rights norms and protections first and foremost aim to safeguard the body from forms of injury.

Above all, human rights are constructed to defend the individual from abuse, torture, pain, suffering, and other corporeal hardship or deprivation. For this reason, the expectation of bodily integrity lies at the core of most definitions of human rights, structuring their larger explanatory architecture. Yet while bodily integrity and its corollary of human dignity are in many ways salutary ideals, they can and have also provided ideological sanction for a vast range of human rights abuses and other failures of social justice, both into the present and over history. As this essay will explain, to be reduced to or trapped within the body is to be relegated to a state of dehumanization, a connection that equates the body with the in- or sub-human. Most liberal theories of the human furthermore treat the body as something to be mastered and transcended through enlightened reason and mind, a teleology of progress that understands embodiment as a condition of immaturity and underdevelopment. Liberal human rights norms in many ways echo and reinforce this broad aversion toward the body. In turn, the premium on bodily integrity smuggles in an array of biases and other exclusions, which have historically authorized, and still authorize today, the denial of human rights to different populations along the lines of gender, race, class, disability, sexual orientation, species membership, and – as will be the focus of this essay – nationality, immigration status, and citizenship.

This essay explores these interrelated paradoxes of human rights through a reading of the award-winning director Alejandro González Iñárritu's 2010 film *Biutiful*. *Biutiful* follows the final months in the life of its protagonist Uxbal (Javier Bardem), as he dies from prostate cancer. In a storyline set in present-day Barcelona, Uxbal earns his income as a middleman who brokers the labor of illegal immigrants, and the film exposes those activities to be fueled by a series of neoliberal fantasies that both sustain contemporary immigration policy and legalize its refusal of human rights to undocumented migrant populations. As such, *Biutiful* lends illustration to Arendt's prophetic cautions about how citizenship and nationality are fated to constrict the ambit of human rights. However, Uxbal's ailment also forces him to confront his own mortality, and that reckoning precipitates a moral awakening about the many human rights abuses on which his own livelihood and prosperity have depended, even while he himself is relatively impoverished. Uxbal's enhanced awareness of human rights is directly fostered by his own experience of bodily disintegration and vulnerability. That embodied self-consciousness is one that González Iñárritu furthermore incarnates within *Biutiful*'s cinematography – with its intensely visceral, sensorily charged aesthetic. Taken together, the film's style, tone, and storyline thus cultivate what I'll describe as an "embodied human rights imaginary" – an imagination of human rights that carries distinct implications for expanding their protections and remedying many of their historical failures.

It is a truism that any legal declaration or other statement of human rights contains within it a particular definition of the fully human. The basic design of a human rights covenant or decree is to enumerate a series of specific entitlements and guarantees. In so doing, however, such catalogues enshrine certain qualities and goals as vital to human flourishing, while omitting or demoting others. From one angle, critics have therefore widely debated whether human rights norms should be critiqued as culturally relative or, even worse, Eurocentric, although such debates are never uncomplicated or straightforward. But beyond the question of their sociocultural or historical particularism, liberal human rights instruments, along with the philosophical traditions that spawned them, presume a relatively narrow and contradictory conception of both human embodiment and the individual's relationship to their own corporeal being. This inconsistent account of embodiment represents a central although relatively unexplored paradox of human rights, a paradox that this essay contends with. In general, human rights norms treat the body as an entity whose anarchic desires must be mastered or disciplined by liberal reason. While rhetorically speaking human rights are devised to protect the body from pain and injury, they do so through norms and standards that link bodily suffering with dehumanization. The liberal emphasis on bodily integrity, in other words, carries with it the inverse presumption that to be reduced to or confined within the body is to be less than fully human – especially since imprisonment within the body is seen to deprive the individual of speech and reasoned self-assertion, the core indicia of the human.[123] The resultant reluctance about embodiment that inflects human rights norms reproduces the very logic that over history has permitted the sociopolitical oppression of a wide range of populations understood to be hostage to the body's appetites and needs and therefore exiled from rational self-possession.[124]

To examine this bias against embodiment from a different vantage, we might say that human rights norms have tended to marshal a thin, normative, and exclusionary vision of the dignified human subject. Although legal statements of human rights codify a wide range of values, "dignity" is commonly explained as the core value that suffuses all of those disparate entitlements and protections, reconciling their internal conflicts and variances. Central to the meaning of human dignity is the notion of bodily integrity, and partner to the dual constructs

---

123 Such an equation, for instance, informs Elaine Scarry's seminal account of trauma in *The Body in Pain*. Moreover, it pervades theorizations of political practice. Even Arendt associates "the loss of the relevance of speech" with "the loss of all human relationship" (1968, p. 297). For another recent example of this linkage, see Giorgio Agamben, *The Sacrament of Language*.
124 For a more extensive discussion of this tension, see Anker (2012).

of dignity and bodily integrity are a collection of what I'll for shorthand term "liberal" expectations about the human – in particular, that legal personhood depends upon a reasoning, autonomous, sovereign, integrated, self-determining subject. Within such a liberal conceptual framework, human rights standards come to operate less as safeguards and more as benchmarks that must be attained before a subject is seen as deserving of rights. This slippage accordingly elucidates one way in which human rights norms not only become compulsory but also legitimize existing sociopolitical hierarchies and patterns of oppression.

In addition, these ideas about the self-possession of the liberal individual are cognate to views about nation-state sovereignty. Much as the rights-bearing subject must claim both a rationally ordered identity and bodily integrity, parallel assumptions undergird contemporary theorizations of the nation-state. Not only is the national community typically imagined as unified and coherent, but state sovereignty is also demarcated and verified by the border and the territorial enclosure.[125] This is to say that the logic through which the expectation of individual bodily integrity serves to disavow human vulnerability, brokenness, and mortality is mirrored in dominant definitions of state sovereignty, which similarly infer a closed, defensive, organic, homogenous national community. Such formulations of political community in terms of integrity and enclosure have under many circumstances directly justified the ostracism or expulsion of populations deemed outsiders – much as the rights bearing individual must rationally subdue and exorcise those bodily energies seen as anarchic, ungovernable, or threats to liberal reason. So we see here a symmetry between, first, how liberalism explains the individual and state alike in terms of sovereign self-determination and, second, how that principle naturalizes an exclusionary logic that can warrant key exceptions to the universal protections of human rights. As such, it offers a nuanced explanation for the very exclusions of citizenship that Arendt alerts us to, while also exposing her own reasoning as complicit with those underlying biases.

González Iñárritu's *Biutiful* poignantly exemplifies many of the foregoing paradoxes of human rights. At the beginning of the film, Uxbal is in key ways a prototypical liberal subject. His initial denial of the physical symptoms of his spreading cancer are what make his untimely death unavoidable, rendering it a direct byproduct of a refusal to acknowledge his own contingency and weakness. With an alcoholic, bipolar wife, he is effectively a single father and therefore must behave as though self-reliant. Much of the film's footage observes him in supervisory roles either cooking, feeding, and caring for his children or attempting to

---

125 See Brown 2010.

provide financially for their futures – in other words, performing different indices of sovereignty. Throughout, Uxbal also fixates on the terms and nature of his own sovereign legacy, relative to both his own and his father's paternal bequests. His illness coincides with the excavation of his father's long dead but embalmed body when the cemetery that houses it will be leveled to create space for a new highway, in a transaction from which Uxbal and his brother expect substantial financial remuneration. Two dream sequences that dramatize his imagined interactions with his father also open and close the film, replaying one another almost exactly. As Uxbal and the ghost of his father encounter one another in a surreally lit dark wood, his father mysteriously cautions Uxbal that "Owls shoot a hairball when they die." Such a line is reminiscent of González Iñárritu's related preoccupation with the precise physiological evidence of death in his 2003 *21 Grams*, the title of which is an allusion to the exact weight that is purported to escape the body upon death and therefore supposedly confirms the existence of the soul.

Relatedly, Uxbal yearns to devise his father's inheritance to his children, a yearning channeled through a ring that he is depicted twice – also in the opening and closing scenes – bestowing on his daughter. Uxbal and his daughter Ana fetishistically meditate over the properties of this classical token of sovereignty, as Ana's observation that "It's bonita" is followed by her related anxiety that it might not be "real." These parallel sequences that bookend the rest of the dramatic action both conclude as Uxbal bequeaths the ring to Ana with the incantatory words, "It's yours now, mi amor." Notably, the final of these two near identical scenes ushers Uxbal into actual death; to the extent the scenes contextualize and explain the rest of the storyline, they therefore impose circularity on it while also suggesting that the entire plot might be one extended hallucination of Uxbal's as he loses consciousness. Yet regardless of their explanatory weight, the debate between Ana and Uxbal about the "realness" or materiality of Uxbal's bequest to his children crystallizes broader desires and uncertainties about not only his own sovereign legacy but also, as I'll argue, European national jurisdiction and dominion in the face of accelerating globalization.

Uxbal's professional activities above all render him an apt figure for the symmetrically constituted neoliberal subject and nation-state alike. Uxbal makes a living dealing in immigrant labor, and the film focuses on his interactions with two different unauthorized migrant groups: Chinese laborers housed by their kingpins in a large, unheated, unventilated, unmarked warehouse and Senegalese street merchants who are continually on the run from the law. Initially, Uxbal facilitates trade between these different nationals by delivering the Senegalese fake Gucci handbags and other pirated goods made in a sweatshop by the Chinese. But when the Senegalese are deported after a raid, Uxbal no longer needs the good manufactured by the Chinese and therefore must find replacement labor for them, which he eventually secures at a construction site. Uxbal's relationship to these two groups becomes newly charged when, toward the film's denouement, he negligently contributes to the mass deaths of the Chinese. Uxbal purchases kerosene heaters, attempting to improve their living conditions in the desolate warehouse, but that gesture backfires as the heaters instead suffocate the laborers while they sleep in the warehouse's enclosed space. This cavernous warehouse that both domiciles and kills them itself offers a metaphor for the claustrophobic, potentially lethal terms to which the unauthorized migrant must consent to gain entrance into the European community. And no doubt, this thread in *Biutiful*'s plot captures actual shifts in both European migration and its economic dynamics in recent years. Indeed, some estimate that human trafficking (the fate of the captive Chinese laborers) has become more profitable than selling contraband in drugs or arms, a change that aptly vivifies how and why violations of immigrant rights can proximately enrich European fiscal prosperity (Dauvergne 2008, p. 71).

Uxbal, however, believes himself to be helping these two groups – a self-deception that mirrors the paternalistic myths sustaining the neoliberal global economy. When the policeman whom Uxbal has been bribing to shield the Senegalese from legal crackdown breaks his agreement and permits their deportation, he explains to Uxbal: "there's not enough money for everyone." This rejoinder compels their characters to debate the circuits of corruption that they jointly participate within. Uxbal insists: "I don't exploit them... I'm helping them to get work." Whereas the law officer defends himself: "I can't keep playing United Nations. I have a daughter to feed." Here, the policeman's more realistic take on the illicit exchanges that enable European prosperity disabuses Uxbal of the fantasies of beneficence that sanction his own reliance on the immigrant labor black market. By indicting Uxbal's feint of benevolence for its blindness to the human rights violations it directly authors, the law officer also exposes Uxbal's façade of autonomous self-reliance as a sham. Uxbal's character accordingly begs to be read as a figure for the corresponding fictions of the self-determining, rights-bearing liberal subject and the neoliberal state – the fiscal welfare of which directly hinges on yet submerges the immigrant labor it preys upon. From a different perspective, Uxbal's ruse of charity covers over the structures of disenfranchisement and violence condoned by the cognate constructs of individual bodily integrity and the territorial enclosure of the sovereign nation. A defensive immigration policy relies on insidious stereotypes about the irrational, underdeveloped status of unauthorized migrants in order to justify the exclusion them. Yet *Biutiful* simultaneously sheds light on the predatory, manipulative transactions that in fact incorporate those populations and their labor into the national body politic, although that labor remains undocumented and omitted from formal economic measures.

Beyond how Uxbal and his family are directly nourished by illegal immigrant labor, it is ironically Uxbal himself, the European national, whose constitutional health and fortitude is ailing. In this way, *Biutiful* simultaneously inverts the usual metaphors through which alien populations are imagined as diseased, corrupt, deficient, and otherwise threats to the welfare and resilience of the national body even while it grapples with the casualties of those very myths. Anti-immigrant sentiment has historically mobilized derogatory prejudices that cast foreigners as not only morally derelict but also physically contagious and lacking – or as beholden to insufficiently integrated or disciplined bodies. In turn, we can here grasp here how the ideal of bodily integrity can license the denial of human rights and other protections to certain populations, marking some categories of lives as sub-standard or insufficiently developed. *Biutiful*, however, reverses these common equations to instead portray the *European* social body in a state of unmaking, with Uxbal functioning as a figure or embodiment of the fantasies that European nationalism tells about itself. Much as Uxbal's welfare is sustained by immigrant lives even while he enters a condition of progressive dysfunction and decay, the European nation-state is both wholly depend on undocumented immigrant labor at the same time as its own internal politics are increasingly lethal, xenophobic, and self-undermining. Within such an explanatory landscape, immigrant labor is simultaneously denigrated as unfit and what prolongs European health to guarantee its insecure future – just as Uxbal's illegal brokering of such labor finances his intended bequest to his children.

To such ends are the features of Uxbal's particular malady especially revealing. Uxbal suffers from cancer of the prostate, a gland that plays a central role in male sexual response and reproductive functioning. Even the etymology of the word "prostate" is here instructive, being derived from the Greek term for "protector," "guardian," or "one who stands before." This symbolism, too, presents Uxbal as a figure for sovereignty in the classical sense, with that term's coeval associations of familial belonging or paternity, individual self-determination, and nation-state jurisdiction. Uxbal's sickness signifies a cessation of the biological processes of reproduction, impairing his ability either to actualize his masculinity or to perpetuate his inheritance. To turn again to the film's allegorical dimensions, *Biutiful* registers European sovereignty in a state of collapse, with Uxbal's prostate cancer denoting the pending failure of the European state and its ability to metabolize change. Uxbal also experiences growing incontinence, and numerous scenes in the film observe him publically soiling himself, accidents that produce profound embarrassment. Likewise, the storyline is interspersed with shots of Uxbal relieving himself, with bloody urine splattering an unclean toilet bowl. Here again, his condition encodes a breakdown in the excretory system of the body politic, which is overly excited and therefore unable to properly regulate or control itself. In *Biutiful*'s political context, this collapse is primarily due to an overly aggressive immigration policy, the defensive mechanisms of which belie fiscal reality.

Yet while *Biutiful*'s subtle but scathing political commentary is astute, I'd like to suggest that its foremost relevance to a theory of human rights emerges on the level of not only its subject matter but also its tone and aesthetics, which enact an embodied human rights imaginary. While Uxbal's demise and the progression of his symptoms anchor the film's narrative, an unusual number of other dead or dying bodies populate the film, and its diegesis enacts visceral encounters with them. One of Uxbal's sham professions is to act as a medium between the recently bereaved and their deceased loved ones, and an opening sequences follows him as he attempts to commune with the corpses of the three dead boys, trying to channel their final wishes to convey to their parents. Relatedly, the plot thread that involves the excavation of his father's corpse requires Uxbal and his brother Tito to identify it at the morgue before its cremation. And while Tito leaves the room gagging, presumably from the stench, Uxbal approaches the embalmed body, is enthralled with it, and ventures to touch it, with the camera lingering over his hand as it hovers over the graphically decayed face. Paired with the suggestion of the corpse's putrid smell, this scene not only immerses the camera's vision within but also activates other affective sensorium as it stages a confrontation with the flesh in a state of wasting and degeneration.

Even more, Uxbal's negligent responsibility for the murder of the undocumented Chinese workers induces a type of epiphany on his part. Although that reckoning is not construed as overtly political, it is nonetheless implied to unsettle certain fantasies that Uxbal maintains about himself (and, by extension, that sustain European nationalism). After Uxbal arrives at the warehouse and is accused of the deaths, the camera pans that enclosed space, lingering over individual corpses, vomit, gestures of desperation, and suggestions of final intimacies. The diegesis protracts its exposure to these dead bodies, rendering the scene excruciatingly painful. Moreover, Uxbal's grief is so profound that he absconds with the dead body of Li, a woman he employed to babysit his children. Uxbal initially carries her corpse into his car presumably to flee with it, although he returns with it in futility, as an ensuing shot watches him tenderly caressing Li's dead body in a type of pieta. In this way, González Iñárritu's cinematography here, too, incites a visceral engagement with these bodies in death, as the camera pans the large room to mimic Uxbal's experiential vertigo, and images like vomit prompt the corporeal response of disgust. The acoustic qualities of this scene further incarnate and amplify the viewing experience. The background noise first fades out as Uxbal rages in regret, again replicating his sense of disequilibrium, and thereafter garbled voices and a rushing noise sonically overtake the natural sounds of the warehouse, as the storyline apparently lapses into one of Uxbal's hallucinations.

But what is striking here is not so much Uxbal's remorse or enhanced moral responsibility, especially insofar as those sentiments might translate into a clear-cut politics. Rather, *Biutiful*'s many dead and dying bodies – including Uxbal's own – foster a highly specific appreciation for human rights. Beyond the film's storyline, the aesthetic features of González Iñárritu's cinematography stage a series of encounters with the flesh in all of its exposure and vulnerability. And that absorption with the sensory and affective qualities of those ailing, decomposing bodies triggers a particular kind of human rights awareness, both in Uxbal and in González Iñárritu's audiences. All in all, *Biutiful* thereby unfolds an embodied account of the human that both overwrites and reveals the folly of the dual myths of human dignity and bodily integrity that, as I have argued, lend ideological coherence to liberal definitions of human rights. By demanding that its viewers viscerally undergo the many physical dimensions of dying and death, *Biutiful* rebukes the expectations of reasoned autonomy and sovereign self-possession that underwrite liberal human rights norms. In their place, it offers up a portrait of the human grounded in precarity, brokenness, and bodily unmaking, and it further gestures toward the ethical-political merit of such an embodied understanding of the human. Notably, it does so not by sensationalizing or encouraging a voyeuristic fascination with that suffering, so as to profit from human misery or manipulate its audience, a strategy NGO's are frequently criticized for employing. Rather, *Biutiful* calls attention to the profound vulnerability that is constitutive of all human experience.

Let me further analyze the slow progression of Uxbal's corporeal unmaking in order to elucidate how *Biutiful* incarnates its conception of the human and thereby generates a more robust account both of the human and of human rights. From the outset, the film refuses its audience emotional distance, instead concentrating on and protracting the throes of Uxbal's suffering. Its storyline begins as he visits the doctor to report his different symptoms. The camera first observes Uxbal's face as he undergoes what is presumed to be a rectal exam and then follows a nurse's extended effort to draw blood. The camera zooms in on the needle, with a female nurse initially trying to find a vein while Uxbal dramatically flinches. Subsequently, Uxbal himself takes the syringe, quickly locates a vein, and punctures his skin (in a seeming allusion to a past heroine habit), with a close-up of blood filling the vial as Uxbal clenches and unclenches the muscles in his forearm. Needless to say, this intense focus on the needle penetrating his skin will make even the most resolute of viewers squeamish. Similarly elongated attention to other signs of Uxbal's spreading cancer consumes much of diegesis, whether outward manifestations of pain on his face or more extreme symptoms such as vomit. Such reminders in effect punctuate and organize the other plot developments, rendering his body and its symptoms independent characters of sorts in the plot. Many episodes find him at the hospital as he submits to chemotherapy or other treatments, for instance in one clip showing Uxbal entering an MRI as its loud hum drowns out all other sound.

As I've already noted, numerous scenes involve him either accidentally soiling or relieving himself, with bloody urine splashing about in an unclean toilet bowl. Notably, the latter such shots are filmed from overhead with a high-level camera angle, simulating Uxbal's own vertigo and prompting a response in the viewer akin to nausea. The affective sensorium that González Iñárritu's cinematography harnesses, as such, activate a corporeal engagement that mirrors Uxbal's progressive agony, aesthetically incarnating his suffering. To such ends, I should further note that much of *Biutiful* is shot with grainy film stock and dark background lighting, and that muted tone often requires the viewer to struggle to perceive the outlines of human shapes, subordinating vision to other sensory stimuli. Relatedly, many of the final segments that depict Uxbal on the verge of death are entirely devoid of dialogue and extra-diegetic sound. In effect, González Iñárritu's cinematographic style demotes the importance of sight to instead animate auditory and other visceral registers of involvement.

The vision of the human that *Biutiful* portrays is, as a consequence, not the abstract, reasoning individual of much social contract, rational choice, or discourse-based democratic political theory. Similarly, the human body that it depicts is not the artificially purified one implied by the twinned constructs of bodily integrity and human dignity. Here, the film's title with its subversion of standard spelling is significant. Much as it phonetically captures the word "beautiful"'s sounds while refusing to abide by standardized spelling, it denotes a conception of human beauty that resists artificial, sanitized conceptions of the human form. The film depicts the flesh in all of its messiness, disorder, and precarity, and it enlists the viewer's participation with that vulnerability on a corporeal level. In so doing, it implicitly attests to the worth of such an embodied portrait of the human.

Biutiful's focus on Uxbal's bodily disintegration, in turn, signals far more than a macabre fascination with human suffering and death. Rather, *Biutiful*'s embodied account of the human contributes to a distinct conception of social justice that works to correct a number of the neoliberal assumptions that, I have maintained, have helped to authorize many contemporary failures of human rights. At this point, Maurice Merleau-Ponty's phenomenology will prove instructive. For Merleau-Ponty, art and aesthetic experience are unrivaled in their abilities to actuate embodied perception, much as I have been arguing about *Biutiful*. In particular, art induces the self's different sensory faculties to collaborate, reversing liberalism's usual privileging of mind and exemplifying how embodied perception can foster community and selfhood alike (see "Eye and Mind"). Within such an understanding of the human, the body offers vital contributions to both selfhood and interpersonal engagement, reversing the conventional stigma that treats the body's appetencies as chaotic forces requiring mastery by liberal reason. For Merleau-Ponty, the body's faculties of involvement productively interpenetrate one another and collude to structure human experience in ways that model the self's relationship to the surrounding lifeworld. Much as the senses intertwine, so, too, is the individual subject embedded within and materially dependent on other lives. A phenomenology of embodied perception thus culminates not with the sovereign, autonomous subject of liberal individualism but rather with an image of interpersonal solidarity grounded in shared vulnerability and brokenness.[126]

Two additional aspects of Merleau-Ponty's thought are helpful for analyzing *Biutiful*. First, while Merleau-Ponty celebrates embodied perception as a route to co-belonging, he does not naively romanticize the human condition or cleanse it of contradiction. To the contrary, corporeal experience remains a source of profound paradox – of the kind that *Biutiful* wrestles with. Indeed, Merleau-Ponty describes the phenomenological method itself in terms of paradoxes that are analogous to those animating embodied perception. He construes the goals of phenomenological inquiry as "thoroughly to test the paradoxes it indicates; continually to re-verify the discordant functioning of human intersubjectivity; to try to think through to the very end the same phenomena which science lays siege to, only restoring to them their original transcendence and strangeness" (Merleau-Ponty 1964, p. 97). Second, Merleau-Ponty's phenomenology carries distinct implications for theorizing political community, even while overt political questions were often peripheral to or submerged within his thought. As I've maintained, one corollary of the premium on bodily integrity is that the nation-state is defined in cognate terms. Whereas within the liberal tradition the individual subject entitled to rights must possess a fully integrated, rationally ordered, and autonomous body, nation-state sovereignty casts political community as closed, insular, and governed by the politics of the territorial enclosure or border. Yet for Merleau-Ponty, the embodied subject is not atomistic or isolated but rather ensnared within the surrounding world and therefore constitutively intertwined with other beings. By extension, then, Merleau-Ponty's philosophy suggests how we might reconfigure political community to instead think about its jurisdic-

---

126 Merleau-Ponty's important works include *The Phenomenology of Perception* and *Nature: Course Notes from the College de France* and *The Visible and the Invisible*.

tional reaches as open, dynamic, and permeable. No doubt, such a formulation of national community as fluid and porous would provide a basis for critiquing the exclusionary immigration policies that trouble Uxbal in *Biutiful* and that are shown to authorize a spate of human rights abuses. The kind of explanatory framework suggested by Merleau-Ponty's thought would not only overturn the conventional stigmatization of immigrant populations as captive to unwell or unfit bodies but also explode conservative figurations of the nation-state as unified, homogenous, and familial – instead envisioning the nation as absorbent, inclusive, and accommodating. In sum, Merleau-Ponty's phenomenology suggests how a greater theoretical attention to embodiment might provide a metric for remedying many contemporary human rights violations and the biases that subtend them.

To conclude, Uxbal's encounters with dying bodies, including his own, overridingly depict embodiment as a source of torment. That said, certain sequences in the film simultaneously present corporeal perception as a font of profound interpersonal connection. Perhaps not surprisingly, Uxbal's interactions with his children above all lead him to experience his embodiment, in all of his vulnerability, as generative of solidarity and hence meaning. For instance, the corresponding sequences that follow his two donations of his own father's ring to his daughter depict their hands and limbs interlacing, with that imagery concretizing their emotional connectedness. Yet perhaps most revealing is the sequence in which Uxbal's daughter Ana first learns of his pending death. As they embrace, the sounds of a racing heartbeat overtake the background noise, and that heartbeat both indexes and heightens the emotional intensity of this exchange, with its sonic amplification inducing a corporeal response in the viewer. Such scenes recruit all of the body's faculties of perception, inciting vision and hearing to collaborate with the physical sensation of touch and causing those sensory registers to interpenetrate one other.

Through such modalities of imagination does *Biutiful* incarnate its own aesthetic to craft an embodied account of the human and, by extension, of human rights. González Iñárritu's cinematography harnesses not only auditory and visual registers of the viewer's engagement but also smell, touch, and other affective sensorium. In the process, the film implicitly demonstrates the value of these habits of participation that liberalism has traditionally denigrated, showing how they nurture a particular awareness of human vulnerability as well as of the larger community that embeds the individual. The recognitions fostered within *Biutiful* thereby stage a rebuke to the myths of sovereignty, autonomy, dignity, and bodily integrity that typically sustain liberal definitions of the human and of human rights. As a consequence, it is not accidental that Uxbal's own bodily disintegration as he faces death is partner to a moral awakening concerning the human rights abuses that have enabled his very lifestyle, with those dual recognitions together unfolding an embodied human rights imaginary.[127]

Bibliography

Agamben, Giorgio (2010): *The Sacrament of Language: An Archeology of the Oath*. Trans. Adam Kotsko. Stanford: Stanford University Press.

Anker, Elizabeth (2012): *Fictions of Dignity: Embodying Human Rights in World Literature*. Ithaca: Cornell University Press.

Arendt, Hannah (1968): *The Origins of Totalitarianism*. New York: Harcourt.

Brown, Wendy (2010): *Walled States, Waning Sovereignty*. New York: Zone Press.

Dauvergne, Catherine (2008): *Making People Illegal: What Globalization Means for Migration and Law*. New York: Cambridge University Press.

Merleau-Ponty, Maurice (1993): "Eye and Mind." In *The Merleau-Ponty Aesthetics Reader: Philosophy and Painting*. Galen A. Johnson (Ed.). Evanston: Northwestern University Press.

– (2003): *Nature: Course Notes from the College de France*. Robert Vallier (Trans.). Evanston: Northwestern University Press.

– (2003): *The Phenomenology of Perception*. Trans. Colin Smith. New York: Routledge.

– (1964): *Sense and Non-Sense*: Hubert L. Dreyfus and Patricia Allen Dreyfus (Trans.). Evanston: Northwestern University Press.

– (1968): *The Visible and the Invisible*: Alphonso Lingis (Trans.). Evanston: Northwestern University Press.

Scarry, Elaine (1985): *The Body in Pain: The Making and Unmaking of the World*. New York: Oxford University Press.

---

127 A substatially abbreviated version of this essay was published in *Frame, Journal of Literary Studies* 26.1 (2014): 11–26.

Artemis Manolopoulou

Why Them and Not I?
An Account of Kalliopi Lemos's Art Projects
About Human Dignity

On the occasion of the Conference on the 'Imagination of Human Rights' in Bielefeld, sculptor and site-specific installation artist Kalliopi Lemos was invited to participate and present some of her art projects that focused on the human condition and human rights, especially about issues concerning physical and psychological displacements and the mistreatment of human dignity.

This work has been largely influenced by Lemos's personal life experiences. She was born in Chios, Greece, an island situated at the eastern part of the Aegean Sea, and grew up in Athens. Her childhood memories are filled with painful, heartbroken stories of her maternal grandparents, their violent uprooting from their homeland Smyrna (modern Izmir, Turkey) and their moving to Chios. In 1922, they had to flee their homes due to the exchange of populations between Greece and Turkey and create a new life in Greece. And Lemos still holds a vivid memory of their tears, the laments and the songs full of longing for a freed country where they could return back one day. The hardships of forced migration and the humiliation of finding oneself with nothing and at the mercy of others have marked the artist's psyche deeply.

Then, at the age of twenty, Lemos herself migrated to London to follow her husband who was already working there. Away from family and friends she had to make home a new country. After time and effort she succeeded in calling London home, but such migratory experiences have been instrumental in her sympathizing with the increasing numbers of people who have been making risky efforts to cross borders and make Europe or the States their new home.

As a result, for the last decade Lemos has focused on the creation of sculpture and site-specific installations that explore psychological and physical passages; the latter in the form of migration and forced displacement, as both are for her a manifestation of the human being's effort to go through life, enduring all the behavior of the social body as it inflicts abuse, pain, cruelty, even hypocrisy.

Crossings: A sculptural trilogy about migration

In 2003, while on holiday in Chios, Lemos came across some abandoned, worn wooden boats in the beach. Although not an unusual site in the Greek shores, the artist could immediately see something different in these boats and soon she found out that these were used to smuggle migrants from the coasts of Turkey to the Greek islands, with the hope of advancing to the Northern European countries. The stories of the efforts of thousands of people from Afganistan, Pakistan, Syria, Tunisia, Somalia and other regions of the Middle East and Africa to cross the European borders were imprinted on those vessels. Instantly Lemos felt the urge to use them in her installations and she started collecting authentic boats used by traffickers and left abandoned throughout the Greek shores. These dilapidated vessels were once filled with hopes and aspirations for a place to live, but also with tears and fears, agony and despair. And although abandoned, they would still bear immense historical and emotional significance and they epitomized human suffering; so, their treatment as sacred objects became paramount for the artist.

Soon the idea of an ambitious three-part project was born. It was titled *Crossings* and it took the form of three public space installations in three different cities, in Eleusis (Greece) in 2006, Istanbul (Turkey) in 2007 and Berlin (Germany) in 2009. It was developed as an interdisciplinary project that aimed to reach out to different countries, from Germany and it's powerful position in policy making, to Turkey, that functions as a mediator between East and West, and Greece, that has become one of the three main points of entry to Europe for undocumented migrants (the other two being Italy and Spain).

Eleusis

Crossing (Fig.11.1) was the first installation of the project and it was shown in Eleusis from 2006 to 2009. An upright, 11 to 12 meters high structure of seven migrant boats was put together with all the vessels facing outwards in a circle, as if they were holding hands and showing their wounds to the world. The structure was reminiscent of a Sign of an ancient Greek public grave or a small chapel. The upright positioning of the boats was meant as the symbolic gesture of lifting up someone who has fallen. Their interior was anointed with pure beeswax as a purifying ritual for the healing and sealing of a wound. Furthermore, Lemos constructed and installed wooden sheds in the surrounding area, drew on them human silhouettes and wrote the first names and dates of birth of actual migrants who had entered Greece that period.

Fig. 11.1: Kalliopi Lemos *Crossing* (2006)

This gigantic structure was installed within the ruins of an old oil and soap factory, where some of the Greek refugees of 1922 got their first jobs after their relocation from Asia Minor to Greece. And the choice of Eleusis as a stage for this first installation was not arbitrary; its archaeological site features one of the most known ancient Greek shrines, the shrine of Demeter and her daughter Persephone. The myth goes that Demeter lost her daughter, but with Zeus' intervention, Persephone would leave the underworld and return to her mother once a year. So this place symbolized strongly the cycle of nature and the connection between life and death. For Lemos it was the perfect space for starting a public dialogue about refugees' experiences, their hardships, their dreams and their inherent rights.

The work remained in this space from 2006 to 2009. It was the artist's first effort to show the world the terrible tragedy of undocumented migration and to initiate an understanding of these people's struggle and agony. Ultimately, according to the artist, the installation belonged to the place it was created and in 2009 it had completed its circle of life, so she decided to burnt it down in a private funeral-like ritual that included a performance with the narration of Yiannis Ritsos' poem 'Persephone' and fragments from T. S Elliott's 'Four Quartets'.

Istanbul

The second installation, *Round Voyage* (Fig.11.2), was staged in Istanbul in 2007, within the grounds of Bilgi University in Eyup, at the innermost tip of the Golden Horn, where East and West meet, where one can find the ancient remains of the first settlers of Byzantium. Two migrant boats were put together and were inverted one above the other, in a form that brings to mind the yin and yang symbol. A steel arch construction, a bridge, was made to hold the boats in place and it was painted in different colours, bringing to mind a rainbow, a symbol for hope and regeneration.

Fig. 11.2: Kalliopi Lemos *Round Voyage* (2007)

This work was shaped in the form of a loose circle, like the cyclical flow of life, reminding us that where one journey ends, a new one starts, and how it must feel to be in between borders, cultures or identities. Still in public view since 2007, it symbolizes unity and the whole of the world where differences are bridged and peaceful solutions to problems are adopted.

Berlin

For the third and final installation of the *Crossings* project, Kalliopi Lemos collaborated with the Akademie der Kunste. The work *At Crossroads* (Fig.11.3) was shown in Berlin, it was presented in connection with the 20th anniversary of the fall of Berlin Wall and it was installed in front of the Brandenburg Gate. It featured nine of the remaining collected migrant boats, one placed on top of the other inverted horizontally and supported by a large-scale wooden structure. It occupied 180 square meters, so it was very effective in the openness of the Platz des 18 Marz.

The installation formed a 13-meters tall cross so as to symbolize Berlin as a crossroads of migration in Europe and a policy making centre. At the same time, this tower-shaped structure became a tower of anticipation and hope, but also of despair and loss. This dark and ominus construction, rising from the shadow of the opulent Brandenburg Gate, challenged the gate's classical beauty and it's symbolism of the power and principles of the Western civilization.

Fig. 11.3: Kalliopi Lemos *At Crossroads* (2009)

Navigating in the Dark: a journey within

Following the highly acclaimed *Crossings* project, in 2011 Kalliopi Lemos turned towards a more introvert approach for the examination of the human condition. It was again a three-part exhibition that took place in Athens, Crete and finally London. Not explicitly connected to human rights, Lemos's new project *Navigating in the Dark* was more about the human journey through life, the navigation towards self-realisation, reminiscent of a migrant boat navigating at night and searching for a light. Its central idea was the search for the base within our self, the move deep within, in order to feel secure and survive in times when things collapse around us (e.g. political and economic systems, environmental changes, borders re-calculated etc). And ultimately what we achieve inwardly eventually brings changes to the outer reality. It was an examination of humans and their relation to the society, but more importantly their relation to themselves – understanding, acceptance and effort for a better life, a life true to the self.

Athens

Placed within the courtyard of the Benaki Museum in the centre of Athens, in the midst of an urban and very busy environment, the first part of the *Navigating in the Dark* project explored the relationship between the collective and the individual and the transition towards an inner journey. According to the artist, when social, political and economic systems are in crisis, we must turn to ourselves and rediscover our base. This first show aimed to create a metaphor for this transition from the social to the personal and for the beginning of the journey within.

The Benaki courtyard was dominated by a platform that featured four large-scale steel abstract sculptures such as *Bear All Crawl* (2008) (Fig.11.4), acting as the four cardinal points, and an hexagonal 'beehive' structure that was filled with water and twelve steel heads. This 'beehive' could be perceived as a place of initiation, with the heads semi-submerged in water, evoking the act of entering the darkness and commencing the journey.

Fig. 11.4: Kalliopi Lemos *Bear all Crawl* (2008)

Rethymon

Located in Ibrahim Khan mosque, in Rethymnon, Crete, the second exhibition explored the spiritual path of the journey. The site, originally a Christian church that was later converted into a mosque, had great significance for Lemos, as it underlined the human need to connect with the spiritual world. The motif of the boat could again be seen in some of the works exhibited and the passage from earth to sky, from matter to spirit and to a deeper self-exploration.

One particular sculpture, the *Odysseus's Boat* (Fig.11.5), was particularly poignant of the process of the life journey and the remnants from the experience;

Fig. 11.5: Kalliopi Lemos *Odysseus's Boat* (2011)

featuring a wooden boat and twelve, semi-abstract salt heads positioned through-out its length, it symbolized the crossing and the lonely search for self-awareness. The salt heads, with their distorted expressions of pain and agony, encapsulated the meaning of life, what remains from this journey and reflected the difficulty of the voyage, the achievement of reaching the destination as well as the experiences of life that shape each person's individuality.

London

The third and final part of the *Navigating in the Dark* project took place at the Crypt Gallery of Saint Pancras Church in London, which was originally a burial place. It focused on the ultimate journey through darkness, the passage through death, the connection with the unconscious and the final transition from an outward existence to an inward self-awareness.

Fig. 11.6: Kalliopi Lemos *Wooden Boat with Seven People* (2011)

The installation was located in an underground space and it aimed to evoke strong feelings, reminding us of the dark side of the unconscious and the intense discoveries that we might dig out while exploring hidden sides of the self. Three boats – found objects (Fig.11.6), stripped down of any colour to expose the raw wood – were each filled with snakes, crows and human figures made of steel and were accompanied by an evocative sound installation. Additionally, a vaulted space in the Crypt was filled with white paper sculptures of semi-transparent bees that hovered in the air like migrating souls.

Pledges for a Safe Passage:
An installation for the 3rd International
Biennial of Canakkale

When Lemos was invited to participate in the 3rd International Biennial of Canakkale, in Turkey in 2012, the theme of undocumented migration was again revisited. The site-specific installation *Pledges for a Safe Passage* (Fig.11.7) focused on this ever increasing global issue and it was dedicated to the struggle and hardships thousands of people endure in the hope for a better life. It marked the process of a passage, a journey from one place to another, from one situation to another, from life to death, from hope to despair.

The work (Fig.11.8) featured an unused boat found in Canakkale that was covered with numerous handmade and readymade votives, called *tamata* in Greek, that had inscriptions with the names, date and place of birth of migrants that entered illegally Greece's borders. These votives, used extensively in the Greek Orthodox tradition, acted as individual prayers for the safe journey and the realization of the dream. Simultaneously, however, they also became a met-

Fig. 11.7: Kalliopi Lemos *Pledges for a Safe Passage* (2014b)

Fig. 11.8: Kalliopi Lemos *Pledges for a Safe Passage* (2014)

aphor for the human drama, expressing the fear, the agony and the uncertainty that each migrant experiences in the effort to cross to another border. Made of recycled aluminium soft drink cans, the votives were also meant to point to the excessive consuming habits of the Western world and the division between rich and poor as one of the causes for the displacement of people.

I am I between worlds and between shadows: A parallel event of the 13th Istanbul Biennial

More recently, Kalliopi Lemos's incessant artistic preoccupation with the human condition and the offence of human dignity has resulted in her latest project *I Am I Between Worlds and Between Shadows*, which concentrated on women's experiences and the frequent abuse of their self-respect. Organised as a parallel event of the 13th Istanbul Biennial in 2013, the exhibition was concerned with the human rights of women and children and it underlined how, in many different ways, women still face, and still have to put up with, behavior that is insulting, wounding, oppressive and overpowering.

The exhibition consisted of an installation that featured seven evocative sculptures, each one positioned in different classrooms of the Ioakimion, an old girls' school in the historic area of Fener in Istanbul. In this way, they stood like remote islands, expressing the psychological isolation and loneliness experienced after violation. A sound installation was also incorporated so as to enhance the atmosphere of the old school, while on the pupils' desk one could find recent newspaper articles with incidents of violence and mistreatment against women all around the world. Made of steel fillings, fiberglass and mild steel, the sculptures referred to the brutal violations directly or indirectly affecting all women. But the story was also about the mundane violations, the struggle to combine and achieve and the daily sacrifice of the feminine that causes so much suffering to the soul, and to society as a whole.

Fig. 11.9: Kalliopi Lemos *Hen on Crutches* (2013)

Fig. 11.10: Kalliopi Lemos *Hanging Hare* (2013)

Among the works, the *Hen on Crutches* (Fig.11.9), with no wings or legs, hangs suspended like a piece of meat, bringing to mind all those countless women that have been victims of trafficking, or the millions of underage girls forced into arranged marriages still in many parts of the world. The sculpture *Hanging Hare* (Fig.11.10), on the other hand, features a multi-breasted hare hung from his ears. The numerous breasts are nothing else from what is expected of women; to be wives, lovers, mothers, professionals and daughters. The expectations are high, diminishing the space and time for a woman to maintain a connection with her inner self. Other sculptures show a mutilated body of a woman on leg stands, a female headed body of a deer that brings in mind the myth of the sacrifice of Iphigenia, or a sculpture of a goat with female breasts placed away from its body, a metaphor of the woman who 'sprints' throughout her life due to all her increasing responsibilities.

The choice of the space was particularly significant as Lemos saw in it the neglect and pain that her sculptures also conveyed. The school offered a stark and disturbing contrast of how life starts full of dreams and expectations and what the reality might later bring. Closed for almost thirty years, the artist found it exactly as it was on its last day of operation, with all its desks, books, maps, and files. So she left it intact as a dramatic stage for her haunting female-animal sculptures, each expressing the distortions of the psyche due to pain and abuse and displayed on its own in one of the rooms of the high school. On the desks of the classrooms the visitor could find the latest newspapers' articles with news about unjust and violent behaviour against women from all over the world. As a contrast to this ghostly environment one could hear, from the sound installation, the sounds of children laughing, singing and reading fairy tales, bringing to life some of the school's past glory.

Epilogue

Art, in all its different forms, can be a powerful tool in raising awareness of social issues and injustices. A thought provoking work can change a person's perception and it can have a great impact on his/her views. An image can sometimes have such a power so as to affect people profoundly and bring them together in a deeper and more meaningful sense than a new law or a new policy. Understanding this, artists of the 20th and 21st century have long used their practice in order to communicate ideas about issues of identity, gender politics, racism, abuse and disrespect of human rights. Who has not felt pain and anguish in front of Pablo Picassos's famous work *Guernica*, inspired by the bombing of the Basque town during the Spanish Civil War?

Over the last decade, sculptor and installation artist Kalliopi Lemos has created works that draw extensively on themes such as undocumented migration, human suffering and a person's journey through life. Central concern in her art is the upholding of human dignity and, with that in mind, she often explores cases of mistreatment, inequality and disregard of human respect. With her projects, Lemos aims at engaging the viewer with such issues and re-evaluating his/her understanding of the world. Through works of art that aim to communicate the desperation, hardships and violence many people endure today, Lemos creates explicit images of suffering and pain. The viewers of her exhibitions are thus confronted with the harsh realities of our world and hopefully, empathise and realize their obligation to protect the rights of both themselves and those of less fortunate human beings. More importantly the artist attempts to awaken the common feeling of humanity and the spiritual quality within all people so that, in spite of the pervasive chaos we are living through, there is beauty and harmony to be rescued and installed back in our lives, and inspire people to imagine a better world.

List of Contributors

Elizabeth S. Anker is Associate Professor in the English Department at Cornell University and Associate Member of the Faculty of Cornell Law School. Her first book is *Fictions of Dignity: Embodying Human Rights in World Literature* (2012), and her recent publications include essays in *New Literary History, American Literary History, Novel: A Forum on Fiction*, and the *University of Toronto Quarterly*. She is currently working on two book projects. The first, "Our Constitutional Metaphors: Law, Culture, and the Management of Crisis," looks to literature, architecture, and film to study popular metaphors for constitutions, examining how they resolve challenges to democracy. Second, she is writing a book on "Human Rights and Critical Theory," that explores the "human rights turn" within literary study. She is also co-editing two essay collections, one on "New Directions in Law and Literature" with Bernadette Meyler and another on "Rethinking Critique" with Rita Felski.

Nina Berman is Professor of Comparative Studies at Ohio State University. She is the author of *German Literature on the Middle East: Discourses and Practices, 1000–1989* (2011), *Impossible Missions? German Economic, Military, and Humanitarian Efforts in Africa* (2004), and *Orientalismus, Kolonialismus und Moderne: Zum Bild des Orients in der deutschsprachigen Kultur um 1900* (1997). A co-edited anthology (with Klaus Mühlhahn and Patrice Nganang), entitled *German Colonialism Revisited: African, Asian, and Oceanic Experiences*, was published in early 2014. Her current project, *Land, Charity, and Romance: Kenyan-German Dynamics on the Coast of Kenya*, is based on extensive ethnographic fieldwork, archival research, statistical data collection, and analyses of cultural representations and public debates, and assesses changes brought on by contemporary migration patterns that flow from nations of the northern hemisphere to nations of the southern hemisphere.

Rüdiger Bittner received the Dr. Phil. from Heidelberg University and the Habilitation in philosophy from Free University Berlin. He taught philosophy at the Universities of Heidelberg, Princeton, Hildesheim, Yale and Bielefeld. He is the author of *What Reason Demands* (1989) and *Doing Things For Reasons* (2001). He has also published articles on moral and political philosophy, theory of action and philosophy of mind, as well as historical studies of Augustine, Hobbes, Kant and Nietzsche. In 2012, the *Gesellschaft für analytische Philosophie* awarded him the Gottlob Frege-Prize.

Michael Bösch is Professor of Philosophy at Catholic University NRW in Germany. He received his Ph.D. in 1993 for his dissertation on Søren Kierkegaard and his

Habilitation in 2002 with a thesis on Ernst Cassirer. Between 2003 and 2008, he was lecturer at the University of Kassel. His publications range from philosophical studies of Kant, Hegel, Husserl, Heidegger and Arendt to critical inquiries into cultural philosophy, political philosophy, social philosophy, hermeneutics, phenomenology and ontology.

Hans Joas is Ernst Troeltsch Professor for the Sociology of Religion at the Humboldt University of Berlin and Professor of Sociology at the University of Chicago where he also belongs to the Committee on Social Thought. He received his Ph.D. (1979) in sociology from the Free University of Berlin and honorary doctorates from the University of Tübingen (2012) and Uppsala University in Sweden (2013). The most recent publications of his include, among others, *The Sacredness of the Person: A New Genealogy of Human Rights* (2013), *War in Social Thought: Hobbes to the Present* (with W. Knöbl, 2013), *The Axial Age and Its Consequences* (with Robert Bellah, 2012), and *Faith as an Option* (2014).

Susanne Kaul is Heisenberg Fellow in the German Department (Literature and Media) at the University of Münster. She studied Philosophy, Linguistics and Literary Studies at the University of Paderborn and Goethe University in Frankfurt am Main and received her Ph.D. and the Habilitation in Literary Studies from Bielefeld University. One of her seven books is titled *Poetik der Gerechtigkeit: Shakespeare – Kleist* (2008) and other publications range widely from film, modern literature, and narratology to ethics, and theories of humor. During the spring of 2012, Kaul was the Max Kade Distinguished Visiting Professor at the University of Notre Dame.

David Kim is Assistant Professor in the Department of Germanic Languages at the University of California Los Angeles. Until 2014, he was Assistant Professor of German and Inaugural Core Faculty of Global Studies in the Arts and Humanities at Michigan State University. He received his Ph.D. in German Studies from Harvard University and his publications explore cosmopolitanism, world literature, transnational adoption, postcolonial and translation theories, contemporary German and *fin-de-siècle* Austrian literatures, and human rights. He is currently finishing a book project, titled *Parables for World Citizenship*. He is also co-editor of *The Postcolonial World* under contract with Routledge.

Oliver Kohns is Attract Fellow at the University of Luxembourg, where he currently leads the research group "Aesthetical Figurations of the Political," funded by the Fonds National de la Recherche (FNR). He studied German philology, sociology and history at the University of Cologne and received his Ph.D. (2006) in Comparative Literature from Goethe University in Frankfurt am Main. His dissertation has been published under the title *Die Verrücktheit des Sinns. Wahnsinn und Zeichen bei Kant, E.T.A. Hoffmann und Thomas Carlyle* (2007). Further publications deal with literary theory, modern literature, and political aesthetics.

Kalliopi Lemos is a sculptor, painter and installation artist, born on the Greek island of Oinousses, near Chios. She studied painting and printing at Byam Shaw School of Art, University of the Arts London, Central Saint Martins, where she also pursued post-graduate studies. She studied the art of Ikebana for 15 years. She lives and works in London. Lemos creates site-specific installations that often focus on human rights, and on issues such as the increasing global undocumented migration and the upholding of human dignity. During the last decade she has exhibited extensively in various international venues like Berlin, Istanbul, Athens and London. Her work can be found in private collections and on permanent display in New York, Istanbul and Canakkale.

Artemis Manolopoulou is an art historian based in Athens and she has a MA in History of Art and MA in Arts Policy and Management, both from Birkbeck College, University of London. After completing her postgraduate studies, she worked at the British Museum as Assistant Curator and as Curator of African Money. Since 2011, she has been working as Projects Manager at Kalliopi Lemos Fine Arts Ltd.

Samuel Moyn is a professor of law and history at Harvard University. Until 2014, he was James Bryce Professor of European Legal History at Columbia University. He holds a Ph.D. in history from the University of California-Berkeley and a J.D. from Harvard University. He is the author of four books, most recently *Human Rights and the Uses of History* (2014). He is also editor of *Humanity*.

Thomas Pogge received his Ph.D. in Philosophy from Harvard University and is currently Leitner Professor of Philosophy and International Affairs and founding Director of the Global Justice Program at Yale. He is a member of the Norwegian Academy of Science, as well as President of Academics Stand Against Poverty, an international network that aims to enhance the impact of scholars, teachers and students on global poverty, and of Incentives for Global Health, a team effort toward developing a complement to the pharmaceutical patent regime that would improve access to advanced medicines worldwide. Pogge's publications include *Politics as Usual* (2010), *World Poverty and Human Rights* (2008), *John Rawls: His Life and Theory of Justice* (2007), and *Freedom from Poverty as a Human Right* (2007).

Paul Slovic is a professor of psychology at the University of Oregon and a founder and President of Decision Research. He holds a Ph.D. from the University of Michigan and honorary doctorates from the Stockholm School of Economics and the University of East Anglia. He co-directs a multidisciplinary initiative at the University of Oregon titled "Genocide and Mass Atrocities: Responsibility to Prevent." His most recent research examines "psychic numbing" and the failure to respond to mass human tragedies. His books include *The Perception of Risk* (2000), *The Social Amplification of Risk* (2003), *The Construction of Preference* (2006), and *The Feeling of Risk* (2010).

Lora Wildenthal is Professor of History at Rice University in Houston, Texas, USA. She studied history at Rice, Freiburg University, and the University of Michigan, where she received her Ph.D. (1994). She is the author of *German Women for Empire, 1884–1945* (2001) and *The Language of Human Rights in West Germany* (2012). She is also the editor of Else Frobenius's memoirs, *Erinnerungen einer Journalistin: Zwischen Kaiserreich und Zweitem Weltkrieg* (2005), and co-editor of *Germany's Colonial Pasts* (2009).

Sebastian Wogenstein is Associate Professor of German in the Department of Literatures, Cultures and Languages at the University of Connecticut. He is the author of a monograph, *Horizonte der Moderne: Tragödie und Judentum von Cohen bis Levinas* (2011), and co-editor of two books: *Globale Kulturen--Kulturen der Globalisierung* (2013) and *An Grenzen: Literarische Erkundungen* (2007). His other publications focus primarily on German-Jewish literature and intellectual history, contemporary German literature and theater, and literature and human rights. Wogenstein is a Faculty Associate of the University of Connecticut's Human Rights Institute.

Daniel Västfjäll, Ph.D., is a research scientist at Decision Research and Professor of Cognitive Psychology at Linköping University. He is the director of Linköping Center of Behavioral- and NeuroEconomics. His research examines how affect influences judgment and decision making – in particular, the role of emotion in charitable giving. He has recently focused on how psychological factors such as singularity, identifiability, and scope influence decisions about resource allocations. A specific goal of this research has been to use multimethod approaches (brain data, physiology, behavior, and self-report) to examine the role of affect in charitable decisions. The research has been published in journals such as *PLoS One*, *Journal of Neuroscience*, *Judgment and Decision Making*, and *Nature*. Västfjälls' basic research on the psychology of charitable giving is funded by awards from the National Science Foundation, the Swedish Science Foundation, and the European Commission.

Index of Persons

Index of Subjects